4⁸⁵

# THE
# SHAMBAA KINGDOM

## A History

# THE
# SHAMBAA KINGDOM

## A History

*STEVEN FEIERMAN*

THE UNIVERSITY OF WISCONSIN PRESS

Published 1974

The University of Wisconsin Press
Box 1379, Madison, Wisconsin 53701

The University of Wisconsin Press, Ltd.
70 Great Russell Street, London

Copyright ©1974
The Regents of the University of Wisconsin System
All rights reserved

Printed in the United States of America

For LC CIP information see the colophon

ISBN 0-299-06360-7

# CONTENTS

# MAPS

# PREFACE

Hundreds of Shambaa helped me during my stay in Shambaai. I owe them all my thanks. Leo Hassani and Hatibu Hassani participated actively in the research. They are really the coauthors of this book, although responsibility for any errors is my own. My "family" at Vugha tolerated my strange habits and provided unfailing hospitality. I owe special thanks to Shechonge Kishasha, Ali Shechonge, and Zekifisha Sheconge of Vugha. My hosts Kazushwe at Bumbuli and Kimea Abdallah at Mshihwi were extremely generous and helpful. I am deeply indebted to them.

This study has benefited from the guidance of Professors Franklin Scott and John Rowe, to whom I am deeply indebted. I owe special thanks and gratitude to Dr. Rodney Needham, whose advice, criticism, and inspiration have guided my anthropological research. I am grateful to Dr. John Beattie, who commented on the manuscript, and who has given valuable advice on my continuing research. While in Tanzania I received the invaluable assistance of a number of members of what was then the University College, Dar es Salaam, including Professor Terence Ranger and Dr. John Iliffe. Dr. Iliffe has allowed me to see a draft of a paper on the Bondei rebellion of 1869. Dr. Isaria Kimambo generously shared his knowledge of the history of the Pangani Valley region. I owe much to my colleagues at the University of Wisconsin, Professors Jan Vansina and Philip Curtin, for encouragement and advice, and for a continuing education in African history.

I would like to thank the archivists of the Tanzania National Archives and of the United Society for the Propagation of the Gospel, the librarians of Rhodes House, Oxford, the Welt-Wirts-chafts-Archiv in Hamburg, the Bethel Mission in Bielefeld, Northwestern University, and Mr. Michael Briggs of the University of Wisconsin Library. I am grateful to the officers of the regional administration of Tanzania, who assisted me in Shambaai. Professors Roland Oliver, Joseph C. Miller, Paul Bohannan, T. O. Beidelman, James D. Graham, Mr. Roderic Lacey, Mr. Thomas Spear, and Mr. Lee Cassanelli have all given me valuable advice and assistance, for which I am grateful. I owe special thanks for hospitality to Mr. and Mrs. Kees Ton, Sister Elfrieda Haase, Father Andrew Grant, Mr. and Mrs. Daniel Pearson, and Mr. and Mrs. Samuel Rea.

The study resulting in this publication was made under fellowships granted by the Foreign Area Fellowship Program and the National Science Foundation. However, the conclusions, opinions, and other statements in this book are those of the writer and are not necessarily those of either fellowship program.

Finally, I owe very special debts to my parents and to my parents-in-law, who tolerated a long absence in East Africa. My wife Elizabeth carried countless gourds of water and built innumerable cooking fires while the research was being done. She helped me in ways that I have not yet begun to understand. With the deepest affection and gratitude I dedicate this work to her.

S. F.

*Madison, Wisconsin*
*August 1973*

# NOTE ON ORTHOGRAPHY

The orthography used in this work is similar to that of standard Swahili, which literate Shambaa use for writing in their own language and in Swahili. Tone markings are omitted. The most notable additions to the orthography, when used for writing Shambaa, are those consonants which do not exist in Swahili (or in English)—the voiceless prenasalized plosives: the labial *mp,* the dental *nt,* the palatal *nch,* and the velar *nk.* Most published works in Shambaa are written in the dialect of Mlalo, because that was where the missionaries who first recorded the language lived. The main difference is the presence or absence of the letter *l,* which is sometimes written as *r.* I have chosen, where possible, to write words the way the great majority of Shambaa say them. They speak of themselves as Shambaa, although written works in the language refer to them as Shambala. For most proper names, however, with the exception of Shambaa and Shambaai, on which I hope a new convention will be established, I have followed the spellings found in the historical literature, and on maps, even when I disagree with the orthography. For example, the royal name which is written here and in the literature as Kimweri is pronounced Kimwei by most Shambaa. Similarly, I have not altered the way in which literate men write their names. For example, in the name Mputa, the *M* is a separate syllable. As it is written now, one would assume incorrectly, from the convention on prenasalized consonants given above, that the letters *mp* are both part of a single syllable. I hesitate, however, to change the way in which the recently retired king of Shambaai writes his middle name.

# THE
# SHAMBAA KINGDOM

## A History

# INTRODUCTION

All of my research on the history of the Shambaa has been an attempt to demonstrate that African history can be written for an audience which is western in orientation, in approach to historical issues and critical method, without losing sight of the point of view of the actors themselves. Every historian, in every field of history, is engaged in this search for authenticity. But African historians, especially those who write about the precolonial period, face an unusual problem. There are relatively few documents written from an African point of view, and the world view of the historical actors is foreign to the research scholar and to his audience.

The reconstruction of the African historical record has proceeded with great vigor, in spite of the relative scarcity of written documents, ever since the publication in 1961 of Jan Vansina's handbook of historical method, which has been translated as *Oral Tradition*. Cultural translation, however, remains a problem at two levels. At the first, there is a need for adequate cultural materials so that the historian can describe actions in their proper setting. At the second, there is the problem of understanding one's sources. The oral traditions are cultural documents which, at their most complex, may be given by the tellers as broad statements of the nature of society, or of the universe. Even when traditions are given as bare narratives which describe the course of events in a dry factual tone, historical and political concepts which are assumed as common cultural knowledge by the tellers are not a part of the historian's knowledge unless he comes from that particular society. A full reading of a simple oral tradition may require a broad understanding of cosmology and social organization.

My own approach, in the study of the history of the Shambaa of northeastern Tanzania, has been to do two separate but complementary research projects at once: the first is the collection and analysis of Shambaa oral traditions, and the second, a general study of Shambaa culture and society. This work on precolonial history is the first of two works, the second of which will be a study of the political culture of the Shambaa.[1] The materials on both culture and history were gathered during one period of field research between June 1966 and July 1968.

While the idea of doing two research projects at once may seem unusual, it was in actual practice a simple and direct undertaking. The men who taught me Shambaa oral traditions were at the same time not uninformed on the nature of Shambaa culture. It was quite natural to consult a single set of informants, now on history, now on society. But perhaps the most important reason for studying culture as well as oral traditions is that the traditions themselves are elements in a living culture.

To a much greater extent than many historians realize, oral traditions provide indirect evidence of the nature of historical events; they are "witnesses in spite of themselves." It will be shown below that the Shambaa are not antiquarians—they remember the past not for its own sake, but in order to preserve special rights, to explain social phenomena which persist in time, to keep a record of friends and enemies. It follows, since the oral traditions are not strictly historical texts, but living social documents, that if we do not understand their social context and their social content, then we cannot understand our sources.

It would be confusing and unproductive, however, to clutter a historical study with a great tangle of terminology and conceptu-

1. This exists in unpublished form as "Concepts of Sovereignty among the Shambaa and Their Relation to Policial Action" (D.Phil. thesis in Social Anthropology, Oxford University, 1972).

alization borrowed from anthropology. Instead of trying to understand anthropologists in anthropological terms, it is necessary to understand Shambaa in Shambaa terms.

In any attempt to understand a foreign culture, one is dealing fundamentally with a problem of language. Language is one of the most central and pervasive elements of culture. Our very perceptions of the world around us are, as in color perception, shaped by the categories into which we divide the world. Because of the importance of language in organizing experience, it is most convenient and efficient, when trying to understand a completely alien world view, to determine the content of significant linguistic categories. It is for this reason that, in Chapter 1, I shall describe Shambaa ecology by defining the words which differentiate the most significant ecological zones. In other words, there are elements in the environment which the Shambaa could use, but which, in fact, they do not. In order to understand indigenous reasons for indigenous actions it is not necessary to make a comprehensive survey of the environment, but only to examine how the Shambaa themselves organize it—what use they do make of it.

This attempt to adopt a sympathetic point of view may seem strange, at times, in actual practice. If a historical figure dies because a magical spell was cast on him, or if a violent and competitive chief restrains himself because of fear of his father's curse, it is not the historian's place to invent pseudopsychological explanations for the events, but rather to describe them as the actors themselves see them. It seems to me that the African historian must have an absorbing interest in what the subjects of his study thought that they were doing.

There is a point, however, at which it is necessary for the oral historian to part company with his informants, just as there is a point at which the historian reading a series of letters stops trying to understand the author and begins to explain what "really" happened. The tellers of Shambaa traditions are not much interested in economic influences on history, but we are. They are not interested in critical comparison of a whole series of traditions, but we are.

While the reconstruction of both culture and history involves a considerable expenditure of research time for the study of a particular people, it is hoped that the procedure will make a contribution of interest to those concerned with a field wider than Shambaa history. There are three possible kinds of contributions which may result from the method used. First, there is the value of microhistory. If broad surveys are published of the history of East Africa, or all of Africa, which are not based on numerous small scale studies, then the summaries and generalizations are not likely to be valid. The reconstruction of the Shambaa historical record is written also for the people of Shambaai, and for historians in East Africa. Second, some of the events discussed in this work are examples of recurrent processes with a broad geographical distribution. The study of state formation in Chapter 3, for example, has the immediate goal of explaining eighteenth-century Shambaa history. But the solution to the local problem is applicable to a wide range of problems outside Shambaai. It is shown that an individual or a group can use institutions for making transitory alliances in order to change the size of functioning political units. Third, perhaps most important, are questions of the relationship between African thought and African history which arise directly from the use of the combined cultural and historical methods. There is, for example, the question of how to interpret oral traditions which are rich in symbolic content, or how a myth which is told in order to teach lessons about the general character of society can at the same time be a repository of historical knowledge. These questions on the nature of oral sources, which are discussed in Chapter 2, are the proper concern of all African historians.

The oral historian finds that he must do two completely separate kinds of research: he must try to understand the categories into which his informants divide their world, to comprehend their expectations of the behavior of both man and nature, and he must collect evidence from which indirect historical inferences can be made. These separate tasks require separate approaches. The researcher who wants to understand the indigenous world view needs to stay in one village, understand it fully, and never move. The historian who wants to construct a critical history of an area needs to travel widely in order to collect the greatest possible number of variant traditions, and to understand a wide span of local histories.

My own field research, accordingly, was shaped by an attempt to balance the need for an intimate understanding of social life in one place with the need for a broad survey of historical traditions over a wide area. The field work was divided into four unequal periods. First, my wife and I had our basic orientation in Shambaa village life between June 1966 and January 1967, in Mshihwi. The area has virtually no road connections with the outside world, and we lived without a car, traveling by foot. During this early period we learned the Shambaa language by living with our neighbors all day every day. We saw, but did not understand, many rites of passage, sacrificial rites, magical ceremonies, deaths, burials. At the same time I began to record Shambaa relationship terms and behavior. And I made tape recordings and transcriptions of the oral traditions of the chiefdom of Mshihwi (see Chapter 4). From the beginning, and throughout field research, I worked in the Shambaa language. I never used an interpreter or an English-speaking informant. From an early stage my knowledge of Shambaa was better than my knowledge of Swahili. All the historical traditions and all my field notes are in the Shambaa language.

Next came a period, between March and June 1967, devoted to the recording and transcription of historical traditions at the former royal capital of Vugha. These were histories of the origin of the kingdom and of nineteenth-century events, including the local history of the chiefdoms of Vugha, Ubii, and Gare. In July and August 1967 I lived near Bumbuli and continued recording oral traditions.

At each stage of field research I was helped by a Shambaa assistant, who was able to reassure local people about the nature of the research and to warn me when I was offending Shambaa etiquette. In addition, his family became my family, both for the sake of companionship, and so that I could learn to understand the everyday life of one lineage from within.

Between October 1967 and July 1968 I lived at Vugha, where

I made a number of studies of Shambaa religion and society: a village census, a study of sacrifice, of warfare, of traditional justice, of inheritance and land tenure, and many others. At the same time I made trips to historically important areas, to record oral traditions. Some trips lasted a day, others as long as two weeks. During this second year of field research I abandoned the use of the tape recorder and recorded texts verbatim in an improvised shorthand.

Mbugu oral traditions were recorded in June 1968. The Mbugu speak a language which is not understood by Shambaa speakers, and yet their history is an important part of the history of Shambaai. I therefore traveled among the Mbugu with a grown man as my guide, in addition to a young man with a seventh-grade education whose job it was to transcribe and then translate the tape-recorded texts into Shambaa under my supervision. Obviously this is not a satisfactory way to record oral traditions, and the section of Chapter 3 on the Mbugu has perhaps suffered as a consequence.

There were a number of ways in which I found informants. Often someone appeared at the doorstep and asked to be heard. At other times neighbors or friends would mention an elder famous for his knowledge of the past. The chiefs of important territories were obvious people to contact, in addition to court officials. And if the traditions already collected mentioned a certain lineage as important in the history of an area, I would search for a qualified member of that lineage in order to record its tradition. Since I have a strong preference for individual interviews, rather than group conferences, it was my policy to make separate visits to two or three men of the same lineage instead of calling them together to discuss their history. The differences between individual testimonies are often extraordinarily revealing.

Shambaa do not speculate on why they use oral traditions: the utility of oral narratives is obvious in a place where people have not until recently been commonly literate. In our society, important records of social relations are in writing—from constitutions to contracts to birth certificates. But in Shambaai, as in most of Africa, land deeds, religious doctrines, constitutional arrangements, and technical data are committed to memory.

Oral traditions are essentially different, however, from written documents. While the original author of a document must obviously believe that his work is useful, that there is a reason for writing about a historical event, the document itself, once it is written, can survive quite accidentally—by lying in a trunk in someone's attic, for example. The usefulness of an oral tradition, however, must be reaffirmed in every generation. Therefore, the oral traditions which survive are collections of facts or ideas considered important by some social group which persists in time.

In the present study two very different kinds of traditions are used, and they are remembered for different reasons. First, there is the myth of Mbegha, a hero tradition which tells of a hunter who came to Shambaai from the south. The myth tells how Mbegha killed wild pigs in Shambaai, and settled difficult disputes. All the Shambaa welcomed him and spontaneously made him king. The myth, as Chapter 2 will show, is a rich statement in which the Shambaa describe the values of their society, and the fundamental, lasting characteristics of Shambaa political life. By describing the broad characteristics of society in the myth of the founding hero, the Shambaa are saying that society as it is known took its shape in the days of the founding of the kingdom.

The second type of tradition is much less interesting as a cultural document, but at the same time more valuable for the reconstruction of the probable course of historical events. There are a great many separate traditions, each of which is remembered by a particular social group; each tradition recalls those historical events which in some way changed or determined the relative status or rights of the group. The first type of tradition, the Mbegha myth, describes the enduring constitution of the society; the second describes the particular compromises, arrangements, achievements of status, within the broad, permanent framework.

A single historical event can, of course, be remembered not only in mythical or epochal traditions but in traditions concerning the status of particular social groups as well. An event of great enough magnitude to be remembered as epochal changes the relative position of a number of social groups, and therefore creates a number of historical traditions. The creation of the kingdom is remembered not only in myth, but also in a number of separate lineage traditions, because political rights, from the time of the kingdom's origin, were defined in terms of the historical relationship between any subject lineage and the royal lineage. Many traditions recount how various subject lineages received the first king. The expansion of the kingdom, on the other hand, was a gradual process which affected different areas at widely varying times. There is no epochal tradition, and no concentrated body of separate group traditions concerned with a single event. In each chiefdom one can learn about the incorporation of that particular area, but because the process itself was discontinuous and fragmented, the body of traditions is not unified and coherent. One king (Kimweri ye Nyumbai) reigned between the second decade of the nineteenth century and 1862. Many of the alliances he made survived until the end of the colonial era, and most of the colonial chiefs were descendants of the men Kimweri ye Nyumbai had installed. For these reasons there are a great many separate traditions concerning the particular arrangements made during the period. In addition, there is a partly formed epochal tradition which mythologizes Kimweri's actions, even though they took place in the relatively recent past (see Chapter 4).

Two points being made here are fundamental for the understanding of oral sources. One is that epochal traditions, or myths, often attribute major features of the form of society to eras when important changes did in fact take place. This will be demonstrated in detail in Chapters 2 and 3. The second is that the traditions of separate social groups are the records in which the groups remember special rights, whether in land or in political status. The separate group traditions are preserved largely because of their present utility; the rights which are being buttressed, however, were themselves created by historical events. The argument here is that the social utility of traditions, which is often taken as evidence that they cannot be true accounts of historical events, is precisely what gives the traditions their historical value. One has only to ask a few questions. What rights are the traditions meant to legitimate? When were those rights created? How have both the rights and the traditions been passed down from that time to the present?

This relationship between tradition, history, and social structure can be demonstrated most clearly by returning briefly to the traditions about the founding of the kingdom. It was mentioned above that the epochal tradition describes how Mbegha, the hunter-hero, was welcomed by all the Shambaa, who spontaneously made him king. Most of the subject lineages of Shambaai merely repeat the official version, and have genealogies only three generations deep; in other words they do not remember their own histories in detail. The Nango clan, located a considerable distance from the royal capital, managed to retain partial political independence. The independent portion of the Nango clan remembers its traditions of resistance to incorporation, and has a genealogy five generations long. The Nango lineages at the royal capital were absorbed into the kingdom; they have genealogies only three generations long, and they do not remember the tale of their own resistance: they merely recite the standard version of the tradition.

The battles of the early years of the kingdom, in other words, determined that some Nango would be thoroughly integrated into the polity and that others would not. The outcome of these battles also determined that some lineages would remember them and others would not. The resulting variations in the levels of political independence led to variations in the length of genealogies: more independent lineages remembered more of their ancestors because the lineages had greater articulation—greater internal differentiation. It is obvious that the articulated lineages had to carry a heavier load, in terms of the functions of self-government.

Although there is considerable differentiation of genealogical depth, detail, and political importance, virtually all separate group traditions in Shambaai are similar in form and in mode of transmission. They are almost exclusively prose narratives describing some aspect of the life of a lineage. The narratives are passed down within a lineage, usually from father to son, but often from grandfather to grandson, or from father's brother to brother's son. The narratives usually begin with the story of a single migrating ancestor who came to the land where the lineage members now live. Little is told of the former homeland, since the lineage has no important links there to define. The traditions of subject lineages often recall whether any particular ancestor had a special relationship to the institutions of government. Traditions of the royal family and its branches are, as one would expect, more detailed.

Because group traditions are records of special rights, there are strong indirect sanctions which work for their preservation. When the tradition tells how an ancestor came to a given village, the teller knows that rights in land are defined by historical precedent. Someone who could prove that his own lineage arrived first might succeed in taking away the ancestral lands. Lawsuits of this kind are usually settled according to the quality of circumstantial detail. Another use of the tradition of immigration is to record the place of sacrifice which has become associated with the memory of an important ancestor. The teller of the tradition knows that if he does not remember the story properly, or if he forgets the names of ancestors, the living will not be able to sacrifice correctly. The children will begin to sicken and die, the whole lineage will wither away because of the anger of the dead.

When traditions record relationships between social groups, strong sanctions are at work to insure their continuity. People remember who their enemies were in the past, and whether the conflict is likely to arise again. Marriage prohibitions between groups must be remembered, together with the story of how they originated. If the prohibition is forgotten and members of the two groups marry, the union will produce deformed monsters rather than human children. Oral traditions also serve as a record of which groups a man may trust. If there has been a long history of cooperation between two descent groups there is a tendency for trust to continue in present relations. Traditions also record oaths taken in the past. The first king, for example, took an oath that neither he nor his descendants would ever enter the town of Ziai. This means that if one of his descendants did enter Ziai, he would die. Such oaths are commonly part of peace settlements and obviously must be remembered carefully.

The sanctions reinforcing the careful preservation of traditions relating descent groups to the institutions of government are obvious. Chiefship brings wealth, power, privilege. The Shambaa have known four kinds of local government within the last eighty years: precolonial, German, English, independent Tanzanian. Many of them feel that the basis of local government might well change again, and they have no idea what the new basis will be. Some of my informants believed, despite my protests to the contrary, that I was collecting materials for the creation of a new set of local government institutions.

There are strong sanctions also for the preservation of traditions associated with royal ritual. And the ritual itself helps to preserve the authentic tradition. While Shambaa sacrifice is normally made to those recently dead, in the royal sacrifice each dead king must be invoked at the royal grave site. Since there is one grave site for the many kings, someone must remember where in the site each of the kings has been buried, in order to know where to bury the present king when he dies.

In assessing the relative reliability of traditions, a sharp distinction must be made between traditions which have gone unchallenged—which have had only a latent practical function—and traditions which have been the subject of dispute. In unchallenged traditions the tellers remember facts which they assume to be of interest in the history of the status of the group. They may exaggerate the group's importance, or hide shameful facts, but this kind of modification is easily allowed for. In a tradition which has been the subject of dispute, on the other hand, the most subtle elaborations may take place as a response to the arguments of the opposing lineage. In the early 1960s, for example, the traditional king was removed by the newly independent government. Many of the former king's enemies took him to court, saying that the royal headdress was not his personal possession but rather the property of all the people. As a result, there is now an elaborate group of new traditions about the history of the headdress. Fortunately, there remain some descent groups which were not involved in the court case, but which had been important in the earlier history of the regalia.

While the Shambaa oral traditions are rich in content, there are five important limitations on their usefulness. First, there are important subjects that the traditions do not mention. Since many of the traditions define the relationship between a social group and institutions of government, few traditions mention historical events before the founding of the kingdom. Most household articles, agricultural implements, seeds, are possessed by all Shambaa alike. Since oral traditions describe special relationships between particular social groups and cultural items, there are no traditions describing the introduction of the most important techniques and implements of everyday life.

Second, sometimes it is in someone's interest to tell the historian a lie. A descendant of Semboja, the greatest slave dealer in Shambaa history, maintained that Semboja had never sold slaves. Blatant untruth is not an insurmountable problem; before making a critical assessment, the historian compares many traditions told from many points of view. Often when one member of a lineage lies, another member of the same group is willing to tell the truth on a different occasion with little self-consciousness. Indeed, I have seen a man falsify a story only to tell what he believed to be the complete truth several months later.

Third, there is the possibility that a group may determine that its story should not be told. In two years of field research I encountered only one such case. The sons of Kinyashi refused individually and as a group to tell their history. Kinyashi had been king during the German period, and again in the 1920s, at the beginning of indirect rule. Terrified by the difficulty of being a local ruler in a colonial situation, he taught his sons to be secretive, and never to seek the chiefship. And so they refused to report any oral traditions.

Fourth, there is the problem of the corruption of oral traditions because of the existence of written history. A few Shambaa today are literate, and many are partially literate. Two written versions of the history of Shambaai are available to Shambaa. The first is *Habari za Wakilindi*,[2] a lengthy Swahili history of the kingdom. The second is the book popularly called "Wogha na Zumbe,"[3] a collection of stories in Shambaa gathered by Ger-

---

2. Abdallah bin Hemedi l'Ajjemy, *Habari za Wakilindi*, ed. J. W. T. Allen and William Kimweri bin Mbago (Nairobi, 1962). This work was translated and published by the editors as *The Kilindi* (Nairobi, 1963). Cited henceforth as *H.z.W.*

3. Bethel Mission, *Ushimolezi: Schambala Lesebuch* (Vuga, 1930), pp. 176–85.

man missionaries. It contains several historical sketches. The number of men who had read "Wogha na Zumbe" was much greater than those who had read *Habari za Wakilindi;* they prefer it because the historical sketches are brief and in the vernacular. I encountered two men who retracted the account of their traditions after learning that a published history disagreed. Informants freely admitted the influence of the published traditions, since they were proud of literacy. The problem of the corruption of traditions is minimized because men old enough to be lineage elders usually cannot read. But it is clear that traditions are being lost as a result of the existence of written history. Many Shambaa insist that oral narration is obsolete, that writing is much more complete. And the result is that they neither remember traditions nor write them down.

The fifth difficulty in the use of Shambaa traditions is that, just as groups have political interests in remembering history, they sometimes have a stake in forgetting. The Nango, whose history is discussed in Chapter 3, are an example. They have a history of conflict with the rulers, and have long tried to hide it. One Nango at Vugha, the royal capital, said that in his youth the old men would say, "Forget that story; if we tell it our lineage will be destroyed." Yet fragments of this body of traditions can be found all over Shambaai, and the history can be reconstructed.

There are several bodies of documentary evidence, described in detail in the Bibliography, which supplement the oral traditions, supply evidence for chronology, and add information where the oral traditions are weak. The main archival resources for precolonial Shambaa history are the records of the Universities Mission to Central Africa, which are preserved in London and Dar es Salaam. UMCA missionaries were present in Bondei, to the east of Shambaai, continuously from 1875 on. The missionaries themselves became involved in local politics, since there was no dominant European or African power with which to come to an understanding, and their letters during the period before colonial conquest are therefore unusually accurate reflections of the regional political situation.

The archives of the Church Missionary Society in London, of which there are microfilm copies at the University of Wisconsin, preserve the journals and letters of missionaries who have lived and traveled on the East African coast near Shambaai since the 1840s, and who visited the Shambaa royal court in 1848, 1852, and 1853. The documents give reliable evidence on chronology and on the superficially observable state of the kingdom at the time. They also provide evidence for testing and verifying the much richer account of history given in the traditions.

The German records are important for a study of the colonial period, and I have read many of them, although the German period is not the subject of this work. The richest body of materials is in the archives of the Bethel Mission, at Bethel bei Bielefeld in Westphalia. The Bethel collection includes numerous letters and diaries, in addition to books of limited distribution. The materials are most useful for Shambaa history between 1891 and 1914, but there are also descriptions of precolonial Shambaai: conversations with Shambaa church members recorded by the missionaries, who made it a point of pride to learn the Shambaa language well.

The most important German government materials for the Wilhelmstal District (Shambaai) were lost during the period of British rule. When I left Tanzania in August 1968 they had not yet been found, and there is no reason to believe that they have since been recovered. Because of limitations of time, I did not consult the archives of the Roman Catholic missions which founded stations in Shambaai; the most important of these are the records of the Holy Ghost Fathers, in Paris.

In addition to the archival materials, many published works are important in reconstructing Shambaa history. The Swahili *Habari za Wakilindi* is an invaluable history written by an Afro-Arab who was involved in the factional disputes of the 1860s in Shambaai; it is a primary document for the period of the sixties, while for the earlier period it is a summary of oral traditions of unknown provenance. The reports of nineteenth-century travelers, including Oscar Baumann, Richard Burton, John Speke, and H. H. Johnston, also provide useful evidence which supplements the traditions and the archives.

# 1 • THE SHAMBAA BACKGROUND

*An Indigenous Definition of the Ethnic Group*

The Shambaa are agriculturalists of West Usambara, a mountain block which rises out of the plains in the northeastern corner of Tanzania. They speak the Shambaa language, one of the many related Bantu languages. In 1967 they numbered 272,000, most of whom lived within or just beyond the borders of Lushoto Area, which had an area of 1,350 square miles.[1]

By their own definition, the Shambaa are the people who live in Shambaai, a cool high area above 3,400 feet. In Shambaa usage, the addition of the final *i* creates the locative form. Thus the Shambaa are the people; Shambaai is their home. The term "Shambaai" is used as the name of the particular mountain block in which the Shambaa live, but it is also an indigenous category for understanding the natural environment. Shambaai is a highland zone with identifiable plants and climate. A number of superficial characteristics of the zone are immediately apparent, even to the casual observer. The mountain rainfall is more abundant than that of the surrounding plains; banana

1. The United Republic of Tanzania, Central Statistical Bureau, Ministry of Economic Affairs and Development Planning, *1967 Population Census,* 5 vols. (Dar es Salaam, 1969–71), 3: 345; 1: 332.

plants, important to the Shambaa economy, grow well; the wild vegetation is green and lush.

Any superficial description of the few most prominent crops of Shambaai conveys, however, a misleading view of the indigenous economy. The Shambaa cultivate dozens of food crops, each of which is specially adapted, in some way, to the mountain environment, and each of which relates to the others as merely one of a total community of crops. A number of varieties of tubers, several kinds of medicinal plants, tobacco, and beans are all interspersed in the shade of banana plants in a typical Shambaa garden.

The complexity of the adaptation of the Shambaa to their own particular physical environment is barely touched by even a complete description of all crops. There are hundreds of wild plants of the forests and meadows which are important to the economy: some for poisons, others for string, still others for medicine, for toothbrushes, for pipe stems. Shambaa often say that their language is spoken only by residents of their special highland zone, and although this is not strictly so, the language itself is a major tool for adaptation there, since it is enormously rich in terms for the classification of the flora and fauna of Shambaai.

The identification of an ethnic group with a narrowly defined botanical environment might seem strange to the modern westerner. This is because western agriculture, as a result of the market economy and modern communications, is a good deal simpler than traditional African agriculture. The American farmer grows only the crops that are most profitable, and buys everything else that he needs. The precolonial African farmer, however, had to grow or make virtually all the products needed to sustain life. The American farmer, while he is not happy in a year of drought or of pests, can support his family in a bad year by borrowing against the profits of future years. The important thing is to maximize the profits of good years. Many traditional African farmers died in a bad year.

For an understanding of why the Shambaa are associated with a limited belt of mountain environment, an appreciation of the vulnerability of the African farmer in a year of famine is central.

Since communications and markets were relatively poorly developed, the farmer had to sow a great variety of crops with a great variety of characteristics, in order to survive no matter what the climatic variations: so that he would not be, in effect, wiped out. By taking a single ecological zone, understanding its complexity with a thoroughness incomprehensible to even a rural westerner, developing a rich and subtle language with a profusion of terms for the understanding of local ecology, planting dozens of crops to which the environment was peculiarly suited, the farmer sought to defeat famine, to cheat death.

Modern western man thrives by developing skills which are, to the greatest extent possible, transferable: the botanist does not study a forest, he studies forests; the engineer learns formulae which can be applied to problems not yet imagined. But the precolonial East African was best able to survive if he learned skills which were local in their application. It is for this reason that one commonly finds ethnic groups, with their own cultures (or bodies of skills), associated with narrowly defined environmental zones. The Taveta, for example, were the people who adapted themselves to life at the side of one river. The Dabida (highlands Taita) and the Asu (Pare) are ethnic groups which live in an environment like that of Shambaai. The Ruvu were a people, related to the Zigula, who developed a body of skills in order to cope with the peculiar problems of river fishing.

Since Shambaai is at once an ecological zone and a cultural district, outsiders are those with strange economic practices as well as strange mores. This is quite different from the ethnocentrism of industrial society. The indigenous distinction, which separates native-language speakers from foreign-language speakers, and those who practice local farming techniques from alien farmers, is one between *nyika* and *shambaai,* the plains and the mountains. I was described, since I was a white foreigner, as a person of the plains. *Shambaai* is preferable to *nyika* in every way. It is healthier, less dangerous, and more fertile.

People knew that since there were no mosquitoes in the mountains, there was no malaria. And so, even before Koch established the link between malaria and mosquitoes, the Shambaa were hesitant to sleep even for one night in the plains, for fear of returning with a fever. *Mbu,* the word for mosquito, is also the word for a fever with chills.[2]

*Nyika* is thought to be barren. A Shambaa song describes the difficulty of life on the plains:

> Shi ya nyika ni nkazu'e,
> Nadika nyamangwa na makonge.
>
> I hunt
> in the waterless *nyika,*
> and cook game
> in juice wrung from wild sisal leaves.

Bananas, traditionally the most important food plant, grow well in *shambaai* and less well in *nyika. Nyika* is dangerous, also; there are wild animals and foreigners. There is a proverb: *Muita nyika, mwauya nyosheni*—"When you go to *nyika,* you must all return together."

While the Shambaa describe the difference between the mountains and the plains in terms which have great emotive force, they are capable of defining the distinction with scientific precision. The wild plant life of *shambaai* is different from that of *nyika.* The farmer, by examining the vegetation of a potential agricultural site, can easily determine whether the farm will support plains agriculture or that of the mountains.

The indigenous definition of the ethnic group is, then, remarkably precise: the Shambaa are people who live in a particular botanical environment. The escarpment of Shambaai rises dramatically from the plains to an altitude of about 4,000 feet, and the area in which the vegetation is purely that of *shambaai* is above 3,400 feet. Pure *nyika* vegetation is found below 2,150 feet. There is a zone between pure *nyika* and pure *shambaai* where the two kinds of vegetation are mixed.[3] In an attempt to define the ethnic unity of the Shambaa with some elegance, one is led,

---

2. This is not just modern usage; see F. LangHeinrich, *Schambala-Wörterbuch,* Abhandlungen des Hamburgischen Kolonialinstituts, vol. 43 (Hamburg, 1921), p. 259.

3. The altitudes given here are approximations, although the altimeter was set at a fixed known altitude when I surveyed the plant life which distinguishes the zones.

finally, to lists of plants; these are the data one finds at the confluence of folk sociology and folk botany:[4]

## Some Plants Characteristic of Shambaai

*Mvumo: Ficus leprieurii* Miq., *F. natalensis* Hochst., *F. thonningii* Bl. (Morac.), Epiphytic fig

*Msasa: Ficus exasperata* Vahl (Morac.), *Acacia mellifera* Benth., *A. goetzii* Harms. subsp. *goetzei* (Mim.)

*Uwenge: Senecio deltoideus* Less. (Comp.)

*Mkongodeka: Grewia forbesii* Harv. ex Mast., *G. truncata* Mast. (Til.)

*Mtonto: Cylicomorpha parviflora* Urb. (Caric.)

*Fuiza: Melothria microsperma* (Hook. f.) Cogn., *M. punctata* (Thunb.) Cogn., *M. tomentosa* Cogn. (Cucurb.)

*Mkulo: Antiaris usambarensis* Engl. (Morac.)

*Mnkwanga: Dialopsis africana* Radlk. (Sapin.)

*Mshihwi: Syzygium cordatum* Hochst., *S. guineense* (Willd.) DC., *S. sclerophylus* Brenan (Myrt.)

*Ntughutu: Veronia subuligera* O. Hoffm. (Comp.)

*Fyofyo: Leonotis mollissima* Guerke (Lab.)

*Mntindi: Cussonia arborea* Hochst. ex A. Rich., *C. spicata* Thunb., *C. Zimmermannii* Harms. (Aral.)

## Some Plants Characteristic of Nyika

*Mfune: Sterculia appendiculata* K. Schum. (Sterc.)

*Mnama: Combretum gueinzii* Sond. subsp. *splendens* Exell., *C. nyikae* Engl. (Combr.)

*Muoza: Sterculia leguminosacea* K. Schum. & Engl., *S. rhynchocarpa* K. Schum., *S. setigera Del.* (Sterc.)

*Mkoma hoya: Canthium rubrocostatum Robyns* (Rub.), *Pygeum africanum* Hook. f. (Ros.)

*Mzue: Chlorophora excelsa* Benth. & Hook. f. (Morac.)

*Mnkande: Stereosperum kunthianum* Cham. (Bign.)

*Mgunga: Acacia polyacantha* Willd. subsp. *campylacantha* (Hochst. ex A. Rich.) Brenan (Mim.)

---

4. Historical traditions: Zekifisha (Hassani Shechonge), 8 May 1968. The botanical equivalents may be found in G. R. Williams Sangai, *Dictionary of Native Plant Names in the Bondei, Shambaa and Zigua Languages with Their English and Botanical Equivalents* (Nairobi, 1963).

The most interesting group of plants are species each of which has a pair of varieties: one for *shambaai* and one for *nyika*. The pairs usually have some visible similarity to one another. Thus the *mshai* and the *mshai mamba,* one such pair, have the same leaf formation, although the leaves of the *mshai* are larger. The *mkuyu* and *mkuyu wa nyika* do not look alike, but each, when cut, exudes a milky substance.

### Paired Plants

| *Nyika* | *Shambaai* |
|---|---|
| *Mshai mamba: Albizia adianthifolia* (Schum.) W. F. Wright, *A. glaberrima* (Schum. & Thonn.) Benth. var. *glabrescens* (oliv.) Brenan (Mim.) | *Mshai: Albizia adianthifolia* (Schum.) W. F. Wright, *A. schimperiana* Oliv. var. *schimperiana* (Mim.) |
| *Mkuyu wa nyika* (or *mkuyu kighaza*): *Ficus gnaphalocarpa* (Miq.) A. Rich. (Morac.) | *Mkuyu: Ficus capensis* Thunb., *F. mucosa* Welw., *F. sycomorus* L., *F. vallis-choudae* Del. (Morac.) |
| *Muungu magoma: Erythrina abyssinica* Lam. (Papil.) | *Muungu* (or *Mulungu*): *Crotonogynopsis usambarica* Pax (Euph.), *Erythrina abyssinica* Lam. (Papil.) |
| *Mtua nyika: ?* | *Mtua: Solanum campylacanthum* Hochst., *S. incanum* L., *S. obliquum* Damm. (Sol.) |

### The Distribution of Shambaa Population

While the Shambaa speak of *nyika* in terms of danger, disease, death, they cannot do without it. Shambaa population is concentrated in those portions of the mountains which are easily reached from *nyika*. If the mountain block of Shambaai is seen as two concentric circles, only the outer circle is the land of the Shambaa. The inner circle, the bull's-eye, is occupied by the semipastoral Mbugu, who have a distinct language and culture.

The Shambaa occupation of the top of the escarpment has been stable over a long period of time. There is clear evidence, from the traditions of the founding of the Shambaa kingdom, that the Shambaa live today where they lived in the eighteenth century (see Chapter 3). It is probable that the present occupation pattern had existed for hundreds of years before that, for the earliest iron age remains discovered so far have been located around the edges of Shambaai.[5]

The pattern in which the important population centers were all in Shambaai, but near *nyika,* led to a peculiar distribution of the chiefdoms within the precolonial kingdom. The political unit did not occupy a single, compact, contiguous territory. There were, rather, two chains of chiefdoms. One chain, the chiefdoms of Mlalo, Mlola, and Mtae, was strung out along the northern rim of Shambaai. In the south, the chiefdoms of Vugha, Ubii, and Mlungui all face out over the plains. The chiefdom of Bumbuli, in the east, appears to be an anomaly, for the plains are distant. But there is a mountainous area within the territory of Bumbuli which is, in ecological terms, *nyika.*

The Shambaa explain their preference for living near *nyika* by pointing out the importance of the plains for their economy, but it is difficult for the historian to project economic patterns back into the distant past. These days men like to farm in Shambaai but leave their livestock in *nyika,* in the care of close relatives or blood partners. Farmers, in the precolonial period, supplemented the family diet with game from the plains. Also, because of variations in the seasonal rainfall patterns and in the relative warmth of the two zones, crop failures affect the mountains and plains at different times and in different ways. A man who has farms at his disposal in both zones has extra insurance in time of famine, for famines are often local. Since famines came, in the precolonial period, at least once every fifteen years, and great numbers died of starvation, the man who could get food from either zone actually increased the chances of survival for himself and his children.

Some crops are grown only in Shambaai, others only in *nyika,* and some, the most important of which is maize, are grown at different times and with differing growth patterns in both zones.

5. R. C. Soper, "Iron Age Sites in North-Eastern Tanzania," *Azania* 2 (1967): 19–36.

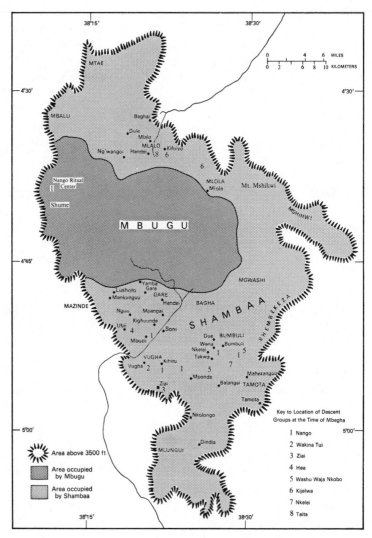

University of Wisconsin Cartographic Lab

Map 1. Shambaai

Maize was grown widely by the middle of the nineteenth century, and possibly much earlier.[6] This crop ripens very rapidly in the plains, but takes weeks longer to mature in the cool mountains. To grow best it needs a great deal of rain when planted, and dry weather after it is fully grown, when drying in the fields. If maize is planted at the same time in both *nyika* and Shambaai, and the rainy season is brief but intense, the plains crop might be excellent, since the plant grows rapidly and needs only a relatively short rainy stretch, but the mountain crop would fail. If the rains go on for a long time, the mountain maize might, because of its long growing period, still get enough sun at drying time, when the plains crop will have already rotted.

In addition, the three rainy seasons of the year differ in duration and intensity, and each rainy season is best for maize growing in a different zone. Besides the zones of Shambaai and *nyika,* there is a third, high in Shambaai, which has the same natural vegetation as the mountain zone, but which has a slightly different growing season. There are three zones for planting maize, and three planting seasons. The relations between zones and seasons vary from place to place in Shambaai. The following relations, which were observed at Vugha, are typical for much of southern Shambaai.[7]

|  | *Ng'waka*<br>March–May | *Vui*<br>Nov.–Dec. | *Muati*<br>August |
|---|---|---|---|
| *Nyika* | Preferred | Possible | Impossible |
| Shambaai | Possible | Preferred | Impossible |
| High Shambaai | Impossible | Possible | Preferred |

In order to live comfortably, a person must plant in more than one season. If a man plants a plot of maize in Shambaai in November, he does not harvest until May or June.[8] The plot is

6. For evidence that maize was being grown in the nineteenth century, see Feierman, "Concepts of Sovereignty," p. 40.

7. Historical traditions: Shechonge Kishasha, 28 June 1968.

8. Manfred Attems, *Bauernbetriebe in tropischen Höhenlagen Ostafrikas,* IFO Institut für Wirtschaftsforschung: Afrika Studien, no. 25 (Munich, 1967), p. 61.

therefore not yet available for sowing during the March rains. If he relied on that one plot, or one group of plots farmed at a single time, he would not have maize much of the year, since methods of storage among the Shambaa are not adequate. If maize is planted in both *nyika* and Shambaai during *ng'waka,* it will be harvested in July in the plains, and in September or October in the mountains. The most skillful farmers exploit these variations, and many others, so that they have both food and farm work all year.

Maize is not the only crop grown by the Shambaa in *nyika.* Cassava is grown in the plains, and because of its hardiness it is very important for famine relief. The area planted with cassava has been expanding rapidly. Pigeon peas and beans are also important plains crops.

The cultivation of maize in both Shambaai and *nyika,* and the importance of the cassava, pigeon peas, and beans of the plains, in addition to the bananas and yams of the mountains, determine the distribution of population in the highlands. All the traditional areas of Shambaa population are, as we have seen, at the edges of the massif: in Shambaai, yet near enough to *nyika* to farm there.

It is difficult, however, to understand the relationship between agricultural practices and population patterns in the distant past, for the population pattern is probably of greater antiquity than the cultivation of maize, and it is almost certainly older than the cultivation of cassava. According to the descriptions of crops in the written documents of the nineteenth century, sorghum, which is no longer commonly planted, was then an important *nyika* crop, along with maize.[9] It is possible that before maize and cassava were ever brought to East Africa from the Americas, the Shambaa lived near *nyika* in order to plant older Afri-

---

9. *H.z.W,* Sura 73; Oscar Baumann, *In Deutsch-Ostafrika während des Aufstandes* (Vienna and Olmütz, 1890), p. 166; Edward Steere, *Collections for a Handbook of the Shambala Language* (Zanzibar, 1867), p. 15; Richard F. Burton and J. H. Speke, "A Coasting Voyage from Mombasa to the Pangani River; Visit to Sultan Kimwere; and Progress of the Expedition into the Interior," *Journal of the Royal Geographical Society* 28 (1858): 188–226, see esp. p. 216.

can crops, including sorghum, pigeon peas, and beans. Maize
gradually took the place of sorghum, which it has now sup-
planted. The point here is that the central feature of the Shambaa agricultural system has remained constant over centuries:
the Shambaa have always made use of local variations in climate
in order to be certain of surviving localized crop failures. While
the central organizing principle has remained constant, the details of implementation have varied over time. Maize replaced
sorghum as a major grain crop. Cassava has become increasingly
important in the Shambaa diet. But now, as before, each Shambaa cultivator consumes the product of dispersed garden plots.

Changes in the crops of Shambaai and *nyika,* resulting largely
from the introduction of exotic crops, have been accompanied
by changes in the locations of the homes of people working in
lowland gardens, as a result of changing political conditions. It is
clear that in the second half of the nineteenth century, a time of
frequent warfare, the only Shambaa who lived in the plains occupied large fortified villages. At that time many Shambaa
walked from their homes in Shambaai to their farms in *nyika.*
Today, and possibly also before the nineteenth century, some
Shambaa live in *nyika* but retain strong ties with villagers in
Shambaai.

In order to confirm the relationship between the distribution
of Shambaa population around the edges of the massif and the
need to have access to farms in *nyika,* I conducted a survey
among the men of a small area near the town of Vugha, which is
near Shambaai but overlooks *nyika.* All of these men could easily choose to farm in *nyika,* since farm land near the plains is
freely available to anyone who clears it. I questioned 135 men,
of whom 63 were cultivating farms in *nyika* at that time. Most of
the 72 who did not have farms in *nyika* had close patrilineal relatives or blood partners who were farming in *nyika.* These relatives or allies would have been obligated to help in a partial famine, of the kind which affects Shambaai but not *nyika.* Of the 72
men, only 18 had neither close relatives nor blood partners
farming in *nyika.* Thirty-six had close relatives but no blood
partners farming in *nyika.* Seventeen had both blood partners
and close relatives. One had a blood partner but no relatives. I

questioned a much smaller group of men (15) on whether they had high Shambaai farms, and all did.

In other words, while the ideal picture of society is composed of all Shambaa living only in Shambaai, in actual fact social ties between Shambaai and *nyika* are quite intense. I knew a man living in *nyika* who had two grown sons; he sent one to farm in Shambaai, and the other to farm in a *nyika* swamp area with an even different set of agricultural characteristics. The distribution of Shambaa population around the outer edge of the massif is a result, and a reflection, of the intensity of social ties between ecological zones.

But even with this regularity established, the locational determinants of the historical chiefdoms have not been exhausted. All of Shambaai is ringed by *nyika,* and one would expect the chiefdoms to be linked in a single circle, but there are actually two chains of chiefdoms, a northern and a southern chain. There were two barriers which broke the spatial continuity of political relations. The western barrier, Shume, had no concentration of Shambaa population because the rains which watered the rest of the mountain area did not fall there. *Ng'waka* (the rains of March to May) and *muati* (August rains) are both brought by the trade winds from the southeast, which blow against the mountains, rise, cool, and deposit their moisture. Most of this rain falls in the southeastern part of the mountains. As the wind passes to the northwest there is less moisture left. The northern rim of the mountains gets much of its rain during *vui* (October to December), from the trade wind which comes out of the northeast. Shume, on the western side of the mountains, gets little rain from either direction. It cannot support Shambaa farming and is therefore part of Mbuguland.[10]

The second barrier between north and south is Mshihwi, in the northeast corner of Shambaai. The soil is rocky: many of the

10. Attems, *Bauernbetriebe,* pp. 20–23, 148. One can see the pattern clearly from the rainfall figures given by Attems. Mombo, in the plains on the southern side of the mountains, has an average annual rainfall of 628 mm. Balangai, at the southeastern tip of the mountains, at 4,600 feet, has 1,718 mm. Malindi shares Shume's climate. Even though the altitude is 5,900 feet, it gets only 666 mm.

mountains are collections of boulders with outcrops of vegetation. Because of its barrenness, Mshihwi is much more sparsely populated than the other parts of Shambaai. Because of its difficult rock-strewn terrain, Mshihwi was easily defended. Early in the history of the kingdom the losers in a succession dispute fled there and defended it against the repeated attacks of the established king. The fugitives founded their own state, a pocket kingdom which survived until modern times.

The borders of the chiefdoms at the edges of Shambaai were stable over long periods of time. Each chiefdom had a permanent town as its capital, as well as a number of permanent villages. A great many Shambaa villages have existed in their present locations for the past hundred to two hundred years, perhaps longer.[11] The spatial stability of the political units, the permanence of the royal towns and commoners' villages, were all related to the cultivation of dispersed garden plots, as described above.

In many African societies, a village moves each time the soil near it is exhausted. The Shambaa villages were permanent because they were residences, and not the actual locations of most economic activities. Each day a village's members would go out in all directions—to a chief's capital or to *nyika,* to a garden high in Shambaai or to another at the same altitude as the village itself. Most daily activities could be carried out within a radius of about five miles: the distance from the center of a typical chiefdom to its borders. I suspect that each chiefdom was a living economic entity tied together by the daily movements of the people who lived in it. Even today, one gets the impression that population is much denser near the center of the old chiefdoms than it is around the edges. This view of the chiefdom as the territory within which individuals moved each day, starting from their villages in the morning and returning in the evening, would explain why the borders of the chiefdoms ran down into *nyika* even when there were no villages there.

Each village and town was surrounded by banana gardens, so that there was a supply of food immediately at hand for the days

11. Feierman, "Concepts of Sovereignty," pp. 37–38.

when people did not go out to their distant gardens.[12] Bananas
were the most important staple at the chiefdom capitals, where
great numbers of people gathered, and where relatively unproductive political specialists spent much of their time.

In a state populated by subsistence farmers there are few
ways to support a town of any considerable size. One is to build
the town on a trade route, so that it can live off profits, commis-
sions, or tolls. Another is to move the town frequently, relying
substantially on raiding. A third is to develop an oasis town—a
town placed in a zone so rich it can support a heavy population,
and whose crops exhaust the soil so little that the population can
be permanent. Shambaa towns were modified oasis towns. They
relied on banana groves which, in the soil and climate conditions
of Shambaai, require little care, and are virtually permanent. In
addition, all the men of the towns had dispersed gardens.

When the explorer Richard Burton visited the kingdom's capital at Vugha in 1857 it had, according to his estimate, 500
houses.[13] The town was supported by banana groves which even
today encircle its site. The groves were public property (*kitaa*),
and a portion of banana garden was given to each new immi-
grant, since the king made it a point of pride to have as great a
town as possible.

The spatial stability of political units was thus related to the
great investment, in terms of labor, required to develop a full set
of dispersed gardens, producing in all the seasons, and the great
labor investment represented by a producing banana grove.
Commoners were less likely to move away from an unpopular
chief than were subjects in places like Unyamwezi where shifting
cultivation was practiced. Borders of chiefdoms were permanent
and precise. A chiefdom changed in importance not by expand-

12. I am following the convention of William Allan, who, in *The African Husbandman* (Edinburgh and London, 1965), p. 161, uses the term
*banana* for both the plantain, which is usually eaten cooked, and for the
table fruit. In fact, it is difficult to distinguish clearly between plantains
and bananas in Africa.

13. Richard F. Burton, *Zanzibar: City, Island, and Coast,* 2 vols. (London, 1872), 2:229.

ing or contracting; it changed with the relative authority of its
chief over other chiefs.

### Descent, Alliance, and Territorial Groupings

Just as the principle for the identification of the community of
Shambaa was a botanical one, the principle for the definition of
social groups within the larger community was one of descent.[14]
The constituent parts of the kingdom, the actors who together
made up the collectivity, were not individuals; they were patrilineal descent groups. In addition, the king and his chiefs were
all members of a single descent group, the Kilindi, and the political relations among them were acted out in a descent idiom, as
will be shown throughout the historical narrative. In other
words, the kingdom can be seen as a territory with a large number of commoner descent groups, over which there was a single
governing descent group.

The Shambaa justification of the most central rules governing
relations in ordinary descent groups is that they bring fertility,
and that they enable individuals to survive as members of the
group. The survival and increase of the group was, and is, the
central good. Each man sought to marry as many wives as he
could support, to beget as many children as possible, and to
keep his dependents secure from illness, enemies, hunger. In order to do this, a man had to have knowledge not only of agriculture, but also of the mystical forces which were thought to bring
life or death. He also needed to have adequate amounts of property, mainly livestock and gardens, to support his dependents.

Everything necessary for survival, including material possessions and skills, was passed on through lines of descent. Every
man was taught skills and given property by his father, and was
expected to pass these on to his sons. Each man could add to the
property his father had given him, but the property a man could
acquire through years of effort was small compared with the size

14. The description of descent and alliance is a summary of detailed
description and evidence given in Feierman, "Concepts of Sovereignty,"
Chapters 2, 3, and 4.

of a typical inheritance. In addition, fathers taught sons about the soils and rainfall of Shambaai and *nyika,* about medicinal plants and spells, about the rites without which it was thought men would die. Smiths taught their sons the heritage of smithing. Medicine men passed on their charms. Kilindi fathers taught their sons to govern. When talking about technology, most Shambaa speak not of new and old things, but of the patrimony of different peoples. I was told that cars were the patrimony (*mila* or *fika*) of the British, but not of the Germans, because there were no cars in Shambaai before the British took over Tanganyika during World War I.

Because a son received essential skills and property from his father, the son's prosperity, and the wellbeing of the son's wives and children, depended on the father's goodwill. The father's curse (*ute*) was dreaded, for it was believed that if a father cursed his child, the child (who might be a grown man at the time of the curse) would wander about Shambaai, behaving like a harmless fool, and would lose all that he had. Even today, there are individuals who wander through the mountain villages trailing vines and babbling harmlessly, whose condition is attributed to a father's curse. There was a sense in which the father retained control over all he had given, even after his death. If the ghost of the father was angered by his son's behavior, the ghost could reclaim the dependents who were really his own. A group of brothers and half brothers who were sons of a single father were therefore thought to share a common fate, for they were all dependent on their father, both when he was alive, and once he had become an ancestral ghost. Daughters too were dependent on the goodwill of their father, but because property and status were transmitted through the male line, the ghost's influence over a daughter's descendants ceased to exist after the daughter's death. The ghost's influence over descendants through male links continued for as long as the ghost's name was remembered, after which the dead man's spirit joined a collectively influential body of ancestors.

There are, then, a few simple ideas which help to make Shambaa descent organization comprehensible. First, many forms of cultural knowledge and of property were seen as parts of a patrimony. Second, a father had great authority during his lifetime, and considerable influence after his death. Third, members of a group which was descended from a single man through male links had a sense that they shared a common fate.

A wide variety of institutional forms were based on these ideas. Different aspects of shared descent were emphasized in groups of different sizes, which were, in other words, varving numbers of generations from their common ancestor. The differentiation of institutional forms depended also on the rules concerning the inheritance of several forms of property. If one takes only livestock as an example, it is possible to see that a man's sons, who had just inherited his livestock, would have had a stronger sense that they must plan together for their joint prosperity, than the man's great-grandsons by different fathers two generations later, to whom the idea that they shared the wealth of a single ancestor was somewhat less concrete and immediate.

It is possible to understand the characteristics of Shambaa descent groups by moving from the smallest and most intimate unit to the largest, and by defining forms of property as well as the rules concerning property at each level. The first step in the distribution of a man's property to his offspring took place before they were even born, for a man allocated gardens to each wife as he married. Each wife worked her own gardens in order to provide herself and her children with food. As her children grew up they would help her to work her gardens, which her sons would ultimately inherit. When each son married his first wife, he would be given an additional garden by his father. Although land is scarce today, it was possible for a young man in the precolonial period to acquire additional gardens simply by clearing the forest. Just as a commoner father gave each wife a garden for the support of her children, the king gave each wife a chiefdom for her children to govern.

While a commoner's wives did most of the repetitive daily subsistence farming, the husband worked to increase his *mai* (or *mali*), which means wealth, in its meaning, as the *Shorter Oxford Dictionary* gives it, as "a collective term for those things the abundant possession of which constitutes riches." Livestock—goats, cattle, and some sheep—were the characteristic form in which wealth was kept. Other goods such as ivory, or, in the late nineteenth century, quantities of trade cloth, were counted as wealth, and could readily be exchanged for livestock. There were a number of ways in which a man could increase his wealth. Livestock were acquired by natural increase of existing stock, and as bridewealth. In addition, Shambaa specialists were usually paid in livestock, or they converted their earnings to livestock. Thus the blacksmith who reduced iron, or who worked iron he bought from the Pare to the west, the medical specialist, the hunter (who sold the meat of each kill), the proficient warrior (who was rewarded with livestock), were likely to be wealthier than their neighbors. Other men could acquire livestock by selling excess staple in a good year, or more frequently by raising and selling tobacco, for Shambaa tobacco was purchased over a wide area of what is today Tanzania, as well as Kenya.

Wealth, as the characteristic masculine form of property, was essential for the survival and increase of the descent group. Bridewealth was given in exchange for wives, without whom the lineage could not increase. Normally, a father paid the bridewealth for the first wife of each son. In addition, the father needed to provide wealth, perhaps a goat or a chicken, as a payment to the medicine man when any of his wives or children became ill. There is a proverb, *Vimba vingi ni vya ushoi*—"Many corpses are the result of not having livestock." In times of localized famine, a man could exchange wealth for quantities of staple from unaffected areas, and thus ensure the survival of his dependents. When an individual committed a breach of law which harmed someone of another lineage, the most common judgement, in the nineteenth century, was that the violator should make a payment of wealth as an indemnity to the injured person or his lineage. If the violator and his relatives were not able to provide the wealth, the chief paid and some member was detached from the lineage and taken to work and live at the chief's court.

A man's wealth was distributed to his children only after his death. For this reason, the unit which was expected to purchase food in time of famine, and to pay indemnities, included all the descendants through male links of any man whose father was not alive. In other words, if there was a very old man with sons and grandsons who were adults, the old man kept the wealth for the entire group, and therefore the group as a whole was required to make payments for the security of any member.

After the old man died, his sons became heads of indemnity-paying units, for the wealth was divided among them. The sons could decide, however, that they had greater security as members of the larger unit which had existed until their father's death. In this case they set aside a portion of their father's wealth as a fund to meet the sorts of emergencies for which they had relied on their father. The sons of the senior wife were expected to provide leadership for the group of half brothers. They were often the largest group of full brothers, in which case they had a strong incentive to provide responsible and just leadership, for they would have the smallest share of the inheritance if it was divided. Property was given in equal amounts to each of the dead man's wives, for her sons. In normal circumstances the few sons of the most junior wife gained the most from dividing the wealth, and the sons of the most prolific wife had the greatest interest in maintaining a common fund. When the process went one step further, and the sons began to die, it was impossible for the grandsons of the original holder of the wealth to leave their inheritance in the common fund. The Shambaa speak of "the unallocated wealth of father" (*kifu cha tate*), but never of "the unallocated wealth of grandfather" (*kifu cha baba*).

One may well ask why descent groups existed which were larger than the group of brothers who were capable of establishing a fund of unallocated wealth. There are two parts to the answer. First, the larger group could, if the quality of their relations was sufficiently good, decide to contribute toward one another's indemnities, and toward the bridewealth payments for one another's first wives, even though there was no formal requirement that they do so. Second, the system of the transfer of wealth and gardens outlined above worked well so long as old men died after their sons had reached maturity. If a man died when his children were young, there had to be some way of ensuring that they would be cared for, and that their inheritance would be preserved for them. It was especially important that

the group of guardians be wider than the brothers and half
brothers of the dead man, for it was the interests of the younger
brothers that had to be protected from the powerful and poten-
tially greedy older ones.

The full lineage therefore included several sibling groups. The
unity of the lineage was seen as the result of the common descent of all the sibling groups from a more distant ancestor. The
lineage was called together after the death of any adult member,
with special importance being attached to the ceremonies after
the death of a grown man. It supervised the inheritance of
wealth and farms, and it chose the individual who inherited the
dead man's widow and personal effects. This heir had to be a
member of the dead man's own generation within the lineage.

The men who gathered at the mourning ceremonies sent messengers to diviners to inquire about the cause of death, and held
conferences to discuss the results. Many of the possible causes of
death were results of disturbances in the realm of moral relations in the lineage or in the village. Among the common causes
of death were sorcery and magical suicide. It was thought that
others in the lineage would die until the cause of death had been
found and "cooled." The personal effects of the dead man were
thought to carry with them something of the moral personality
of the man who had owned them. For this reason, the lineage
member who inherited the personal effects along with the widow
was thought to be in the greatest danger. The widow inheritor
also acquired special authority over the children of the dead
man. I knew sons who were very deeply impressed by the fact
that they saw in dreams the ghost of their father wearing the
same clothing which their mother's inheritor wore in the daytime.

There are several important points which have been made and
conclusions which can be drawn. A living father and his sons
shared responsibility for indemnities, and this means of course
that they had relations as a group, and not as individuals, with
their chief. The active political unit could be expanded when a
set of half brothers decided to keep a fund of unallocated
wealth. The lineage at its largest extent had a sense of shared
mystical fate, and it acted in the mourning ceremonies to ensure
the survival of each small reproductive unit. There was a strong

sense of the equality of members of a single generation who could, after all, inherit one another's wives and children. And there was a corresponding sense that the respect due to one's father should be extended to the other members of his generation, who were all potential heirs to one's mother.

The qualities of these relations within a generation and between generations had important consequences for the character of royal rule. When the king was the father of his chiefs, his authority as father over sons reinforced the authority associated with his office, and the kingdom was characterized by tight centralization. When the chiefs were half brothers of the king, however, the habitual equality between men at one generation led to chiefly insubordination. Thus the power relations within the kingdom were dependent on the descent relations of those who governed, rather than on the expansion or contraction of territorial units.

There were groups in Shambaai which were larger than the full lineage, and which were based on putative descent rather than fully traceable links of relationship. These groups can be called clans. It is impossible to give a simple brief sketch of their characteristics, however, because of the variety of clan forms. It appears that clanship was one of the bases of political organization in Shambaai before the creation of the kingdom in the eighteenth century. There are divergent forms of organization because a homogeneous Shambaa people as we know it today did not exist at that time. Kingship replaced clanship as the basis of political organization, and so the clans which remain have not evolved new structures to face new challenges over the past two hundred years. The nature of the process by which the clans were dominated will be discussed in Chapters 3 and 4.

A typical Shambaa village was (and is) spread along the crest of a ridge, with banana gardens running downhill from the homesteads. Strangers were welcome to join the village, extend it a bit farther along the ridge, and buy or start banana gardens beneath their piece of the village. Shambaa enjoy living in large villages where people of several lineages reside together. The great majority of villages today have people living side by side who, when they moved together, had been strangers. There is no reason to think that these composite villages are twentieth-century innovations. Within the villages, and stretching beyond them, there are networks of marriage relations, relations through women (that is nonlineal relations, for example, father's sister's son), and relations through the blood pact which overlap in a complex way to produce tightly woven communities rather than loose collections of separate lineages.

It is a remarkable feature of the villages and neighborhoods that no one is completely conscious of the way in which networks are formed. Individuals choose mates and blood partners in what seems to them a reasonable and attractive manner, and a regular pattern of relationship springs up as a result of the individual choices. Fathers do not dictate the choice of marriage partners to their sons, who marry out of what they describe as feelings of personal affection, yet significant alliances between lineages grow up as a result of the choices by the young people.

The most important rules are negative rather than positive: proscriptions rather than prescriptions. One is told whom one should not marry, and individual choice, enlightened by a perception of self-interest, takes care of the rest. It is wrong to marry members of one's own lineage, even when they are distant relations. It is unwise to marry outside one's own neighborhood; in precolonial times it was even more strongly disapproved than it is today. Marriage to a cousin, even one outside the lineage, such as a mother's brother's daughter or a father's sister's daughter, is strongly disapproved. The individual young man is put into the position of choosing a wife from within a circumscribed area while being careful not to marry someone who is already a kinswoman.

There are some regularities of choice which result from the perceptions of young men about their own self-interest. There are a number of advantages to choosing a wife whose home is not distant, and whose close lineal relatives already have good relations with the young man's own relatives. If the girl's father sees the marriage as an attractive one from his own point of view, he is unlikely to make great difficulties over bridewealth negotiations. If the young woman is to be a first wife, then the young man's father is expected to pay the bridewealth. The father can, unless he is enthusiastic about the proposed marriage, argue that it is not yet time for his son to marry, or that he does not have the wealth immediately available. Virtually all women, once married, run away to their parents at some time, after arguing with their husbands. If her parents value the ties created by her marriage, they are more likely to encourage her to return to her husband. A woman is usually happier if she lives nearer to her parents' home, so that she can visit them when they are ill, and can remain involved in the affairs of her own lineage.

The marriage rules, and the perception of self-interest, lead to a broad scattering of marriage ties among the lineages within a circumscribed area. They also lead, in about a third of the marriages, to the creation of overlapping ties of marriage and the blood pact between two lineages. When two men make the blood pact, they swear that if either one ever acts to harm the other, the guilty one will die as a result of the oath. They then exchange hospitality more freely than their other neighbors (who are all quite hospitable themselves), and a relationship of trust develops because serious betrayal of trust is thought impossible. A young man knows that if he marries his father's blood partner's daughter, he will reduce the possibility of friction between the two families and will have the cooperation of his father and wife's father. In other cases, if one of a group of brothers makes a successful marriage with the daughter of a local lineage, his brothers will choose their wives from the same lineage. By the next generation, of course, the pair of lineages will have developed blood relations, through the children born to the marriages. The children are not then encouraged to make more marriage ties between the two lineages. Instead, they either scatter their marriages, or they create a new complex of overlapping marriage ties, or marriage ties following in the path of the blood pact.

The marriage pattern outlined above has great significance for the creation of solidarity based on common residence of a village or chiefdom. Qualitative descriptions of precolonial villages indicate that the pattern was similar in the nineteenth century. It has already been shown, in the second section of this chapter, that precolonial chiefdoms were important economic units. It is now possible to see that the lineages within a territory were bound to one another in a complex network of alliances.

# 2 · THE MYTH OF MBEGHA

## The Problem

The traditions which describe the founding of the Shambaa kingdom tell how a hunter named Mbegha was welcomed and made king by the people of Shambaai. The style of the Mbegha traditions is one which, in other contexts, has caused profound difficulties to African historians who work from oral sources. The myth is one which is overwhelmingly ideological in content, and yet contains a germ of historical truth. The historian faces the choice, when working with such a myth, of either rejecting the value of its evidence altogether, or searching for substantiating facts in other traditions or in the archaeological record. The central question, the one that scholars presumably ask first, is evaded: namely, why does the source exist in this form, and what is the meaning of each element (both historical and mythical) in the tradition? Here is one kind of source that historians have not generally examined on its own terms.

Anthropologists meanwhile, building on the accomplishments of Claude Lévi-Strauss (who was himself building on the accomplishments of Vladimir Propp and Ferdinand de Saussure), have been developing sophisticated techniques of myth analysis. Lévi-Strauss has shown that in any single telling of a myth there are some elements which are contingent and others which are structural. The contingent elements—the embellishments of a skilled teller, or his particularly apt choice of language—vary from one telling to another. The structural elements are those relationships which remain constant no matter how many times the myth is told. The relationships are of two kinds: those among component units irrespective of their place in the narrative, and relationships established as a result of the particular order of the narrative. For example, it is possible to discover relationships among the species of animals which are prominent features of the Mbegha myth. One set of species is herbivorous, another carnivorous. The analyst can construct these sets only by removing every mention of an animal from its context in the myth and considering the relationships among species at one time. The teller mentions a lion at one point in the myth, a wild pig at another; but he and his listeners share cultural assumptions, so that when he mentions either one its relationship to the other is implicit. The analyst explains these implied relationships by creating an arbitrary simultaneity, as though the two animals were mentioned at once. The second set of relationships emerges from the order in which the component units are strung together. A crucial change in the hero of the Mbegha myth takes place when he goes from hunting wild pigs to killing a lion.

The attempt to find the underlying structure which persists no matter how many times the myth is told has a number of advantages in actual practice. It encourages one to examine a great number of variants and to separate those elements which persist from those which are transient. It encourages systematic analysis, for the structure of the myth is to be found in the sum of the relationships. It should be clear that a systematic method is preferable to an illustrative method, where a few apt examples are chosen to show the value of an interpretation of a myth. In a systematic analysis all the persistent elements of a myth are explained. In an illustrative analysis the explanation extends to only a few selected elements.[1]

1. For a symposium on the structural method of myth analysis, see Edmund Leach, ed., *The Structural Study of Myth and Totemism* (London, 1967). The literature of Bunyoro provides one example of how structural analysis can proceed side by side with historical study of the

Myth analysis, then, is one of those areas where disciplinary boundaries have gotten in the way of complete understanding. The historian, in order to understand his sources, should try to analyze all the symbols of a myth systematically, to find the key to the mythical code before deciding on the historical value of a text. The anthropologist needs to be made aware that myths can encapsulate historical data. In this chapter I shall attempt to determine the meaning of all the symbols of the Mbegha myth, and to discern the underlying structure. The next chapter will be an attempt to establish the history of the actual event.

The exercise of myth analysis is important for its own sake, in addition to its usefulness as a study of an historical source. For in Shambaa society, which had no written constitution, the myth preserved, in a simple and pleasing form, some of the most important conceptions of Shambaa government. As a result, this analysis, which starts as a technical exercise, will end as an exploration of Shambaa concepts of government.

In order to apply the structural method of analysis, I collected twenty-six versions of the Mbegha myth, and I will attempt to interpret all of them together.[2] The assumption here is that since

---

same materials, and remain quite separate. See R. Oliver, "The Traditional Histories of Buganda, Bunyoro, and Nkole," *Journal of the Royal Anthropological Institute* 85 (1955): 111–17; R. Needham, "Right and Left in Nyoro Symbolic Classification," *Africa* 37 (1967): 425–52; J. Beattie, "Aspects of Nyoro Symbolism," *Africa* 38 (1968): 413–42.

2. The variants of the Mbegha myth are, Historical traditions: Abdallah Mweta, 13 June 1968, text 1, 15 June 1968, text 2; Avuniwa Titu, 11 July 1966; Boaz Mjata, 15 July 1967; Hemedi Mbogho Wakanali, 6 February 1968; Idi Kibarua, 30 October 1967; Kasimu Kimweri, 1 February 1968; Kimweri Kibanga, 3 June 1967; Kimweri Magogo, 24 March 1967; Mahimbo Kihedu, 1 February 1968; Makao Sangoda, 10 May 1967; Makuno (Hamisi Ng'wa Nyoka), 5 April 1967; Mbaruku Jambia, 8 November 1967; Mbwana Mkanka Mghanga, 7 May 1967; Mdoe Barua, 12 March 1967; Mdoe Loti, 12 May 1967; Mdoembazi Guga, 15 June 1967; Mika Kimweri, 13 July 1966; Mnkande Kimweri, 13 September 1966; Ng'wana Aia, 20 March 1967; Ng'wa Paula, 12 July 1967; Nkinda Kimweri, 6 June 1967; Salehe Ali (Salehe Mzungu), 11 November 1967; Senmpeho Kimea, 27 December 1966; Shebughe Kingazi, 17 August 1966; Waziri Nyeghee, 1 July 1967.

I am not including the published versions of the myth, all of which were written by outsiders and are not relevant to this study.

the symbolic configurations are embedded in Shambaa assumptions about the nature of society and cosmology, one would expect every version of the myth told by a Shambaa in the Shambaa language to arrange the symbolic elements in a manner similar to every other version.

Since any given symbol has a series of possible meanings, it is difficult to determine the meaning of a single symbol in a single context, but one can reliably determine the meaning of two paired symbols in relationship to one another. I shall attempt to interpret all twenty-six versions at once, in order to determine which elements are contingent and which are part of the enduring structure of the myth. This can be done by requiring that wherever a pair of symbols occurs in any one of the versions, it must always occur in the same order and in the same context in any other version. For example, I will contend that there is an important symbolic opposition between Mbegha as a provider of meat and the Shambaa as providers of plant foods. If any one of the versions maintained that Mbegha was a provider of plants, then this pair of symbols could not be accepted as an opposition inherent in the myth itself. But if an abbreviated version of the myth merely omitted to mention the opposition, this is no reason to eliminate it.

The story can be summarized briefly: Mbegha was a hunter who used dogs to hunt wild pigs in the land of Ngulu, south of Shambaai. He was denied his rightful share of an inheritance by his lineage mates who said that he was a *kigego,* a mystically dangerous being. Because as an infant he had cut his upper teeth first, his presence was causing his kinsmen to die. Mbegha fled at night and sought refuge soon after at a place called Kilindi, where he made blood partnership with a son of the chief. His partner begged to go along with Mbegha on a wild pig hunting expedition, and was killed. Mbegha, fearing the retribution of the chief, did not return to Kilindi but went on through the bush, living in caves and rude camps, hunting all the while.

Mbegha finally crossed the Pangani River, and lived in a cave on the face of the southern escarpment of the mountains, below the town of Ziai. One day the women of Ziai were going down to the plains to collect firewood, and they saw the smoke of Mbegha's fire. Their husbands investigated, and Mbegha assured them that he meant no harm and gave them gifts of meat. The people of Ziai reciprocated with gifts of starch. Because of his generosity, and because of his skill at killing wild pigs, he was welcomed by the Shambaa and taken to Bumbuli. He killed many wild pigs there and was given a wife in gratitude. Then the people of Vugha came to get him, and he killed all the wild pigs at Vugha. Mbegha also helped to arbitrate disputes: people found that when he reasoned with the parties to a dispute they resolved their differences amicably. One night at Kihitu, near Vugha, a lion attacked some cows that were being kept in an outdoor enclosure. Mbegha appeared with his dogs and his spear and killed the lion. The following morning the Shambaa decided to make him chief of Vugha.

The structure of the Mbegha story is remarkably like the structure of a rite of passage, as described in van Gennep's classic work: the story can be divided into a period of separation from one status, a stage of transition between statuses, and a stage of incorporation into a new status.[3] In the stage of separation Mbegha disagreed with his lineage mates and fled from Ngulu. In the period of transition he passed through Zigula and crossed the Pangani River. In the stage of incorporation he was welcomed by the Shambaa and ultimately was made chief. This is the stage that is most extensively elaborated in the myth, since it describes the relationship between Mbegha and the Shambaa. The similarity between the Mbegha myth and a rite of passage is not merely one of superficial form: in the myth, as in a rite, there is a transition between total social statuses. Mbegha's transition, like the transition of a ritual initiate, was a change of all statuses at once. He went from being an outcast in his own lineage, who was denied even his rightful inheritance, to being king of all Shambaai, who was given wives without paying bridewealth. Yet both before and after he was alone. Before, he was alone among his enemies. And afterwards, he was alone among his subjects.

There are two sets of relationships at the heart of the myth:

---

3. Arnold van Gennep, *The Rites of Passage*, trans. Monika Vizedom and Gabrielle Caffee (London, 1960), pp. 10f.

one between the hero's attributes as an outcast and his characteristics as king, the second between the king and his subjects. An analysis of the tradition should clarify the meaning of Mbegha's attributes and define the relationship between the hero and the Shambaa. But the interpretation of symbolic statements is not easy. They are by their very nature ambiguous. V. W. Turner has put this well: "Many . . . symbols are *multivocal* or *polysemous,* i.e., they stand for many things at once. Each has a 'fan' or 'spectrum' of referents, which tend to be interlinked."[4] The shape of the myth itself provides us with a method. By examining each of Mbegha's attributes in the stages of transition and incorporation, it is possible to isolate pairs of linked symbols. In transition, for example, the hero lived in the wilderness while in incorporation he lived at homesteads. The meaning of the dyad wilderness:homestead can be elucidated by an examination of a number of the contexts, in Shambaa thought, where wilderness and homestead are brought into relationship with one another. Similarly, the pairs of symbols parallel to the dyad king:subjects can be examined systematically.

### The Humanization of Mbegha

The history of the founding of the kingdom is the story of the humanization of Mbegha. It will become clear that in the wilderness he was a wild, obscene, dangerous man; in Shambaai he became a kind, protective prince. This transformation is shown clearly by the change in Mbegha's environment. He changed from a wild creature, who himself lived in the wilderness, to a protector of villages. For Mbegha's life at his place of origin (Ngulu), in the stage of separation, three variants describe how he hunted in the bush (*tunduwi*).[5] None describes his hunting near a garden or settlement, although he lived in a village. In the period of wandering in Zigula, nine traditions mention that the

4. V. W. Turner, "Three Symbols of *Passage* in Ndembu Circumcision Ritual," in *Essays on the Ritual of Social Relations,* ed. Max Gluckman (Manchester, 1962), p. 125.

5. Historical traditions: Kimweri Magogo, 24 March 1967; Mbaruku Jambia, 8 November 1967; Waziri Nyeghee, 1 July 1967.

hero hunted in the bush and lived in rude open camps and caves.[6]
None mentions his living or hunting near a homestead or garden.

Once Mbegha entered Shambaai and began to live among the
Shambaa, he hunted near farms and villages. Sometimes when
all the wild pigs had been killed near a farm, he hunted in the
forest. But he soon returned, and even his forest hunting was
important simply because it protected farms.[7] In one text, when
the people of Bumbuli were trying to convince Mbegha to go to
their town, the discussion took a form which illustrates the importance of the change: "When they came up to the Tekwa hilltop the men said, 'That's the town of Bumbuli, over there.'

" 'Pigs?'

" 'We've got them.'

"Then Mbegha said, 'Men, I won't be able to go to Bumbuli. I
love the forest. That's where I like to live.' "[8] But in the end
Mbegha lived in towns.

*Kaya,* home, is the word most commonly used to describe
Mbegha's hunting grounds in Shambaai. During his progression
from Ngulu to Shambaai he changed from one who lived at home
(*kaya*) but spent most of his time hunting in the wilderness
(*tunduwi*), to one who lived altogether in the wilderness, and
finally to one who lived altogether at home. We can see that this
is a transformation fundamental to the meaning of the story because all variants, when they mention milieu, describe exactly
the same transformation.

The content of the transformation can be found in the meaning of the pair of terms, *tunduwi* and *kaya*. Here again clear
meaning resides not in single terms but in pairs, for in Shambaa

6. Historical traditions: Abdallah Mweta, 15 June 1968, text 2; Avuniwa Titu, 11 July 1966; Boaz Mjata, 15 July 1967; Kasimu Kimweri, 1
February 1968; Mdoe Barua, 12 March 1967; Mdoembazi Guga, 15 June
1967; Ng'wana Aia, 20 March 1967; Senmpeho Kimea, 27 December
1966; Waziri Nyeghee, 1 July 1967.

7. Historical traditions: Avuniwa Titu, 11 July 1966; Hemedi Mbogho
Wakanali, 6 February 1968; Kasimu Kimweri, 1 February 1968; Kimweri Magogo, 24 March 1967; Mbaruku Jambia, 8 November 1967;
Mdoe Barua, 12 March 1967; Senmpeho Kimea, 27 December 1966; Waziri Nyeghee, 1 July 1967.

8. Historical traditions: Mdoe Barua, 12 March 1967.

one can discuss the difference between home and farm, but when talking about the difference between home and wilderness, farm is included in home. Similarly *mzituwi,* the forest, is subsumed under the term for wilderness.

It is possible to demonstrate the meaning of *kaya:tunduwi* only by examining the contexts in which the two are brought into relationship with one another, as in *ghaso.* This is a storage place for very dangerous medicines. Often, in Shambaai, one sees an anomalous patch of forest when traveling through an area of dense population where all arable land is in use. In the middle of fields which stretch to the horizon (itself as near as the next mountain peak), is an area of dense wild forest. This is usually a *ghaso.* The *ghaso* is a small area of wilderness kept near home so that medicines too dangerous to keep in the homestead may be stored. I know of one medical practitioner who, following a related custom, keeps his curative drugs at home and his most dangerous sorcery drugs in a cave in *tunduwi* (wilderness). When medicines are stored in animal horns, those of domestic animals may not be used for fear that the medicines will affect the household. The medicines are kept instead in the horns of wild animals, or *mazama ya tunduwi* (animals of *tunduwi*).

Formerly, dangerous corpses were disposed of, together with their personal effects, in *tunduwi.* When a man died of "natural causes," or as a result of a sorcery attack in which the harmful charm could be "cooled," so that its effects were removed, he was buried near his home. But if the cause of death was contagious and frightening, if it could not be "cooled," he was "thrown away" in *tunduwi.* The bodies of lepers and of women who committed magical suicide were disposed of in *tunduwi* because they were still capable of harming people. In some cases a small patch of forest, very much like a *ghaso,* was maintained for the disposal of dangerous bodies. In these cases it was called a *kitundu wantu.*

It is said that witches, in the days when all homesteads were fenced, were the only people who would be found outside the fences at night. Witches were driven out of the homestead or village, and curiously the word for driving out a witch is *kuingata,* to hunt. I asked one informant why there was this coincidence in usage, and he said, "It is one word. The man resembles an animal. He hates people."

In distinguishing between *kaya* and *tunduwi,* the wilderness (*tunduwi*), is where dangerous things are located: sorcery charms, uncontrolled forces, wild animals, witches. *Kaya* is a secure place where danger is an intrusion and must be hunted out (*kuingata*). While Mbegha was in the wilderness he was one dangerous being among many. One elder told me that when the women of Ziai first saw Mbegha they fled "because it was *tunduwi.*" When Mbegha entered Shambaai and hunted at the homesteads, he became a bringer of order and a protector of territory. Thus at the heart of the story is a transformation of Mbegha from a hunter in the wilderness to a hunter at the homestead, from a dangerous enemy to a strong friend.

To this point the meaning of only one dyad has been examined as evidence for the humanization of Mbegha, wilderness: homestead. A second is meat eater:eater of starch and meat. Mbegha produced little aside from meat. According to a normal Shambaa definition of nutritional needs, a man cannot subsist on meat alone. Thus Mbegha specialized in one form of economic activity, and one of less importance than farming. He could live only by exchange. By examining the kinds of exchange in which the hero engaged, one can learn something of the quality of his social relations.

In Ngulu, his original home, Mbegha was undoubtedly involved in reciprocal exchange, although the traditions are not explicit. At the same time his position with regard to property rights was irregular, for he was denied an inheritance. As he fled he was joined, according to one variant, by his sister Mboza Mamwinu who brought along starch for the hunter to eat with his meat.[9]

During the period of transition, when Mbegha lived in the wilderness in Zigula, he ate only meat and did not share his kill. In only one episode of transition, when he made an alliance with the people of Kwa Mbiu in order to use their magical charms to

9. Historical traditions: Mbaruku Jambia, 8 November 1967.

ford the dangerous Pangani River, did the hero share meat.[10]
And the relationship with Kwa Mbiu belongs partly to the period of incorporation, for a man of the town became Mbegha's
Mlughu (chief minister) as a result of the alliance. For the
greatest part of his stay in Zigula, the hunter simply killed an
animal then ate its meat alone or with his fellow hunters.[11] Mbegha and his friends, in one variant, "went with their dogs to the
wilderness. They lived two months without ever coming near a
dwelling place. They killed wild pigs and they ate. For starch
(*nkande*) they ate pig. Their staple food (*nkande*) was meat.
They ate like that and went on through the bush. And they
pushed on through the wilderness."[12]

This pattern was transformed when Mbegha reached Shambaai. He gave gifts of meat and got starch in return. All the
foods in Shambaai are divided into two categories: *nkande,* or
starch, and *mbogha,* which is a relish of meat or vegetables. No
meal is complete without both *nkande* and *mbogha,* both starch
and relish. The amount of starch consumed is greater than the
amount of relish. A meal of starch without relish is thought un-
pleasant. But a meal of meat without starch is spoken of as
"famine" or "hunger" (*saa*). When Mbegha reached Shambaai
he gave gifts of meat and generally received *nkande* in return.
Thus, in the tradition by Boaz Mjata, he gave meat and received
sugar cane, bananas, and *viungu* (a root plant) in return. In the
version of Kasimu Kimweri, he exchanged meat for unripe bananas, and then later the Shambaa decided to farm for Mbegha.
In the variants by Ng'wa Paula, Senmpeho Kimea, Avuniwa, and
Hemedi Mbogho, we again have the exchange of meat for
starch. In only one unusual version is there a mention that Mbegha exchanged meat for domestic animals, an exchange which is

10. Historical traditions: Waziri Nyeghee, 1 July 1967.
11. Historical traditions: Abdallah Mweta, 15 June 1968, text 2;
Avuniwa Titu, 11 July 1966; Boaz Mjata, 15 July 1967; Mdoembazi
Guga, 15 June 1967; Ng'wana Aia, 20 March 1967; Senmpeho Kimea, 27
December 1966.
12. Historical traditions: Mdoe Barua, 12 March 1967; see also Kasimu Kimweri, 1 February 1968.

understandable in terms of the hunter's move from wilderness to homestead.

The record of exchange shows that Mbegha and his fellow hunters were alone in the period of transition. They did not exchange anything with anyone. In the period of incorporation they were involved in a form of solidarity through exchange. In the period of transition Mbegha ate only meat, while in the period of incorporation he ate both meat and starch. In order to understand the nature of the transformation Mbegha underwent, one has to understand two pairs of terms:

one who consumes alone:one who engages in exchange
meat eater:eater of starch and meat.

In Shambaai one who eats alone brings death; one who engages in exchange brings life. I am saying that Mbegha ate alone in the wilderness in spite of the fact that some versions mention his hunting companions. This is because they all engaged in a single productive activity and simply shared the product. To take a parallel case, a man who farms with his brothers and never engages in exchange with other descent groups is considered to be eating alone. In virtually all life-giving ritual in Shambaai it is necessary for people of different descent groups to eat together, or to exchange wealth. The idea that social solidarity is created through exchange is at the heart of marriage, sacrifice, rites of passage.

Rights in women are exchanged for livestock in order to unite groups in marriage. If you ask a Shambaa why incest is bad, you are told it is because an incestuous person eats his own cattle himself, without exchange. If all the secrets of a rite of passage are explained to the initiate but the community is not called to feast on starch and meat, then the initiate is considered not to have completed the ritual.

Perhaps the clearest example of the opposition between eating alone and exchanging is the sacrificial rite. A deceased relative is dangerous before the ritual is performed because he is alone between the world of the living and the world of the spirits. At the sacrificial rite the dead man's progeny give their entire house, in a figurative action, to a medical practitioner, who must be of an unrelated descent group. The practitioner calls up his own ancestors. The owner of the ritual then calls up his ancestors. After a night of dancing and drinking the ancestors of the two separate lineages are given a meal of starch and meat to eat together, while the living eat a mere image of the feast. At the end of the rite the lone dead man has joined the group of ancestors and is no longer dangerous.

This rite shows the importance of exchange and the danger of eating alone in three ways. First, a man cannot sacrifice to his ancestors alone. He must call in a member of another descent group for the sacrifice to be effective. An outsider is an essential part of every Shambaa ritual. Second, the dead spirit himself is dangerous only so long as he is alone. Yet it is not sufficient to unite him with the other dead members of the lineage. Spirits belonging to two separate lineages must partake of the communion, accepting the dead man into their midst. Thus the sacrificial rite (*fika ya chekecheke*) is the transformation of a dangerous spirit into a harmless one through the transfer of meat and beer between two groups of living people, and the consumption of a common feast by two groups of ancestors.

The third and most vivid way in which the sacrificial rite shows the dangerousness of a man who eats alone is in the witch's sacrifice (*ushai wa fika*). The witch's dead ancestor is not joined to the larger group of ancestors until the witch performs his sacrifice. But instead of calling the members of another group to eat his meat and sacrifice for him, the witch steals naked to the house of strangers at night and while they are asleep performs his ritual acts. At the same time that he secretly performs the sacrificial rite, he ensorcells the members of the village he has entered. In this case it is not the entire lineage which sacrifices as a group, but rather one member of the lineage, without the knowledge of his fellows. The witch is dangerous because he is alone, and because he secures the unknowing participation of a second group while refusing to give them the meat which is their due.

Mbegha was a witch when he ate alone, a man revered when he exchanged. There are strong parallels with a myth which was told far from Shambaai: "The demons said: 'To whom can we bring our offerings?' They set them all in their own mouths. But the gods set the gifts in one another's mouths. Then Prajapati, the primal spirit, gave himself to the gods.' "[13]

Two pairs of terms have been examined, so far, which describe the humanization of Mbegha:

> hunter in the wilderness:hunter at homesteads
> one who eats alone:one who lives by exchange.

In both cases the death-giving attributes were transformed to life-giving ones. There is a final dyad which has a similar meaning, but which is more difficult to interpret fully:

> one who eats meat:one who eats meat and starch.

These terms are difficult to interpret simply because the Shambaa abhor the idea of eating meat alone, so that there are very few customs which have as a central feature the consumption of meat without starch.

One has to turn to another myth to get a clear parallel to the dyad in question. It is the myth of Sheuta. In one version Sheuta, before he was accepted into the society of people, lived in a cave in the wilderness. He was fed meat by his friends the lions. His sex partner was an elephant. Later Sheuta joined the society of people and was normal in every respect. In the portion of the myth where Sheuta ate only meat, he was bestial in character. If he did not become completely animal, he was at least in the liminal area between animal and human. The idea that the border between animalness and humanness can be crossed is a recurrent one in Shambaa thought. Those who resemble animals bring death to their fellow men. (See below, p. 67.)

There are some kinds of rituals in which meat is eaten alone, and in those cases it is roasted. Roasted meat is called *mbishi*, raw, as opposed to boiled meat which is cooked, *mbizu*. In the rite of passage called *ng'waiko wa kaya*, which has been integrated into the adolescent boys' initiation rite, each boy is held down and a medical practitioner with a knife pretends to circumcise him. In fact, the boys have been circumcised in early

---

13. Martin Buber, *I and Thou*, trans. Ronald Gregor Smith, 2d ed., rev. (Edinburgh, 1959), p. 61.

childhood. Immediately after the "circumcision," while the boys are still in the mystically dangerous stage of the rite, each one is offered a pointed stick with a single piece of roasted meat near the tip. The meat quite obviously represents human flesh, and it is eaten without starch. When the dangerous portion of the ritual is over, and the boys are being reintegrated into the larger body of family and friends, the young initiates are given a bit of meat together with starch to eat in communion with the others.

There is only one circumstance in which a Shambaa would choose to subsist on meat or vegetable relish alone, rather than the normal diet of relish (*mbogha*) and starch (*nkande*). In case of famine, livestock are sold to those neighboring peoples who have a surplus of a staple crop. Only in a famine so severe that there is no starchy food available in any neighboring area would a Shambaa think of eating meat alone.

The examination of Mbegha's transformation from one who, in transition, ate meat alone, to one who ate meat and starch during the stage of incorporation into Shambaai reinforces and amplifies the general picture of the domestication of the hero. Mbegha changed from a person apart, mystically dangerous, associated with famine, a wild beast, to one who ate both meat and starch and was associated with the whole range of ritual feasting and everyday commensalism.

## Mbegha and the Shambaa

The examination of Mbegha's transformation, as he moved from Zigula to Shambaai, has emphasized the humanization of Mbegha, his shedding of bestial characteristics and his assumption of the attributes of a human being. Nothing has been said of the relationship between Mbegha and the Shambaa, between the first king and his subjects. The description of this relationship occupies the greatest portion of most of the texts, and is considered the paradigm of ideal kingship. Shambaa ideas of how a king *ought* to act are revealed in the symbolic statements about the relationship of the hunter king with his farmer subjects.

Mbegha was transformed from an eater of meat to one who ate starch and meat, and from one who ate alone to one who lived by exchange. In modern market exchange whoever has a surplus of meat sells some, and whoever needs meat buys it. The man who sells today may buy tomorrow. But the form of exchange between Mbegha and the Shambaa was much more highly ritualized. In every instance Mbegha gave meat and received starch. In every instance the Shambaa gave starch and received meat. In addition, reciprocity was more important than equivalency. That is, Mbegha did not sell meat for a price but gave it away. The Shambaa did not demand so many portions of meat for a bushel of maize. They too gave freely.

To understand the relationship between Mbegha and the Shambaa one must understand the meaning of the dyad,

provider of meat:providers of starch.

An obvious set of meanings is associated with this pair of terms. At any Shambaa feast, whether a major ritual or a minor celebration, every woman comes with some cooked starch, while the men cook the meat at the house of the "owner of the feast." In addition, while every woman brings some food, the "owner of the feast" provides all the meat.

There are two overlapping meanings. First, in the relationship between a provider of meat and a provider of starch, the one who gives the meat is the man. Second, there is one man giving meat while many women bring starch. Similarly, in the everyday arrangements of a polygamous household, the lone man provides the meat but each wife brings starch from her own fields. Mbegha was alone, and the Shambaa were many. At the same time Mbegha was masculine while the Shambaa were feminine. The masculine:feminine opposition is a Shambaa figure of speech describing a hierarchical relationship in which Mbegha was the stronger. In our own language we say that Mbegha had power over the Shambaa, instead of talking about masculine and feminine.

I shall quote a fragment of actual Shambaa conversation to elucidate the terms under discussion:

"Who is the man here?"

"There is no man. The only man is that one, who makes the rain." The meaning of this as explained by the speakers, is: "He has made his fellows into women. They have not been able to make magic more powerful than his." If Mbegha made all the Shambaa into women, it means that he was stronger than they were. Mbegha went through all his transformations, from death giver to life giver, when he acquired power over the Shambaa— when he made them all women.

The idea that Mbegha's humanization came as a result of his power over the Shambaa widens the field of discussion so that many of the important ideas about politics are relevant. But each of the concepts is a nexus, about which whole groups of symbols are ranged, many of which have been examined already. Therefore, although discussion will still be restricted to the symbolic content of the myth, the closer we get to the heart of the problem, the more discursive the analysis will become.

A logical place to begin a general analysis of political concepts is with the idea of territoriality, which can be studied systematically by examining the categories of animals Mbegha hunted. He hunted many different animals, and the same animals for different purposes, at separate stages of the myth. In Ngulu and Zigula, Mbegha is said to have hunted mainly wild pig (*nguuwe*), but also "other animals." In the period of transition he hunted buffalo and bushbuck also, in one version.[14] For incorporation into Shambaai, most of the versions mention the hunting of wild pig. In addition, one version mentions "dangerous animals" (*mazama madaa*),[15] one mentions bushbuck and waterbuck;[16] also mentioned are "animals which destroy food,"[17] and baboons.[18] Mbegha was made chief of Vugha, in many of the versions, immediately after killing a lion.[19]

14. Historical traditions: Abdallah Mweta, 13 June 1968, text 2; Avuniwa Titu, 11 July 1966; Boaz Mjata, 15 July 1967; Mdoembazi Guga, 15 June 1967; Ng'wana Aia, 20 March 1967; Senmpeho Kimea, 27 December 1966; Waziri Nyeghee, 1 July 1967.
15. Historical traditions: Boaz Mjata, 15 July 1967.
16. Historical traditions: Waziri Nyeghee, 1 July 1967.
17. Historical traditions: Senmpeho Kimea, 27 December 1966.
18. Historical traditions: Mbaruku Jambia, 8 November 1967.
19. Historical traditions: Boaz Mjata, 15 July 1967; Kasimu Kimweri, 1 February 1968; Kimweri Magogo, 24 March 1967; Mdoe Barua, 12 March 1967; Salehe Ali (Salehe Mzungu), 11 November 1967; Senmpeho Kimea, 27 December 1966; Shebughe Kingazi, 17 August 1966; Waziri Nyeghee, 1 July 1967.

A sharp distinction was made in late precolonial Shambaai between animals which eat meat and those which eat only plants. Herbivorous animals, which resembled the domestic animals raised for meat, could be eaten; carnivorous animals could not. These beliefs survive today, but in addition some European and Muslim ideas have been superimposed on Shambaa notions.[20] Thus ratlike rodents and pigs, which were commonly eaten eighty years ago, are rejected as food today. It is still thought, however, that anyone who eats prohibited meat will break out in open sores (*-umbuka*), the most extreme form of which is leprosy.

Mbegha hunted edible herbivorous animals for meat. These included buffalo, bushbuck, waterbuck, and wild pigs. Their meat is eaten by the Shambaa, and they are dangerous in varying degrees. All of them were hunted by Mbegha as a provider of meat, a consistent attribute of the hero in all parts of the myth. All of them show that Mbegha was a courageous man.

Another group of creatures important in the myth are the ones which destroy crops. Of these, only baboons and wild pigs are mentioned specifically. Other farm pests common in Shambaai are ravens and monkeys. Wild pigs alone, of all the creatures known in Shambaai, are the only farm pests which are at the same time edible and dangerous. Thus the descriptions of Mbegha as a hunter of wild pigs express all of the hero's characteristics: he was courageous, he provided meat, and he protected gardens.

In transition Mbegha hunted pigs for their meat. In incorporation he chased them as farm pests and in addition distributed their meat. The protection of farms is mentioned explicitly in a number of the variants as the reason for Mbegha's popularity with the Shambaa. In one version the people said, " 'Let's go with him to Bumbuli.' And he killed wild pigs. . . . Kill, kill, kill,

20. It is possible to construct a picture of Shambaa animal categories with the help of the memories of old men, scattered references in the written sources of the first two decades of colonial rule, and observations in areas like Mshihwi where alien ideas have had the least impact. A more detailed description of the evidence, and of animal categories, is given in Feierman, "Concepts of Sovereignty," pp. 238–44.

kill. The country of Bumbuli became a good one. Sweet potatoes [*viogwe*] were undisturbed in the fields. All the crops remained untouched, in peace."[21] The change to the hunting of wild pigs in order to protect crops is adequately explained by considering it as part of Mbegha's transformation from hunter in the bush to hunter at the homesteads.

While the transformation has been described, we have not yet explored Mbegha as killer of farm pests in his relationship with the Shambaa as tillers of the soil. According to the division of labor in Shambaai, women do repetitive work, while men worry about the irregular events which disrupt fertility, health, and plenty. One elderly Shambaa informant put it this way: "The man has to do with disturbances. He has many worries. A woman thinks only about going to her farm and cooking. A man can go from here to Moshi, just because he is worried. Every day has a new problem. A woman only cooks. She can say, 'I have nothing to cook,' or 'I have no relish.' But it is the man's place to consider why she has none."[22] Land is a possession of men, and wild pigs violate the man's territory. It is the man who sits up at night on the farm, with bow and arrows ready for the wild pigs.

The image of Mbegha as the wild pig hunter and the Shambaa as farmers, then, is yet another context in which Mbegha is the man and the Shambaa are women, Mbegha is powerful and the Shambaa dominated. This is the same meaning as that of the exchange of starchy foods for meat. But here there is an additional element of territoriality: the hunter of wild pigs who guards the territory against the depredations of wild animals is the possessor of the land. He worries about the unusual while the "women" take care of daily tasks. Two of the texts state that the Shambaa did Mbegha's daily farming so that he could devote

21. Historical traditions: Mnkande Kimweri, 13 September 1966. Other texts which describe how Mbegha freed the farms of pests are: Kasimu Kimweri, 1 February 1968; Kimweri Magogo, 24 March 1967; Mbaruku Jambia, 8 November 1967; Senmpeho Kimea, 27 December 1966.

*Viogwe* are identified by G. R. Williams Sangai, *Dictionary of Native Plant Names*, p. 85, as *dioscorea* sp. (Diosc.).

22. Historical traditions: Zachaia, 3 March 1967.

himself to the hunting of wild pigs.[23] The Shambaa were like
wives of a village elder, while Mbegha was the elder, the owner
of the land. In fact, one of the descriptive titles of the king in
Shambaa is *ng'wenye shi*—the owner of the country or land.

Mbegha's last act before becoming king was the killing of a
lion. According to the text of Kimweri Magogo:

> At night a lion came, and fell upon a cow at Kihitu. The
> people shouted, "Li-on, li-on, lion's got a cow!" Mbegha
> went out with his spear, because he was accustomed to
> hunting. He wasn't afraid of the lion. He hurled the spear
> and hit it just right on the side, at the heart. It fell there and
> did not get up again. He didn't remove his spear. It stayed
> there until morning. When the people gathered they saw
> that the lion was dead. Ah, how amazed they were. "It's
> true! The man has really killed a lion. The man is a lion."[24]

Because he killed a lion, Mbegha was made king.

At the heart of the myth is an opposition between lion and
pig. There is a formalized Shambaa phrase which describes a decline in the quality of rule: "Where once a lion sat, there is now
a pig." One who understands this phrase knows one of the most
important concepts of Shambaa kingship. A lion eats meat. In
this tradition the lion was killing a cow. The wild pig, as we have
seen, roots up food plants. Mbegha killed pigs in the daytime,
but he killed the lion at night, a time of dangerous occurrences,
death, witchcraft. Mbegha hunted wild pigs, but he *was* the lion.
"The man has really killed a lion. The man is a lion."

The king in Shambaai is said to "eat the whole country," *aja
shi ngima.* This means that all of the wealth of all the people in
the country is his, to take at will. Just as the lion kills cows at
will, so does the king. And the king is dangerous. One informant
described how the king is like a buffalo (an image from the accession rites): "My reason for saying the king is dangerous, is
that he can do a deed which he tells no one. He doesn't tell his
chief minister. He goes at night with his club. They go on a trip.

23. Historical traditions: Kasimu Kimweri, 1 February 1968; Senmpeho
Kimea, 27 December 1966.
24. Historical traditions: Kimweri Magogo, 24 March 1967.

A wife of the king goes on ahead. When they get out on the path the king kills his wife."[25] Later in the same conversation the informant said, "At night the whole country resembled the wilderness (*nyika*). There is darkness. A person cannot move. Night is danger. But he rules even at night. He does not sleep. In the darkest hours of the night the ruler listens. He sleeps in the afternoon. . . . He goes to his chief minister in the middle of the night. 'Awaken the bachelors. Go and look.' When they come to a place they see people drinking beer. They say, 'All right, there's nothing wrong here.' "

The justification for the king's right to destroy is that a rain magician, a magician of the fertility of the land, must possess and dominate the entire land in order to be effective. When Pare rain magicians, the Mbagha, came to make fertility magic, they were free to take any livestock they saw.[26] The notion that a magician must have full possession in order to cure is an important concept in Shambaa sacrifice and magic. So if the king is a lion, if he eats the wealth of the whole countryside, then the land will be fertile. If the king is not strong enough, if the hierarchical principle is not adhered to, then there will be famine—pigs, not people, will eat the crops. The idea that absolute hierarchy leads to fertility elucidates the meaning of the phrase, "Where once a lion sat there is now a pig." That is, where once there was an absolute ruler, there now is famine.

The notion that a magician only successfully heals things which are his own is the explanation of why Mbegha was transformed from a hated man to one held dear, from a bringer of death to a life giver as he went from Ngulu to Shambaai. His personal attributes did not change, only the context in which they worked. Take for example Mbegha's sexuality. In Ngulu he was a man who broke the norms of sexual behavior. In one version Mbegha was driven out because he and his blood partner used to run off with other men's wives.[27] In another variant, Mbegha was driven out of Ngulu because he made his sister

25. Historical traditions: Mdoe Loti, 1 May 1967.
26. Historical traditions: Kimweri Magogo, Mdoe Barua, and Ng'wana Aia, (group testimony), 27 July 1968.
27. Historical traditions: Mbaruku Jambia, 8 November 1967.

pregnant.[28] Yet in Shambaai his behavior was not different, only the response to his actions changed. In the version that describes Mbegha's incestuous behavior, he lived with his sister in Shambaai, and his sister gave birth while living among the Shambaa. Then he got a girl pregnant, and was given her as a wife, free of bridewealth.[29] Many versions mention that Mbegha was given wives without having to pay bridewealth.[30]

Mbegha's sexuality knew no bounds. When he saw a woman he wanted, he took her. The people of Ngulu would not tolerate his licentiousness. They drove him out. Yet the Shambaa gladly gave him their daughters. This anomaly can be resolved only by reference to Mbegha's position as owner of the land in Shambaai. Marriage is the exchange of certain rights in women for livestock. It is defined not by ritual but by the transfer of wealth. And as king all the wealth of the land was Mbegha's. Therefore Mbegha could not marry because he would have had to transfer his own wealth to himself. This is not just a sophistical explanation of the anomaly, but the description of a principle which is at the heart of Shambaa social structure. The kings of Shambaai never paid bridewealth. This was not simply an unusual form of taxation, for a Shambaa man who married the king's daughter did not pay bridewealth either. The king, because he owned all wealth, existed outside it.

The contrast between Mbegha as a dispossessed person in Ngulu, and as the possessor of all wealth in Shambaai, is significant. Shambaa normally share some rights in wealth with other members of their own lineage. But Mbegha was first dispossessed, and came to the Shambaa outside any group. When he was given the wealth of the land he received it outside any descent group. The country is never the possession of a lineage. It is the possession of a person. It is my contention, as already expressed above, that there is a necessary relationship between the two sets of transformations:

28. Historical traditions: Senmpeho Kimea, 27 December 1966.
29. Historical traditions: Senmpeho Kimea, 27 December 1966.
30. Historical traditions: Avuniwa Titu, 11 July 1966; Hemedi Mbogho Wakanali, 6 February 1968; Kasimu Kimweri, 1 February 1968; Kimweri Magogo, 24 March 1967; Mdoe Barua, 12 March 1967; Mdoembazi Guga, 15 June 1967; Mnkande Kimweri, 13 September 1966.

dispossessed person > owner of the country
   bringer of death > bringer of fertility and life.

In Ngulu and in the period of transition in Zigula, Mbegha was a bringer of death. In two versions, Mbegha is described as a *kigego* (pl. *vigego*).[31] This is a child who cuts his upper teeth before any of his lower teeth appear, or one whose molars come through before his incisors. Twins are also *vigego*. In traditional practice a *kigego* is killed. If he is not killed, members of his lineage will die one by one until he is either driven out or murdered. One informant described *vigego* and why they are dangerous: "When an infant's molars appear first he is a *kigego*. He is transformed. He is not in the same category of beings that we are in. Animals teethe irregularly. Maybe we will become sick because of him. . . . Goats have twins, but people do not. He is like an animal."[32] Mbegha was half man, half animal: a dangerous creature who existed between categories. Mbegha's name carried the same implication, for it is that of a kind of hairy monkey (*Colobus palliatus*).[33] The *mbegha* is the only herbivorous monkey in Shambaai, and the only kind of monkey that was ever eaten. One informant mentioned that Mbegha was hairy like the monkey. Hair in many contexts in Shambaa symbolism is unclean, ritually dangerous. A great medical practitioner, who was of necessity also a great sorcerer, often wore a lock of long hair on top of his head (*ushungi*) as a sign of his powers. We have already seen how Mbegha in the first and second stages of the myth was something of a wild man and a witch. There is another example of his destructive character in the death of the chief's son who went hunting with Mbegha.

Yet it is clear that the Shambaa welcomed Mbegha because of his life-giving qualities. In everyday conversation in Shambaai one often hears that rain magic, the key to fertility, began with Mbegha. His magical powers, which were the powers to kill, and which derived from his wildness, were also the powers to bring fertility to Shambaai. That magical power is ambivalent, that it

31. Historical traditions: Kimweri Magogo, 24 March 1967; Salehe Ali (Salehe Mzungu), 11 November 1967.

32. Historical traditions: Mdoe Loti, n.d., text 4, "Accession Rites."

33. LangHeinrich, *Schambala-Wörterbuch*, p. 256.

can be used to help or to harm, is axiomatic in Shambaa medicine. In order to cure illnesses caused by sorcery one must know the sorcerer's art. Mbegha had the power to destroy and the power to bring fertility. When all Shambaai became his possession, he was transformed from a killer to one whose powers led to the increase of life.

The ambiguity and ambivalence of power in Shambaai is clear also from the place of dogs, which are so important a part of the myth, in the rites performed by the descendants of Mbegha. Dogs are used mainly for hunting in Shambaai. It is thought that plant foods are their proper diet, since they are domestic animals. They are commonly fed on leftover porridge. But it is clear that dogs like meat. Whenever an animal is slaughtered, they wait to eat the scraps and bones left behind. Because a dog is both a domestic animal and omnivorous, dog meat is one of the most dangerous foods. It is said that one who eats dog meat will become a leper. Yet there was a kind of royal sacrifice, performed by the descendants of Mbegha, in which the meat of a dog was roasted and eaten. This would have been thought to cause illness, and possibly death, in any other descent group. For the Kilindi, however, the polluted and disgusting meat of the dog was associated with mystical power. Once again, the power to harm was the power to rule; the power to cause death was the power to bring life.

The entire preceding discussion can be summarized as two sets of oppositions. The first expresses the relationship between Mbegha and the Shambaa:

| *Mbegha* | *Shambaa* |
|---|---|
| provider of meat | providers of starchy foods |
| stranger | natives |
| man | women |
| powerful | weak |
| protector of territory | performers of repetitive work |
| king | subjects |
| owner of the country | inhabitants of the country |
| possessor of women | providers of women |
| judge | litigants |

The second set of oppositions describes the transformations Mbegha underwent when passing from life in the wilderness to life in Shambaai.

| *Mbegha in Zigula* | *Mbegha in Shambaai* |
|---|---|
| hunter in the wilderness | hunter near homesteads |
| dangerous being | bringer of order |
| eater of meat | eater of meat and starchy foods |
| lone eater | one who lives by exchange |
| famine | plenty |
| witch | bringer of social solidarity |
| hunter of meat | protector of territoriality |
| steals wives | given wives |
| hated | liked |
| outcast | king |
| bringer of death | bringer of life |
| *kigego* | rain magician |

The superficial intention of the teller of the Mbegha myth is to describe the wonderful qualities of the first king. But there is a serious problem. If all the qualities of the king are taken from the column "Mbegha in Shambaai," then what is the purpose of demonstrating the opposed qualities of Mbegha in Zigula? Perhaps some comments by Shambaa elders, taken verbatim from field notes, will help to clarify the ways in which the terms were complementary.

"Historian: 'But Mbegha was an evil man. He stole people's wives. Why did the Shambaa like him?'

"Mbaruku Jambia: 'Mbegha gave up all his evil ways. But his notoriety did not disappear. His descendants the Kilindi did things just like Mbegha's deeds in Ngulu' "[34]

I can quote a very similar conversation with a second elder.

"Historian: 'Kingship in the days of Mbegha was not associated with death. What happened?'

"Mdoe Loti. 'You might be a kind person and a father, for you have a wife. And your wife can have a son who is completely vicious.' "[35]

34. Historical traditions: Mbaruku Jambia, 8 November 1967.
35. Historical traditions: Mdoe Loti, 12 May 1967, "Mbegha."

I interpret this as meaning not merely that Mbegha's children did not have his personal qualities of goodness, but that
kingship necessarily is power, and power can be used either for
great good or for great evil. The king, when he used his power
for evil, resembled Mbegha in Ngulu—a man of great and destructive mystical power.

Mbegha, in other words, encompassed within his person opposed but related possibilities of kingship in Shambaai. Mbegha
as king was the embodiment of all the ideal virtues of a Shambaa
ruler. Yet each aspect of his beneficial power had a complementary opposite—the same power used to bring death and destruction. In fact, in the course of Shambaa history there were kings
who were given wives, and others who stole wives, kings who
dealt death through the countryside, and those who brought life.
There were kings who brought famine, and others who created
plenty. But when the kingdom was truest to its good principles it
was based on a relationship between king and subject for which
Mbegha's relationship with the Shambaa was the paradigm.
Thus the story of Mbegha is both an intellectual's and a moral-
ist's model of the Shambaa kingdom. For it told how the kingdom should work, and at the same time how the kingdom, in evil
times, does work.

## Myth and History

By this point in the analysis the reader might well doubt that
the Mbegha myth has any historical relevance at all. If the structure of the myth is determined by the logic of Shambaa symbols
and by the social relevance of that logic, then where can historical materials be found? The case against using the myth as a historical document is made even stronger by the fact that similar
myths and configurations of symbols exist across East Africa.

There are a number of separate questions which must be
asked, and kinds of analysis which must be made, in order to use
the Mbegha myth as a historical document. First, and least satisfying historically, there are fragments of data embedded in
the myth which have no symbolic justification, and in which the
myth-tellers appear to be making statements about the succes-

sion of events. There is, in the Mbegha myth, the interplay between symbolic and historical statements which is so often found in oral tradition. What is in question here, it must be emphasized, is the historical intent of the teller.

The traditions generally agree on the route which Mbegha took as he traveled from Ngulu to Shambaai, and then as he moved within Shambaai. He started at Ngulu and went to Kilindi, nearby, to its east. He crossed the Pangani River at Maulwi. From Maulwi he followed what is now the railway line northwest to Makuyuni. He then went northeast to Vuruni, where the plains form an indentation in the mountains. He climbed to Leopard's Cave (*Mpanga ya Shuwi*) just below Ziai. From Leopard's Cave he went to Bumbuli, and from there to Vugha. When he retired from public life, Mbegha lived at Shashui, near the modern town of Soni.

The tradition tells, also, about some of the important groups with which Mbegha had contact, and the areas within Shambaai in which his influence was greatest. Different variants tell of Mbegha's early impact at Ziai, Manka, and Mlungui. These place names describe an arc along the western side of the southern tip of Shambaai. From Ziai, Mbegha went to Bumbuli. Here, also, different versions mention different place names. The traditions speak of Mbegha's influence at Shembekeza, Ngulwi, Funta, Tekwa, Ng'wavula, Balangai, Mpaau, Due, Nkongoi. There seem to be at least a few informants who filled in village names to add verisimilitude. But it is clearly the intention of the tradition to describe Mbegha's influence in the country around Bumbuli. He had relations of some sort with the Nango lineages at Bumbuli. At Vugha, Mbegha had close relations with the lineage of the Wakina Tui. Mbegha had at least one wife from Shambaai, and at least one son. He traveled with one or more comrades from Zigula, of the lineage of the Wakina Mbiu, from the village of Kwa Mbiu.[36]

In addition to the historical elements embedded in the structure of symbols, there is a second important sense in which

---

36. Historical traditions: Ng'wana Aia, 20 March 1967.

Mbegha is connected to the continuing history of the Shambaa people. Mbegha's descendants were the dynasty that ruled Shambaai. The kingdom itself was seen by the Shambaa as evidence for the hero's historicity; it was Mbegha's temporal creation.

One of the most striking achievements of the myth is that it managed to combine, in a single neat form, both the historical and the timeless symbolic elements. Mbegha's transformation from death bringer to life bringer was at the same time a progression from Ngulu to Shambaai. The transformation was symbolic, the progression historical. As Mbegha moved through real time and space he was transformed by moral forces.

While the statements outlined above appear to be historical, the critical history of Mbegha depends on a comparative analysis of the myth with evidence which is outside it, and relatively independent of it. This evidence will be examined in the next chapter. There remains, however, a crucial question which must be answered before any historical analysis will be convincing. There are myths told all across East and Central Africa about heroic hunters who founded dynasties. There is also a myth about a hero who had been half man half beast before he became king of Bunyoro, in Uganda. Since similar myths appear to exist with different place names and personal names in other societies, how is it possible to treat Mbegha as a historical personage?

Any historical judgment about Mbegha depends on a judgment about the history of the myth. There are a number of bits of evidence which lead one to believe that the ideas and images, and perhaps the myth, existed long before the founding of the Shambaa kingdom. The broad distribution of the myth throughout East Africa is itself evidence for the tale's considerable age. The image of the pig hunter occurs in Ngulu initiation rites with much the same meaning it has in the Mbegha myth (see Chapter 3, note 18).

In addition, there is a myth common to the Zigula, the Bondei, and the Shambaa, which all those who tell it insist is of the greatest antiquity, and which in at least its Shambaa version resembles the Mbegha myth in form and content—the myth of

Sheuta. Indirect evidence supports the claims about the myth's antiquity. Sacrificial rites among all three peoples include invocations to Sheuta, who is named as the primeval ancestor. The broad regional distribution of the rites and of the myth, taken together with the claims of antiquity, the lack of evidence for recent diffusion, and the fact that Islam was spreading among the Zigula and to a lesser extent among the Bondei in the nineteenth century, all support the notion that the Sheuta myth originated long before the creation of the Shambaa kingdom in the eighteenth century.

In one version of the myth which I collected from a very old Shambaa, who lived on the border between the Shambaa and the Zigula, Sheuta was described as a hunter who lived in a cave in the wilderness. He was befriended by a lion who shared his meat with Sheuta. One day Sheuta went out hunting with his dogs and met an elephant who grabbed hold of Sheuta's penis and stretched it until it was long enough for Sheuta to sleep with the elephant, and who then gave Sheuta a magical charm for making his penis longer or shorter at will. At this time, there was a woman named Bangwe who killed men once they had slept with her. Men from all over Shambaai were dying until Sheuta came and murdered Bangwe by lengthening his penis as he was having intercourse with her. The Shambaa were so happy at having rid the land of its scourge that they made Sheuta chief.

In another version, collected by a Shambaa-speaking German planter in the first decade of the twentieth century, Sheuta came through the wilderness from the south to an island in the middle of the river, in the land of the women. A woman was chief. Sheuta hid himself because he was naked. He had with him his bow and arrows, roasted meat, and honey. When the women discovered him, Sheuta gave each one a taste of honey from his finger, which he dipped and then offered. At night Sheuta slept in one part of the great house with the chief of the women, while those who served her slept in another part. The chieftainess became familiar with the masculine body, and with the functions of the various organs. The next morning, when she explained to the women what she had seen, heard, and felt, the women demanded that they be given men of their own. When their leader refused, the women decided to make Sheuta their chief, and their former leader became his wife.[37]

There are striking similarities between the myth of Sheuta and the myth of Mbegha. In both, the hero is a wild man who lives by hunting and who eats only meat in the wilderness. Mbegha was mystically dangerous; Sheuta was naked in one version, and lived with lions in the other. Mbegha arrived in a land where he was the only man and all the others were, in a figurative sense, women. Sheuta came to a land dominated by women. In one version of the Sheuta myth there were only women in the land. In both the myths, the hero's masculinity and magical power led to his domination. Sheuta's magical organ in the one version, the simple fact of his masculinity in the other, led to his ascendancy. Mbegha's masculine occupation as a hunter led to his assumption of the chiefship. Sheuta's essential masculine characteristic, aside from his sexuality, was his work as a hunter. The name *Sheuta* means "father of the bow."

The important difference between the two myths is in the kind of government which appears to be justified. The Sheuta myth justifies the patrilineal and patriarchal regime within the villages: the domination of men over women. Sheuta's place as the primeval masculine ancestor in sacrificial rites to the ancestral ghosts of each lineage reinforces the notion that the Sheuta myth explained and justified leadership by the heads of the separate patrilineal descent groups. This is the form of organization which existed in Shambaai before Mbegha (see Chapter 3). The Mbegha myth, in its turn, justified the domination of the separate descent groups by territorial chiefs.

The point being made here is a speculative one which goes just a bit further than conservative critical reasoning can support. It is that the Sheuta myth existed before the Mbegha myth; as Mbegha receded into the past as a familiar figure, his history was grafted on to the Sheuta myth because the changes Mbegha had made in Shambaa political organization required a revision of the society's central political myth. This view is supported by

37. A Karasek, "Beiträge zur Kenntnis der Waschambaa," ed. A. Eichhorn, *Baessler-Archiv* 1 (1911): 155–222; see esp. p. 221.

the fact that the Sheuta myth was much more widely known and told seventy years ago than it is today. Its place as the tale which explains the nature of politics has been taken by the Mbegha myth. Today almost no one knows the tales of Sheuta outlined above. The most striking support of the position taken here is provided by the existence, in the first decade of the twentieth century, of a transitional form between the myth of Sheuta and the myth of Mbegha. In this version Sheuta was the first Kilindi, who came from the land of Ngulu to Shambaai, and then returned to his homeland to report to Mbegha that there were many women in the land of the Shambaa.[38]

Thus the larger Mbegha-Sheuta myth has its own independent history as a cultural phenomenon. Mbegha's transformation of Shambaa society led to a transformation of the myth. The full work of the creation of the kingdom went on for several generations. The substitution of Mbegha for Sheuta also took generations. One of the most difficult problems for the historian who deals with myth is to imagine how heroic attributes could have been associated with the hero during his lifetime. If, on the other hand, the myth was created in its entirety after the hero's death, then there is no reason to accept that the heroic age existed. The analysis presented here solves the problem by showing that historical information can be integrated into a preexisting myth. This accords with the commonsense view that complexes of cultural ideas are not created all at once, no matter how significant the historical period in question. The evidence which shows that the myth existed before the event, and that descriptions of historical events were integrated into the myth, makes it especially important to study the historical events which led to the myth's transformation.

38. Ibid., 208. Hubert and Mauss describe how historical figures were integrated into preexisting European myths. Their work remains the indispensable classic on conceptions of time; see "Étude sommaire de la représentation du temps dans la religion et la magie," in M. Mauss and H. Hubert, *Mélanges d'histoire des religions* (Paris, 1929).

# 3 • THE HISTORY OF MBEGHA

After the examination, in the preceding chapter, of the symbolic content of the Mbegha myth, it may appear to the reader that a myth so rich in ahistorical cultural meaning could not possibly be used as a source for the reconstruction of a probable chain of historical events. But it can be. Many of the historical issues have been hidden, however, because the myth describes the unity which emerged from a momentous era of Shambaa history, rather than the conflict which led up to it. The myth is not only a description of the unity of all the people of Shambaai under a Kilindi king, it is one of the greatest supports of that unity.

The myth refers to two sets of historical realities: the events surrounding the coming of Mbegha, and the social reality of the time in which the myth is told. If the Mbegha myth were the only evidence, it would be impossible to separate the current social truths from the historical truths. The problem is made even more difficult by the subtlety with which the mythmakers played with the debris of time. To take one example, the myth maintains that Mbegha was welcomed by the Shambaa. It will be shown below that there were some groups in Shambaai which did not welcome Mbegha, but most of these groups were not thought of as Shambaa, even though they have since been absorbed into the Shambaa population. Thus the statement that the

70

hero was welcomed by the Shambaa is neither true nor false, but true in a special sense.

The historian's task is to separate those emphases and implications which are true only as social ideas of the tellers, from those which are historically probable. The materials for critical analysis are to be found in those separate traditions which have not become part of the collectively accepted picture of Mbegha. There are two kinds of these traditions. First, there are private traditions which are the property of individual descent groups within the kingdom. Members of these groups accept the standard version of the myth as "true," yet they remember details of their own special position during the events. Second, there are the traditions of groups which remained outside the Shambaa kingdom but which had been involved in the events. The Mbugu of central Shambaai, for example, were never brought into the kingdom, but they had been present at its creation.

Each separate tradition has, like the Mbegha myth, a social relevance, and each is built on historical fact. Critical analysis is possible because the biases of the separate groups are identifiable, and because each group interprets the historical reality in a different way. The greater the number of independent traditions analyzed, the more probable the historical reconstruction. This cannot be a simple numbers game, however. It was shown in Chapter 2 that the many versions of the Mbegha story were in fact a single myth. Additional traditions shed light only if they are told from different social viewpoints, and if they have had separate chains of transmission from the time of the historical event.

## Shambaai before Mbegha

A comparison of all the historical sources available reveals that the time of Mbegha's arrival was a time when the centuries-old ethnic unity of the Shambaa had been challenged by the entry of large groups of immigrants. The immigrants came from outside the region into which the Shambaa were integrated, from beyond the lands of neighbors with whom the people of the mountains had intimate long-term culture contact.

Shambaai, at the time of Mbegha's arrival some time in the eighteenth century, was, then, divided between two major ethnic groups, one old, one new, one deeply integrated into the culture of the region, one which danced, literally, to the beat of a different drum.

The real unity of the older Shambaa population is clear, in spite of an apparent diversity of origins, for it derives from the cultural unity of the region. There are two separate categories of neighbors who have significant affinities with the people of Shambaai, and virtually all the early population of Shambaai came from peoples in one or the other of these categories.

The first category includes the Zigula and the Bondei. These peoples have languages which can easily be learned by Shambaa speakers. The language differences are just a bit more pronounced than mere dialect differences. Rituals are often similar throughout the cultural region which includes the Zigula, the Shambaa, and the Bondei (see Map 3, p. 97).

The second category includes neighboring peoples whose ecological settings are similar to Shambaa ecology. These are people like the highland Taita and the Pare. In these cultures medical knowledge, folk botany, agricultural techniques, even ritual, were very strongly tied to the highlands environment. The cultural similarities were intensified by the effects of centuries of migrations of small groups of people back and forth between the highland areas, since it seems clear that migrants who came from the highlands preferred to find new homes in highlands. Because agricultural knowledge was so specifically tied to a particular kind of environment, it was easier for migrants to seek out a familiar environment than to learn a whole new body of agricultural techniques.

The people of Ngulu—one of the major sources of the population of southern Shambaai—were included in both groups of related peoples. Many Ngulu live in a highlands environment. At the same time their culture was part of the Zigula complex.

The overwhelming majority of the early Shambaa descent groups claim to have come from Ngulu and other hilly portions of Zigula, from Taita, and from Pare. The people of Ziai, for example, the very first ones to welcome Mbegha into Shambaai, originated in Ngulu. The Wakina Tui, who gave Mbegha his royal capital, also came from Ngulu. Thus Mbegha, who was himself from Ngulu, came, in a very general sense, to kinsmen.

The Hea of Ubii came from the mountain of Hea in Zigula. The Washu Waja Nkobo, one of the most important groups in Bumbuli at the time Mbegha arrived, claim to have lived in Shambaai since time immemorial. Taita and Pare origins are most commonly found in northern Shambaai.

The unity of highlands peoples exists not only in Shambaai,

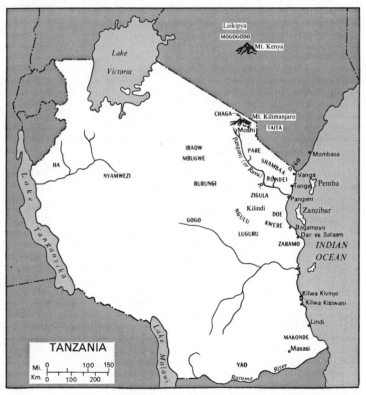

University of Wisconsin Cartographic Lab

Map 2. Peoples and places mentioned in the text

but also, quite probably, in all the areas from which the early Shambaa population came. Kimambo has shown how Ngulu and Taita were important dispersal areas for Pare population.[1]

Into this small world of related highlands peoples there burst, shortly before Mbegha's arrival, two great bodies of immigrants who had their origins hundreds of miles away, probably on the Laikipya plateau, northwest of Mount Kenya. These were the Mbugu and the Nango. It was their arrival which set the stage for the creation of the kingdom.

The events which led to the founding of the kingdom began, in other words, decades earlier and hundreds of miles away. They involved the interaction of all three of East Africa's major linguistic units—Bantu, Cushites, and Nilotes.

The evidence for the events is complex but, briefly stated, the arrival of the Mbugu in Shambaai was a rather distant effect of the expansion of the Nilotes into the Laikipya plateau. Before this time much of the plateau above the Rift Valley was inhabited by Cushitic-speaking peoples.

With the expansion of the Nilotes, the earlier inhabitants were either absorbed into the new population or fled to defensible positions where they survived as small isolated remnant populations. The Mbugu are one such remnant population; they fled all the way from Laikipya to Shambaai before finding adequate refuge. Mbugu is a name assigned by their neighbors to people who actually call themselves Vama'a. They say that they fled from their original home in "Lukipya," and went to Mbugwe, and ultimately, of course, to Shambaai.

A similar remnant people, who also originated in Laikipya,

1. Isaria Kimambo, *A Political History of the Pare of Tanzania* (Nairobi, 1969), p. 41. The statement that Taita, Pare, and the hilly portions of Zigula are the most frequent places of origin of early Shambaa groups is based on hundreds of fragmentary conversations. For some of the evidence, see Historical traditions: Asumani Abdallah, 4 August 1967; Athumani Mdoe, 5 February 1968; Idi Kibarua, 30 October 1967; Lihani Shemnkande, 12 June 1967; Makao Sangoda, Idi Kibarua, and Selemani Shebawa (group testimony), 10 May 1967; Mbaruku Nyika, 21 March 1967; Mdoe Zayumba, 8 June 1967; Mhammadi Kika, 20 April 1967; Mwejuma Ngoda, 5 August 1967; Mwokechao Gila, 10 August 1967; Rajabu Msumai, 5 August 1967; Singano Tundwi, 8 February 1968.

are the Mogogodo. These are a Cushitic-speaking people who live in the foothills on the north side of Mount Kenya, and who recall in their traditions how they were driven out of their original home by the Laikipiak. While neither the Mbugu nor the Mogogodo language has been adequately recorded, there are some remarkable similarities between the basic vocabulary of the Mogogodo and the Mbugu, similarities which emerge from the scattered word lists currently available.[2]

Just as the similarities between Mogogodo and Mbugu support the identification of the "Lukipya" of the traditions with Laikipya, so do linguistic relationships confirm the statement in the traditions that the Mbugu lived for a time at Mbugwe. Meinhof long ago noted the similarities between the Mbugu language and that of the Burungi, not far from Mbugwe.[3] Once the

2. Some similarities between Mogogodo and Mbugu are:

| English | Mbugu | Mogogodo |
|---------|-------|----------|
| Blood | Saxo | Sogo |
| Country | Di | Dimin |
| Cow | Uwa | Wuat |
| Eye | I'ila | Ila |
| One | We | Wehet |

An Mbugu word list is available in E. C. Green, "The Wambugu of Usambara," *Tanganyika Notes and Records,* no. 61 (September 1963), pp. 175–89. The Mogogodo are discussed in Joseph H. Greenberg, "The Mogogodo, a Forgotten Cushitic People," *Journal of African Languages* 2 (1963): 29–43. The Mogogodo tradition of origin is given by C. W. Hobley, *Ethnology of the A-kamba and other East African Tribes* (Cambridge, 1910), p. 146. One Mbugu tradition, among many, which specifies "Maasai" attacks as the reason for leaving Lukipya, is recorded in Historical traditions: Singo Kumoso, 19 June 1968.

3. Carl Meinhof, "Linguistische Studien in Ostafrika, 11. Mbulunge," *Afrikanische Studien,* Mitteilungen des Seminars für Orientalische Sprachen, part 3 p. 325. See also section 10 of the same work, "Mbugu," pp. 294–323. The relationship between Mbugu and Burungi has been confirmed more recently by W. H. Whiteley, "Linguistic Hybrids," *African Studies* 19 (1960): 95–97. He also mentions Mbugu in *A Short Description of Item Categories in Iraqw* (Kampala, 1958), p. 2. Whiteley calls the Mbugu language Bantoid, a linguistic hybrid. It is clear from the nature of migration, however, that the language must have been more strongly non-Bantu before the Mbugu came to Pare and to Shambaai. Joseph H. Greenberg classifies Mbugu as a Cushitic language in *Studies*

Mbugu had moved southwards to escape conflict, Maasai-speaking peoples (Nilotes) pushed on southwards, and the conflict was renewed. Mbugu traditions do not make clear distinctions between the pastoral Maasai and the Iloikop Maasai.[4]

From Mbugwe the Mbugu fled eastwards, to the neighborhood of Shambaai. The Mbugu migration was not a unitary movement as it approached Shambaai. It was, rather, a complex series of movements, with some groups going to Zigula and others entering Pare at various points, settling, and slowly being assimilated to the Pare way of life.[5] All the Mbugu who came to Shambaai had lived in Pare for some time. At a number of points along the way they fought Maasai. One of the great attractions of mountain life, no doubt, was ease of defense.

The first Mbugu to enter Shambaai were a splinter group who have become known as Nango. They entered Shume, on the western side of Shambaai, at least a generation before the coming of Mbegha. All the traditions agree that the Nango were originally Mbugu of the Gonja lineage, and that the split occurred during a migration of the Gonja from Pare to Shambaai. Just

---

in *African Linguistic Classification* (New Haven, Conn., 1955), and in "The Languages of Africa," *International Journal of American Linguistics* 29 (1963), no. 1, part 2. The clearest explanation of the issues, and of the difficulty of classification in this case, is by Morris Goodman: "The Strange Case of Mbugu," in *Pidginization and Creolization of Languages,* ed. Dell Hymes (Cambridge, 1971), pp. 243–54. I have persisted in calling them a Cushitic-speaking people for the sake of clarity, since they have entered the literature of East African history as Cushites. See Christopher Ehret, "Cattle-keeping and milking in Eastern and Southern African History: the Linguistic Evidence," *Journal of African History* 8 (1967): 1–17, see esp. p. 11. See also B. A. Ogot and J. A. Kieran, eds., *Zamani: A Survey of East African History* (Nairobi, 1968), pp. 8, 85, 162.

4. Alan Jacobs, "The Traditional Political Organization of the Pastoral Masai" (D.Phil. thesis, Oxford University, 1965), Chapter 2.

5. Historical traditions: Abdallah Mweta, 13 June and 15 June 1968; Father Andrew Grant, October 1967; Haimasi Kipingu, 2 August 1967; Ishika Kibabu, 19 June 1968; Ishika Kumoso, 10 June 1968; Mavoa Shambo, 19 June 1968; Mbura Kidala, 19 June 1968; Mcharo Mizighi, 12 June 1968; Nyaki Sempombe, 21 June 1968; Rere Komba, 15 June 1968; Salimu Mhina, 15 June 1968; Singo Kumoso, 19 June 1968; Zahabu Mrindoko, 19 June 1968.

as they were about to enter Shambaai there was a disagreement, and the Gonja turned back to Pare while the future Nango continued on their way to Shume, where they established their main settlements. There is some disagreement in the traditions as to the cause of the split. The Nango maintain that the Gonja leader turned back when two of his cows had broken legs. The Mbugu maintain that there was a quarrel over losses of livestock sustained in raids by the Iloikop Maasai. Later the Nango took up hunting, began to ignore the prohibition against eating the flesh of wild animals, and were in the end permanently excluded from Mbugu society.[6]

Some time after the arrival of the Nango, the Mbugu lineages themselves began to enter Shambaai. There were six lineages of Mbugu, and each entered the mountains by a slightly different route. Each, in the end, settled in an area of the mountains which was unattractive to the Shambaa population, either along the dry western side of the mountains at Shume or in the high inaccessible central mountain region.

Once the Mbugu had entered Shambaai, the Nango, who retained their main settlements in Shume, spread to all parts of the mountains. The Nango began to learn the Shambaa language, while the Mbugu until this day speak a separate language which is unintelligible to the Shambaa. The break between the Nango and the Mbugu over whether to respect the taboo on the flesh of wild animals was probably part of a broader disagreement over the propriety of adapting to the Shambaa economy. The Nango chose to live the Shambaa way, and so they had to live among the Shambaa, exploiting with them the resources of the Shambaa environment.

The division of the new immigrants into Mbugu and Nango groups, and further into a number of competing lineages, is clear evidence that while the new population of Shambaai had common origins, they did not enjoy an unambiguous sense of political unity. The older Shambaa population, in much the same

6. Historical traditions: the most complete statement of the Nango position is the text of Mbogho Mzao, 9 February 1968. The Mbugu position is given is the following texts: Abdallah Mweta, 13 June 1968; Nyaki Sempombe, 21 June 1968; Salehe Mbaruku, 11 June 1968.

way, enjoyed the advantages of a deep-rooted cultural consensus while riven by factional disputes which arose from the interaction of competing descent groups.

With the entry of the Nango into areas of Shambaa population, the unspoken bases of Shambaa unity were challenged. At the heart of the tension between the old and the new population were divergent definitions of the extent of the political unit. Shambaa ideas of the importance of cooperation among neighbors came into conflict with Nango and Mbugu ideas of the importance of cooperation among men who share common descent wherever they may live.

Among the older Shambaa population the basic political unit was the single village, built on a hilltop or along the crest of a ridge. The leader of the village was the head of a lineage, and the largest group of his followers were his sons and grandsons. Strangers could settle in an established village, but the man whose ancestor had first settled there had the greatest authority because it was his ancestor who had first cleared the site, and who had to be propitiated. It was his ancestor whose medicines protected the village against witches, thieves, warfare, natural calamities. At some places the controlling lineages of a number of neighboring villages thought of themselves as sharing patrilineal descent. In these cases, the men of the related lineages often acknowledged a single ritual leader who presided in sacrificial rites for the larger descent group, and in protective rites for the set of villages.[7]

Since the self-sufficient political units were so small, there was a need for cooperation over a larger area, for the purpose of common defense, trade, the exchange of marriage partners. It is clear, even from the sketchy traditions which survive, that there was a complex web of relationships and institutions which tied together a group of villages into a neighborhood.

7. For a detailed description of pre-Kilindi descent groups, see Feierman, "Concepts of Sovereignty," pp. 51–60, and Chapter 3. The argument is based on general descriptions from the historical traditions, inferences from the distribution of clan forms, and historical traditions describing events which affected particular groups during the period, as in the traditions of the Hea, which are mentioned below, pp. 86–89.

Rites of passage were performed by the people of a neighborhood. No one descent group was permitted to hold initiation rites for its own members to the exclusion of outsiders. As these rites are performed today, the initiation is not considered valid unless a number of participants from a number of lineages take part. There is strong evidence that the same rule existed at the time of Mbegha, for as we shall see in the history of the Hea descent group below, the early Kilindi used the relative freedom of movement during the rites to send assassins to kill important enemies.

Internal trade drew the members of a neighborhood together, regardless of their village and lineage affiliations. Iron working was the specialty of a few descent groups; an entire neighborhood might rely on one or two iron-working centers from which implements and weapons were purchased. In addition, a hunter who had made a big kill could divide up the meat and trade portions of it.[8]

Another institution, probably the most important one, which tied separate villages into a coherent neighborhood network, was marriage. In modern Shambaai, marriage ties create intricate patterns of interrelationship within neighborhoods (see pp. 37–39); institutions similar to the modern ones undoubtedly existed in the eighteenth century. Any descent group, no matter how isolated and independent, had to find wives for its sons and to send its daughters into other villages as wives. The long-term payment of bridewealth together with family rites which had to be performed together by the husband's and the wife's families meant that the marriage relationship was not merely a transfer of rights in women, but the establishment of permanent ties between two groups.

When a neighborhood was threatened from the outside, it was usual for all the villages to unite behind the leadership of the most powerful local group. Warnings of raids and other disasters were transmitted over a large area by drums, which were in the possession of preeminent groups. The two most important drums of southern Shambaai were in the possession of the people of

8. Early trade is described in detail in Chapter 5.

Bumbuli and those of Vugha (the Wakina Tui). In northern Shambaai the most important single pre-Kilindi group was that of the Kijelwa.[9] While the largest groups provided leadership in time of common danger, the power to settle disputes or to redistribute wealth could be exercised only within a single descent group.

A distinction can be made between the solidary institutions which united the older Shambaa descent groups, and those of the Nango and Mbugu. Among the older Shambaa, united action which transcended the village polity was rooted in ties of neighborhood. But the Nango, even once they had spread into Shambaa neighborhoods, retained an allegiance to their own widely ramified group wherever it was. The tension between this new political pattern and the older one led ultimately to Shambaa acceptance of Mbegha.

The overriding allegiance of the Nango to their own large group and of the Mbugu to theirs, in spite of territorial dispersion, can best be seen in the patterns of marriage and of ritual. A Nango could marry another Nango. Mbugu, to this day, tend to marry within Mbugu society.[10] There were six lineages of Nango, each of which claimed to be descended from a separate ancestor, yet all of which acknowledged their common origin. While a person could not marry someone of his own lineage, he could marry a Nango of any other lineage. The Mbugu had a similar structure of six lineages. Shambaa, on the other hand, could not marry members of their own descent groups. Thus, while every Shambaa marriage tended to unite local groups into an integrated neighborhood, each marriage of a Nango to a Nango intensified the cohesiveness of the group at the expense of neighborhood integration.

9. Vugha's drum is described in Historical traditions: Kimweri Magogo, 1 December 1967. See also *H.z.W.*, Sura 14, on the competition between the Vugha and Bumbuli drums. In Mlalo, when the Kilindi sacrifice at the royal grave site, they invoke the name of a Kijelwa leader before the name of the first Kilindi chief. See Historical traditions: Nasoro Maghembe, 18 July 1968.

10. There is a tradition which describes a dispute between two Nango lineages over bridewealth at about the time in question, in Historical traditions: Shemzighua Rupia, 7 February 1968.

This would not have been presented a serious political problem had it not been for Nango and Mbugu initiation rituals. In order for any individual Nango to be initiated, *all* Nango had to assemble at Shume. The rites, called *mshitu,* could only be completed at a gathering of the total Nango community.[11] While the Nango lived in many parts of Shambaai, interspersed with the Shambaa, they were not drawn into neighborhood rituals, and they reaffirmed their unity as Nango by holding great mass meetings periodically at Shume.

The Mbugu case was slightly different. The Mbugu lived in areas which were isolated from the Shambaa, and so they were undoubtedly a less disturbing element within Shambaa society. But the Mbugu may well have presented an external threat, for they gathered in Pare to complete their *mshitu* rites, reuniting the Mbugu of Pare and of Shambaai in one ritual community. Four lineages of Mbugu went to Suji, on the western side of South Pare, for their initiation. (These were the Ombeji, Gonja, Nkanzu, and Ngarito.) Two lineages participated in the rituals of Vudee, just north of Suji. (These were the Nkwangwana and Ombweni.)[12]

There were, in other words, two separate points of tension, one with the Mbugu, and the other with the Nango. The Nango would not be integrated into Shambaa localities. The Mbugu were potential fifth columnists. Mbegha entered a society, in other words, in which an ancient consensus on the proper organization of stateless politics had been challenged, and which, in addition, felt itself threatened by outside forces.[13]

11. All Nango traditions agree on this point. The most detailed description is given in Historical traditions: Mbogho Mzao, 9 February 1968.

12. Historical traditions: Father Andrew Grant, October 1967; Haimasi Kipingu, 2 August 1967; Ishika Kibabu, 19 June 1968; Mavoa Shambo, 19 June 1968; Mbura Kidala, 19 June 1968; Mcharo Mizighi, 12 June 1968; Nyaki Sempombe, 21 June 1968. Dr. Isaria Kimambo has informed me that the Mbugu *mshitu* at Vudee was quite separate from Pare *mshitu* rites (personal communication, 28 November 1967).

13. According to *H.z.W.,* the Mkina Tui said to the men of Bumbuli, "Bring Mbegha to Vugha, because we have a great war with the people of Pare and we are in expectation of attack every day." Tui himself

Yet we must not assume, in spite of the presence of two competing political systems in Shambaai at the time of Mbegha, that either the old or the new populations enjoyed a sense of monolithic unity. There were clearly tensions among the older Shambaa: the evidence seems to show that the Hea of Ubii were irreconcilable enemies of the Wakina Tui of Vugha. And in the ultimate conflict between the Shambaa and the Nango, the Nango were to be defeated by conflicts within their own society, not by the strength of their enemies.

## The Founding of the Kingdom

It was at this time of disunity that Mbegha entered Shambaai. The society was divided at its core. There was not merely surface conflict between established groups—there were differing views on the way in which conflict should be acted out.

Mbegha started his journey from Ngulu. This is significant, for Ngulu was the place of origin of much of the older population of southern Shambaai. And Ngulu itself is a society which, within living memory, has had no centralized political institutions. Each small area and lineage has stood independent of the others.[14]

---

"boasted how he slew the men of Pare with his spear" (Suras 10–11). This war with Pare was not mentioned by any of my informants in any of the traditions collected.

14. T. O. Beidelman, *The Matrilineal Peoples of Eastern Tanzania,* Ethnographic Survey of Africa, East Central Africa, part 16 (London, 1967), p. 58. Three of the twenty-six variants of the Mbegha myth describe Mbegha as either an Arab from Ngulu, or the son of an Arab who went to Ngulu. It is extremely improbable that these describe historical reality. *Habari za Wakilindi,* written by a man the Shambaa called an Arab, and based on traditions which he began to hear by the 1860s, does not describe Mbegha as an Arab. Quite probably the Arabic connection was created in the second half of the nineteenth century as a fictional genealogical link to be referred to in dealings with coastal traders. Of the three traditions I collected which make the connection, one was told by a Kilindi who dresses like an Arab, carries a sword, and is proud of the fact that he looks like an Arab. Another was told by a Kilindi who takes Islam very seriously and is married to the daughter of an Arab. One of the traditions creates a set of genealogical links of which the Arabic connection is only one. According to this tradition, three Arabs who were

The first place Mbegha established a relationship which was to endure through his years in Shambaai was Kwa Mbiu, in Zigula, before he ever came to the mountains. He made blood partnership with one of the people of the village, one of the Wakina Mbiu, before continuing on his way. The two men entered Shambaai together. Later, when Mbegha became king, the Mkina Bbiu became his Mlughu, or hereditary chief minister.[15]

When Mbegha arrived on the borders of Shambaai he stayed at Leopard's Cave (*mpanga ya shuwi*), below Ziai. The members of the Ziai lineage report, in their tradition, that their leader at that time, Shenyeo, reacted initially to Mbegha's presence with fear. Then he and Mbegha tested one another's magical powers, with no clear outcome. Finally the two men took the oath of blood partnership.

The Ziai tradition clearly indicates that Mbegha was powerful —a man to be feared—when he entered Shambaai, for they made an unusual form of blood partnership, a form used only for potential enemies. In the common form, the oath is a conditional curse. Two men who decide that they need to be able to trust one another pronounce the curse and then consume each other's blood. Each man says, "If I come to your house at night when you are not there, I will sleep in it. I will ask your wife to

---

kinsmen in Mombasa separated from one another. One remained in Mombasa, one went to Zanzibar, and one went to Ngulu, where he fathered Mbegha and Mbegha's brother Meli before going to Zanzibar to die. Mbegha and Meli left Ngulu together, but separated at the Pangani River. Mbegha went on to become king of the Shambaa, Meli to become chief of Moshi. It is chronologically impossible for Mbegha and Meli to have been contemporaries. The tradition is, however, a masterpiece of diplomacy, for it creates links with Mombasa, Zanzibar, and Moshi. These portions of the traditions were not discussed in the analysis of the myth of Mbegha because they are an example of historical material woven into the myth, of a kind easily changed without altering the myth's structure (see pp. 64–65). The variants which describe Mbegha as an Arab do not vary any of the structural elements. They describe Mbegha in Ngulu as an outcast, ritually dangerous, a bringer of death, a hunter with dogs, an eater of pig meat, a man of boundless sexuality.

15. Historical traditions: Mdoe Barua, 12 March 1967; Ng'wana Aia, 20 March 1967; Ng'wa Paula s/o Ng'wa Kimungu, 12 July 1967. Ng'wana Aia is an Mkina Mbiu.

cook, and eat your food. But if I touch your wife, may I die, or if I steal your possessions may I die." Mbegha's partnership with Shenyeo took a different form. Mbegha swore that he would never enter Ziai, either to eat or to sleep. This shows that Mbegha was a man to be feared for his great powers as a magician and as a hunter-warrior.[16]

All the traditions, including those of the Ziai themselves, agree that Ziai was relatively weak and unimportant among the villages of the older Shambaa at the time of Mbegha's coming. A test of strength with the Ziai leader might have established Mbegha's reputation as a powerful man, but it was not sufficient to overawe the leaders of Bumbuli and Vugha. If the leaders of the southern Shambaa chose to ally themselves with Mbegha, it was because he was useful to them, for there is no tradition of conquest in the areas of Mbegha's earliest influence, Vugha and Bumbuli.

Mbegha went northeastwards from Ziai to Bumbuli, and then at Bumbuli he was invited by the men of Vugha to their village. The Wakina Tui recall that they were delighted to welcome Mbegha and make him their leader. Mbegha married an Mkina Tui. The traditions of Mbegha's enemies confirm that the relationship between Mbegha and the Wakina Tui was one of alliance.[17]

All the independent traditions from the area which initially accepted Mbegha stress the importance of two mechanisms he used in building his power—marriage and blood partnership. Even today these are the two relationships any outsider uses to establish alliances with local groups. Mbegha did not initially, in other words, achieve permanent heritable power as a political leader; he did not create an office. Instead, he made personal alliances with some of the main groups of southern Shambaai. These were groups, moreover, which had important interests in common as members of the older Shambaa population.

16. Historical traditions: Idi Kibarua, 30 October 1967; Makao Sangoda, Idi Kibarua, Selemani Shebawa (group testimony), 10 March 1967.

17. Historical traditions: Abdallah Mweta, 13 June 1968; Athumani Mdoe, 5 February 1968; Yeremia Muati, n.d.

Mbegha was ultimately able to consolidate his power because he had forged personal alliances within the two areas which had been in bitter competition with each other, and yet which had a great deal to gain from union—Vugha and Bumbuli. These have traditionally been the two most densely populated areas of southern Shambaai. Bumbuli could not accept the leadership of Vugha; Vugha would not be ruled by Bumbuli. But both made alliances with a powerful outsider in order to reestablish the internal unity of the Shambaa way of life. In the end they were ruled by him.[18]

18. Two arguments on the creation of the Shambaa kingdom have been rejected here, but deserve comment. Professor Roland Oliver has argued that Mbegha brought at least some elements of kingship with him from Ngulu. He has pointed out that the skill in hunting wild pigs ascribed to Mbegha was "attributed to the founders of ruling houses from Ugogo all the way south to the Nyakyusa." See Oliver, "Discernible Developments in the Interior *c.* 1500–1840," in *History of East Africa,* vol. 1, ed. Roland Oliver and Gervase Mathew (Oxford, 1963), p. 197.

There are two difficulties with this argument. First, there is no record of the existence of the institution of kingship in Ngulu. Second, T. O. Beidelman has shown, in an essay which appeared after the publication of the Oxford history, that pig-hunting is a key symbol in an Ngulu initiation rite which has nothing to do with politics. See Beidelman, "Pig (*Guluwe*): an Essay on Ngulu Sexual Symbolism and Ceremony," *Southwestern Journal of Anthropology* 20 (1964): 359–92.

The second argument has been presented by Edgar Winans in his ethnography of the Shambaa. He has put forth the hypothesis that *gao,* the men's initiation rite, was imposed on the Shambaa by the Kilindi, and that before the Kilindi ruled, each group had a different rite. He says, "It seems quite clear that *gao* is a Kilindi rite, for it is controlled by the Kilindi." See Winans, *Shambala, the Constitution of a Traditional State* (London, 1962), p. 97. This seems to be a misunderstanding of the phrase *gao ja Kikiindi*—"Kilindi *gao.*" There were, in fact, two kinds of *gao* in the precolonial period, those sponsored by a Kilindi, and those sponsored by any other wealthy commoner. Those sponsored by a Kilindi had several additional *vihii,* or mysteries.

Because I had read Winans' hypothesis before doing field research, I asked dozens of elders about the rites practiced by the Shambaa before the coming of the Kilindi. All said that *gao* was the ritual of most Shambaa before the coming of Mbegha.

Winans has also argued that the similarity between *gao* and the rites of the Ngulu and the Zigula is evidence that the rite came to Shambaai with Mbegha (*Shambala,* p. 97). The correspondence is, in fact, striking,

The process by which Mbegha converted his personal influence into permanent power is not mentioned in the traditions. The problem may, in fact, be somewhat less significant than it initially appears to be. Southall has shown that in many African states the central authority was able to enforce its will throughout the area nominally subordinate to it if it was able to call on the self-interest of one quarter of the realm to crush recalcitrance in another.[19] This was true of Mbegha as an informal leader, just as it was true of many of the kings who were Mbegha's successors. Once this is said, there remains an important unsolved problem, a hard kernel of ignorance, about the way Mbegha's position in an ephemeral alliance network was transformed into an enduring office. It is clear, at any rate, that Mbegha achieved considerable power during his lifetime, and that he expanded his kingdom by conquering the most important group of Shambaa (as opposed to Nango and Mbugu) in southern Shambaai who did not accept his authority. These were the Hea of Ubii.

The Hea had lived in Vugha before even the Wakina Tui arrived in Shambaai. They had moved to Ubii only afterwards. It is quite possible that the Hea had been hostile to the Wakina Tui since the time they were displaced at Vugha. Ubii, the Hea village and the surrounding area, was the buffer which protected the Nango center at Shume from the immediate pressure of Mbegha's forces.

The Hea say that when Mbegha had been installed by the Wakina Tui he began to plan his attack on Ubii: "There was the mountain of the Hea, and there was the mountain of the Mkina

---

but *gao* is also similar to the *alama* rites of the Bondei; see Godfrey Dale, *An Account of the Principal Customs and Habits of the Natives Inhabiting the Bondei* (London, 1896). Zigula, Bondei, and Shambaai are closely related culturally, and are geographically contiguous. We seem to be dealing with a cultural province which is so large as to transcend any political unit. One would have to use unusual historical reasoning to conclude that a rite which is in general use over an entire culture area came into use in a small part of that area because it was imposed by a local political force.

19. Aidan Southall, *Alur Society* (Cambridge, 1956), pp. 251–52.

Tui. Then Mbegha thought about Mhina [the head of the Hea], and he began to consider putting an end to Mhina's power." Mbegha swore partnership with a girl who knew Mhina, and they decided that the best time to kill the Hea leader was during a ritual, when people would come and go freely. First Mbegha made countermagic to destroy Mhina's protective charms. On the day of the celebration, the girl went, and she approached Mhina affectionately: "Grandfather has such a long beard," she said to the young men, "and you do not shave him. Don't you know that today is a celebration?" She sat down with the old man to shave him, and when he raised his chin to expose his throat she slit it. The girl escaped, in the ensuing confusion, to Vugha.[20]

Even after Mhina's death, the power of the Hea did not decline, and so Mbegha plotted again. Mhina's successor, Shemdola, was invited to a hunting party. Under Mbegha's instructions, the hunters strangled Shemdola and then reported that he had been killed by a wild pig. When the Hea saw what had happened they split up and fled in all directions.

Before their defeat the Hea had been renowned for their rain magic. They had a pot, called a *kiza,* filled with water and herbal medicines which ensured that rain would fall at the proper season. When the Hea were defeated, Mbegha took their rain charms. Later, when it was clear that they were powerless, a Hea was made councillor at Vugha so that the famous Hea protective medicines would be used to guard the great house of the king.

Mbegha's confiscation of Hea rain magic was an important step in his consolidation of power. Rain magic is thought not to work unless one person has an effective monopoly over the magic for a given area. The Shambaa believe that famine is caused by the competition of rain magicians. Mbegha could extend his power over the territory of the Hea only after he had

20. Historical traditions. The quotations are from the tradition of Athumani Mdoe, 5 February 1968. The discussion of the Hea is derived largely from this tradition and from that of Mwokechao Gila, 10 August 1967.

taken their rain magic, for otherwise there would be no effective monopoly of control of the magic within the kingdom.

The Hea traditions make one additional point about how their social structure changed with the advent of Kilindi political control. One informant has said that until the Kilindi conquest all the Hea had one basket (*mfuko*) for use in sacrifice. After the conquest the Hea split up, and there were two baskets, and later possibly even more. While it is difficult to collect evidence on changes in social structure which took place two hundred years ago, the multiplication of sacrificial baskets was probably a common phenomenon. This is, admittedly, a speculative point.

In Shambaai today a group which possesses a single sacrificial basket performs the sacrificial rite together; its members inherit wives from one another; and marriage is prohibited among members. When quarrels or geographical distance split the group, each part gets its own basket, often with a bit of the old one woven into it. The members of the separate groups may then marry one another. Let us assume, for example, that all the descendants of an ancestor five generations ago cooperate within a basket-sharing descent group. If the group then splits, the cooperative units might each be descended from a different ancestor only three generations ago, and the number of people actually cooperating would decrease.

It seems that before the coming of Mbegha it was in the interest of exogamous descent groups to maintain large memberships —for many people to have one basket. In case of any kind of dispute, the more armed men a group could provide, the more likely it was to win. With the coming of Mbegha, however, the strongest groups were attacked. One tradition states that "Mbegha looked around to see who the strong people were" so that he could eliminate them.[21] The ritual leaders of large descent groups were capable of competing politically with Mbegha and his successors. They were therefore attacked. It is possible also that in some areas the large descent groups became less important as individuals moved away from the ritual centers to find land. Thus larger descent groups than those which are active and

21. Historical traditions: Athumani Mdoe, 5 February 1968.

important today were probably characteristic of the pre-Kilindi era, and the division of the Hea basket was probably paralleled by the splitting of many sacrificial baskets.

When Mbegha died, some time after the conquest of the Hea, the battle with the Nango had still not been joined. The creation of the kingdom had, however, had a profound effect on the Nango. The ritual leader of the Nango, whose name was Mbogho, attempted, in response to Mbegha's rise at Vugha, to convert his position of ritual authority into one of political power.

First Mbogho attempted to establish the principle that members of his lineage, the Wavina Mpaa, did not have to pay bridewealth. In the Shambaa view the king's right to marry without bridewealth was equivalent to his right to collect tribute: it was an expression of sovereignty. The Nango move toward centralization came when a member of Mbogho's lineage married a Nango of another lineage (Mvina Mpuku), and refused to pay bridewealth. After a long bitter dispute a member of the bride's family who was sent to collect a cow was killed. The two lineages broke off relations (even today they may not intermarry), but Mbogho did not succeed in establishing his right to tribute.

After Mbegha's death, the Nango leader Mbogho made his final and disastrous attempt to rule the Nango as Mbegha had ruled the Shambaa. The exact nature of the dispute which led to open conflict is unclear, since the Nango are defensive about it, and hesitate to tell the complete story. It is clear, however, that Mbogho killed a Nango of the Mvina Nkima lineage, and that this lineage, in anger, went to Vugha with an offer to kill Mbogho, who was their own leader. Mbegha's son and successor, Bughe, was delighted to accept.

The decline of the Nango came about, in other words, because the Wavina Nkima preferred to cooperate with Mbegha's son Bughe rather than be ruled by their own ritual leader. The Nango were destroyed by internal jealousy. Mbogho was killed because he said, "If you think the Kilindi are the only ones who marry without bridewealth you don't know me. . . . Anyone who objects to my rule will be killed."[22]

22. Historical traditions: Kiluwa Shemhina, 9 February 1968.

After the Nango subgroup (Wavina Nkima) had succeeded in killing Mbogho, Bughe carried out a campaign of persecution. The only group of Nango treated well by Bughe were the Wavina Nkima, who had killed their leader. But the others were hunted down: "If a Nango told the story of Mbogho he was killed. . . . Some called themselves Kwavi so that they would not be wiped out. We hid ourselves in the bush like wild animals."[23]

Just as Mbegha had first defeated the Hea and had then drawn them into the kingdom, Bughe was careful to integrate at least some of the Nango into the kingdom. The Wavina Nkima, the Nango who had conspired to kill their own leader, enjoyed a favored position within the kingdom. In the accession rite, a new king would stop at the Nango town of Tekwa, near Bumbuli, in order to go through a series of Nango rituals with the Wavina Nkima. The Kilindi adopted *kilulumo,* a form of sacrifice which the Nango say was originally theirs. Quite often the great wife, and therefore the mother of the future king, was a loyal Nango of Bumbuli.

By integrating the Nango into the kingdom, Bughe took the final step in solving the problem of pre-Kilindi Shambaai. When Mbegha appeared at Ziai, the Shambaa seemed unable to coexist with the Nango. By the time of Mbegha's son, the Nango were not only defeated, they were also being drawn into the political life of the kingdom. Mbegha, Bughe, and their Shambaa supporters had succeeded in creating a larger synthesis. They not only defeated the Nango; they include Nango culture at the heart of the kingdom.

23. Historical traditions: Saguti Shekiondo, 21 July 1967. The account of the Nango is based on a number of traditions: Gottfried s/o Salomon Shangali, 7 February 1968; Hemedi Mbogho s/o Wakanali, 6 February 1968; Kiluwa Shemhina, 9 February 1968; Kimweri Magogo, 1 December 1967; Mbogho Mzao, 9 February and 19 July 1968; Mhammadi Shekashiha, 8 February 1968; Saguti Shekiondo, 30 July 1967 and 14 February 1968; Shemzighua Rupia, 7 February 1968; Sylvano Shekaaghe, 27 July 1967; Zachaia Shekighenda, 2 August 1967.

# 4 • THE GROWTH OF THE KINGDOM

The rapid movement of the borders outward from the circumscribed limits of Mbegha's kingdom presents a picture of the early generations of centralized rule as an unmitigated success. But the driving force of expansion was the tension between two contradictory conceptions of politics: on the one hand royal rule was seen as a defense of the unity of Shambaa culture; on the other hand the body politic was defined territorially, and within the borders there was always a diversity of culture.

The conceptions of kingship which existed two hundred years ago in a period without written records are very difficult to know. But there is one remarkable body of evidence which survives from the time of Mbegha's son Bughe, and which supports in great detail the notion that royal rule was a glorification of traditional Shambaa culture: this is the royal capital at Vugha. The capital took its form at about the time of Bughe, and it was treated in the nineteenth century as an archaism. Once the form of the capital was determined, no significant change was allowed. If the way of the ancestors were changed, the capital would be overrun in war.[1]

1. A number of pieces of evidence support the contention that the capital had taken its form by the time of Bughe. The traditions state that Mbegha was the founder of Vugha. He established his capital a short

The culture of the capital was prescribed in the most minute detail, and the importance of traditional Shambaa culture was the dominant theme throughout. The houses of Vugha had to be built in the style of the ancestors; only the beehive hut was acceptable. The beds could be constructed in only one manner, the traditional Shambaa manner.

While it was a town which had a great population, Vugha was built as a replica of a Shambaa village. The king was like a village elder, but much more powerful. Just as a Shambaa village occupied a hilltop, with banana gardens spread beneath, so Vugha was a hilltop encircled by banana groves, with the "owner" at the center. The king's houses at the center could only be thatched with dried banana sheaths. The commoners' houses in the outer circle could only be thatched with wild grass. The thatch was a metaphor: just as a village elder owned the territory of his banana garden but not the wild areas of grass, the king owned Shambaai.

In addition Vugha was a representation in microcosm of all Shambaai. An imaginary north-south line which divided the town into halves was seen as equivalent, in a figurative sense, to the Zimui river which divided Shambaai into halves, east and west. The court officials who lived in the eastern half of town concerned themselves with the affairs of Shambaai east of the Zimui. The officials of the western part of town were the king's representatives west of the river.[2]

---

distance from the original village of the Wakina Tui. Bughe's generation was the first to be buried at Vugha. In addition, there were a number of sets of five in the organization of the town. There were five main poles in the construction of the king's house, and five sets of five rods each in the construction of the door. These are said to represent the five main chiefdoms, and at any time after Bughe there were considerably more than five chiefdoms.

2. A full study of the organization of Vugha, which cannot be included within the scope of this work, can be found in Feierman, "Concepts of Sovereignty," Chapter 6. Some of the most important oral sources on Vugha are in Historical traditions: Kimweri Magogo, Mdoe Barua, Ng'wana Aia (group testimony), 22 July 1968; Mdoe Barua, 15 March, 7 December 1967, and 9 May 1968; Ng'wana Aia, 1 April, 19 May, 7 December 1967, and 24 May 1968.

While it may not have been as self-conscious a case of Shambaa chauvinism, even Bughe's machinery for the administration of the kingdom was modeled on local forms, not exotic imports. The relationship between the king and his subordinate chiefs was quite simply that between a father and his sons. Bughe made his sons chiefs of a number of territories: Bumbuli, Gare, Shembekeza, Mkaie-Tamota.[3]

There was a serious contradiction within Bughe's regime, however. His capital glorified traditional Shambaa culture, but at the same time it was politically expedient for him to bring the alien Nango into the kingdom. Bughe took a Nango of Balangai (near Bumbuli) as one of his most important wives. As a result the Nango were given the hope of becoming the maternal uncles of the next king, and thereby rising to a position of great influence.

Bughe's attempt to bring the aliens into the kingdom succeeded during his lifetime: it enabled him to consolidate his rule of southern Shambaai. But after he died, sometime in the second half of the eighteenth century, he left Shambaai with two groups, each of which expected to capture the position of king.[4]

3. For the histories of the separate chiefdoms, see the Appendix, below in this chapter.

4. From the time of Kimweri ye Nyumbai, Bughe's grandson, we have written records for reconstructing chronology. Kimweri ye Nyumbai acceded to the throne about 1815 (for this date see note 12, below). Virtually all Kilindi oral traditions agree that Kimweri ye Nyumbai was in the fourth generation of Kilindi—that he was a great-grandson of Mbegha. According to the Kilindi, there have been eight generations from the founding of the kingdom to the present, including both Mbegha and the most recent ruler, who is a grandfather at the time of writing.

There are a number of ways of confirming the accuracy of the number of generations listed. In 1852 Johann L. Krapf recorded that Kimweri ye Nyumbai was the great-grandson of the founding king (*Reisen in Ostafrika* [Stuttgart, 1964], part 2, p. 289). Mbugu genealogical data indicate that there have been six to seven generations since the first contact between the Kilindi and the Mbugu; again the most recent generation is represented by a living adult with grandchildren (Historical traditions: Abdallah Mweta, 13 June and 15 June 1968; Rere Komba, 15 June 1968). Pare traditions also confirm the length of the genealogy. Kimambo mentions a Sangi tradition according to which Kimweri's troops

In the dispute over succession the Nango of Balangai fought for control of the kingdom against the forces of Bughe's daughter Mboza Mamwinu. The Nango, in other words, had become convinced of the value of participating in the kingdom. But the tension between the Shambaa and the Nango was reinterpreted as a battle between factions of Shambaa for control of the levers of power.

At the death of the old king the leaders of the subject lineages of Vugha called a meeting to discuss the succession. It was a quiet meeting; its existence was mentioned only where responsible elders gathered in private, for the children were not to know the king was dead until a new king had been installed. Mboza Mamwinu was invited. She was the oldest of Bughe's children, and she had a reputation as the most forceful.

Two names were seriously discussed. The first was Kinyashi

---

fought in Pare seven generations ago (*Political History of the Pare*, p. 112). According to the Kilindi naming system, Kimweri was one of the names of every member of Bughe's generation.

The royal grave site at Vugha provides additional evidence. During royal rituals, the names of the dead kings must be recited in the order in which they lived, and at the grave site the unmarked burial place of each must be remembered. This evidence shows that two sons of Mbegha became king: first Bughe, then Maua. According to this source, the early king list begins with Mbegha, followed by his son Bughe, and then his other son Maua. Maua was succeeded by Bughe's son Kinyashi Muanga Ike, whose son was the next king, Kimweri ye Nyumbai. (Historical traditions: Kimweri Magogo, Mdoe Barua, and Ng'wana Aia (group testimony), 22 July 1968. Maua is virtually always excluded from the traditions. He is probably the same king mentioned in *H.z.W.* as the first Kimweri, who had a short, weak, and unpopular reign (Sura 31).

If we knew some of the events of Maua's reign, the interpretations presented in this chapter might be modified considerably. He is not mentioned in the body of the text simply because the sources are not sufficient for any reliable analysis. Thus, the interpretation presented is merely the most probable one based on currently available sources. The sources are quite extensive, in fact, but there are necessarily big gaps in our knowledge of eighteenth-century events.

The Mshihwi traditions offer an additional confirmation of the number of generations which have passed since Mbegha. Mshihwi split off from the kingdom in the time of Kinyashi Muanga Ike. The traditions of this small state have been transmitted independently since the secession, and they confirm the genealogical details given in the traditions of the main group of Kilindi. The sources are listed below, as sources for the history of the secession.

Muanga Ike, the Nango of Balangai. And Limo, the son of a Shembekeza woman, was the alternative. The elders of Vugha supported Kinyashi. Mboza Mamwinu argued hotly that Limo should be king.[5]

The elders of Vugha finally agreed to make Limo king. It was a dangerous decision, for the elders had acted out of fear of Mboza's anger rather than through real consensus. And the decision threatened the existence of the kingdom. Mbegha had created the kingdom at a time when Nango separatism threatened the unity of Shambaa society. Bughe had succeeded in bringing some of the Nango into the kingdom, convincing them to act in concert with the Shambaa. But if the elders agreed to bypass Kinyashi, the whole Nango question would be opened again. Limo's succession might destroy the unity of the kingdom.

Once Mboza Mamwinu had left Vugha, the elders began to discuss their decision slowly and carefully. It was a very difficult time, for either decision was certain to lead to conflict. While the courtiers were discussing the problem, elders arrived from Balangai to argue their case. These were the mother's brothers of Kinyashi Muanga Ike. Quite probably they had been invited by one faction at Vugha. The discussion continued, with the Nango represented, but not the elders of Shembekeza. Finally the courtiers accepted a gift of two cows from the men of Balangai. This sealed their alliance.

The men of Vugha indicated their decision, at a time of succession, by sending for the new king. The trip from Bumbuli to Vugha, retracing Mbegha's footsteps, was an important part of the accession ritual. The king, like the new moon (they would say), comes from the east. Just as the moon dies only to rise again, so the king dies, and yet he still lives.

Once they had decided on Kinyashi's succession the men of Vugha sent two messengers—one to bring Kinyashi to his accession, the other, with instructions to be late, to bring Limo. While Kinyashi retraced Mbegha's steps, Limo, unsuspecting, retraced Kinyashi's. When Limo came near to Vugha, walking westwards

5. Limo is sometimes described as chief of Shembekeza, and in other traditions he is listed as chief of Mlungui. Also, in some traditions the name Maghembe rather than Limo is used. At any rate it is clear that Limo's supporters were the Shambaa of Shembekeza.

with the sun rising behind him in the early morning, he heard the sound of cheering in the distance, at the capital: "Mbogho! Mbogho!"—"The buffalo, killer of men!" Kinyashi was being compared to a dangerous wild buffalo. He was king, the one man in Shambaa society who could kill men as he wished.

With Kinyashi's succession the Nango problem ended as a serious threat to Shambaa society. One Nango expressed the ambiguity of their position when he insisted that the Nango, as mother's brothers to the king, could tear down the fences of the royal enclosure at Vugha to use as firewood. Vugha was alien, the Nango outsiders, but still they had an enormous stake in the kingdom.[6]

When Mboza heard what had happened she went to Vugha, swept into the royal enclosure, took the regalia, and left. Mboza and Limo made a sad ceremony at Shembekeza, imitating the accession ritual amidst Limo's maternal relatives. Limo put on the king's ostrich-feather crown, and the people cheered, "Mbogho! Mbogho!" Before long Kinyashi's warriors came, and after a few engagements Limo and Mboza moved north to the most isolated and inaccessible part of Shambaai. They crossed the valley beyond Mgwashi, climbed the steep mountain of Bumba, and prepared to defend themselves. Kinyashi's armies came again; even at Bumba they could not be resisted.

Mboza moved on westward to the mountain of Mshihwi, which rises sharply up from the valley. Mshihwi is like a truncated cone, with barren boulder-strewn sides and a small crest of green arable land. Mboza settled there, for the place could easily be defended. Her forces merely had to stay on top and roll boulders down onto an attacker. She had come with a great herd of cattle which she distributed to eminent elders of Mshihwi to gain local support. Kinyashi's forces attacked Mshihwi on three separate occasions. Each time the climbing soldiers were crushed by the boulders which roared down the mountainside. Mboza succeeded in creating a new political entity which was parallel in structure to the Vugha kingdom, but independent.[7]

6. Historical traditions: Saguti Shekiondo, 30 July 1967.
7. There are a number of conflicting traditions on the origins of Mshihwi. Generally, the traditions of the Mshihwi Kilindi are more detailed and circumstantial than those of Vugha. Among the Historical tra-

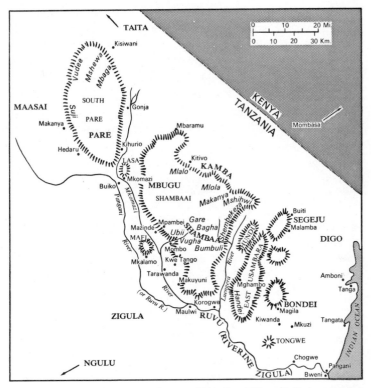

University of Wisconsin Cartographic Lab

Map 3. Shambaai and its neighbors (after Mbazira)

The warfare between the Mshihwi and Vugha kingdoms continued intermittently through Kinyashi's reign, and affected the pattern of political action throughout the kingdom. Kinyashi was unable to dominate the chiefs of southern Shambaai, the original homeland of the kingdom. When he came to the throne his half

ditions, those of Mshihwi include: Mnkande Kimweri, 13 September 1966; Shebughe Shemnkande, 17 August 1966; Yonatani Abrahamu, 20 July 1966. Some of the most important Vugha versions are: Kasimu Kimweri, 1 February 1968; Kimweri Magogo, 24 March 1967; Mbwana Mkanka Mghanga, 7 May 1967; Mpira Sanju, 31 January 1968; Waziri Nyeghee, 1 July 1967. See also *H.z.W.*, Suras 32–38.

brothers were in control of the chiefdoms, where they had been
placed by their father, Bughe. They saw no reason to accept the
authority of a sibling, and they were able to resist successfully
Kinyashi's attempts to remove them. Kinyashi had to face the
grim possibility that the king of Mshihwi would make an alliance
with any chief who felt himself threatened. The extent of the
king's failure in southern Shambaai is obvious from the following chart of the relations between Bughe and Kinyashi and the
heads of the chiefdoms:

| Chiefdom | Bughe | Kinyashi Muanga Ike |
|---|---|---|
| Southern  Shambaai | | |
| Bumbuli | Son | Son |
| Shembekeza | Son | None? |
| Mkaie-Tamota | Son | Brother |
| Ubii-Gare | Son | Brother |
| Bagha | None | None |
| Mbugu  forest | | |
| | Scattered indigenous tributaries? | Scattered indigenous tributaries |
| Northern  Shambaai | | |
| Mlalo | Indigenous  tributary | Son |
| Mtii | Indigenous  tributary | Son |
| Mlola | None | None |
| Mshihwi | None | Brother (rival claim-ant to throne) |
| Eastern Provinces (see Map 3, p. 97) | | |
| Chiefdoms of East Usambara | None | Sons  or  tributaries (unclear) |
| Chiefdoms of Bondei | None | Sons  or  tributaries (details unclear) |
| Districts of Digo | None | Indigenous tribu-taries |
| Coastal towns | None | Indigenous tribu-taries |

Kinyashi Muanga Ike's situation was made more desperate by the need to keep his supporters at Vugha supplied with tribute. Vugha was the main source of the king's fighting men. The alliance between the king and the common people of the chiefdom of Vugha was maintained throughout the history of the early kingdom. The town, unlike all other Shambaa towns, had no defensive palisade. A proverb explains that the people of Vugha are the king's fortifications.

In return for their loyal service, the people of Vugha helped consume the tribute that poured in from all over Shambaai. But with the chiefdoms of southern Shambaai independent, Kinyashi faced the threat that his support at Vugha would melt away.

Rather than see his kingdom disintegrate, Kinyashi took the offensive, using the army he had assembled for the Mshihwi war against his other, weaker neighbors. The kingdom expanded very rapidly, even while it remained weak at the center. The interaction between territorial government and ethnicity entered a new stage. Bughe's attempts at territorial integration had failed, leading to the Mshihwi conflict. In response, Kinyashi expanded his realm enormously, taking in people of several ethnic groups, and widening the arena of future conflict.

Kinyashi Muanga Ike added the people of the northern rim of Shambaai to his kingdom, except for the territory of Mlola, which was adjacent to Mshihwi. He conquered the mountain people of East Usambara, subjugated the Bondei of the hill country which falls away toward the sea, dominated the Digo of the immediate coastal hinterland, and collected tribute from the Swahili speakers of the coastal towns.

Kinyashi is remembered in northern Shambaai for his concern with tactful, diplomatic expansion. But his conquest of the non-Shambaa areas to the east was violent. One distinguished Kilindi gave this vivid description of the acquisition of the eastern provinces:

> You can't go there and have the Bondei like it. You have to break their resistance. When Kinyashi went traveling, if he arrived at Pangani, the men of Pangani would say, "Who is this man?" He would answer, "It's me, Kinyashi; Are you going to do anything about it?" "Nothing, your highness."

The king would say, "All right. In that case bring tribute to
Vugha so that I know you are my people." When he left
there and went to visit the Digo, he would say, "Here I am
lads!" They would answer, "Ai! Ai! My lord! There is not
one of us who wishes to offend your majesty."[8]

It is clear that Kinyashi was less interested in the careful integration of new peoples into the kingdom than in collection of tribute from a great mass of outsiders.

Once conquered, the east was regarded as distinctly inferior to
Shambaai—less deserving of good government. Krapf noticed
this in a later period, when he traveled through the area (in the
middle of the nineteenth century). He wrote: "Since the Shambaa were the original inhabitants . . . of [the king's] realm, and
the Shenzi were added by conquest, it is natural that the Shambaa see themselves as free people, and treat the Bondei harshly,
as slaves." He defined the Shenzi as all those who lived east of
the Luengera valley.[9] It is clear, however, that the people of
northern Shambaai were treated well, as Shambaa, even though
they joined the kingdom at the same time as the eastern subjects.

Even once they had Shambaa chiefs, the people of the eastern
provinces were adversely affected by the pattern of tribute. Subjects all over the kingdom paid tribute in food and livestock to
their local chiefs, who sent a portion of it on to the king. But it
was those who lived near the center of the kingdom who consumed the tribute. Casual laborers at the royal court were rewarded for several days' service with great portions of meat. The
king's ministers and his relations by marriage were very liberally
rewarded. The wealth quickly filtered down to the subject population. The tribute which had collected from commoners at the
fringes of the kingdom was consumed by commoners at the center.[10]

8. Historical traditions: Boaz Mjata, 15 July 1967 · For the history of
the North, see the Appendix.

9. Krapf, *Reisen*, part 2, pp. 111, 114f.

10. The picture of tribute collection and expenditure is drawn mainly
from Historical traditions: Batimayo Mbughuni, 11 April 1967; Boaz
Mjata, 15 July 1967; Gottfried Salomon, 7 February 1968; Kasimu Kimweri, 1 February 1968; Mbwana Mkanka Mghanga, 13 November 1967;

Kinyashi's expedient of conquering the areas to the east of Shambaai supplied his hard-pressed capital with tribute, but it also added a great body of subjects who could not have been loyal, for they were not considered true Shambaa subjects. When the kingdom was ultimately destroyed, two generations after Kinyashi's conquest, it was destroyed by the eastern subjects. Kinyashi, by expanding his Shambaa kingdom into an alien area, sowed the seeds of the kingdom's decline.

In the period which followed Kinyashi's death, however, the kingdom was given a long respite. Kinyashi's son Kimweri ye Nyumbai was a master of Shambaa statecraft, and so the contradictions in the organization of the kingdom remained latent, as Kimweri established firm control in all parts of his father's far-flung territories.

Kinyashi died in a war against Zigula. Having subjugated his eastern neighbors, his last act before his death was to attempt the conquest of the area south of Shambaai. He died without having conquered any part of Zigula.[11]

Kimweri ye Nyumbai succeeded to the throne about 1815.[12]

---

Mdoe Barua and Ng'wana Aia, 18 April 1967; Mhammadi Kika, 20 April 1967; Mnkande Kimweri, 2 December 1966; Nkanieka Mdoe, 30 December 1966; Semnguu Koplo, 16 November 1967; Yonatani Abrahamu, 15 November 1966. See also Krapf, *Reisen,* part 2, pp. 276, 281.

11. Historical traditions: Kasimu Kimweri, 1 February 1968; Kimweri Magogo, 24 March 1967; Mbwana Mkanka Mghanga, 7 May 1967; Mdoembazi Guga, 15 June 1967; Mpira Sanju, 31 January 1968; Nkinda Kimweri, 6 June 1967. While the Zigula were the first to get guns, the traditions are unanimous in saying that guns were unknown at this time, and were not the reason for Shambaa defeat. The war was fought with bows, arrows, and spears (Historical traditions: Boaz Mjata, 15 July 1967; Jaha Mtoi, 28 November 1967).

12. The year 1815 is only an approximation of Kimweri's date of accession. The estimate is based on four sets of facts. First, when Krapf visited Vugha in 1848 and 1852, Kimweri was a mature man who still had not become senile, but who had then been ruling for many years. Krapf distinguished between the king as he was then known, and the young active ruler of the early years (*Reisen,* part 2, p. 289). Second, Burton met Kimweri several years later, in 1857, and he had aged quickly. Burton gave the following description: "The Simba wa Muigni— Lion of the Lord—was an old, old man (un vieux vieux), with emaciated frame, a beardless, wrinkled face like a grandam's, a shaven head, disfur-

His reign is remembered in traditions told all over Shambaai, by
royals and commoners alike, as the golden age of royal rule. The
descriptions of the history of the kingdom during the reign of
Kinyashi have had to be thought out as critiques of the Kimweri
traditions, which assert that Kilindi rule never spread to the
many chiefdoms until Kimweri ye Nyumbai became king. The
traditions say that the first Kilindi chief in each of the many
local capitals was a son of Kimweri ye Nyumbai. The tone of
historical opinion on Kimweri can best be conveyed by selec-
tions from the oral traditions:

> You have seen that the Kilindi spread over the whole of the
> land, becoming rulers everywhere. The real expansion was
> carried out by the children of Kimweri ye Nyumbai. . . .
> But Kimweri didn't make his sons chiefs by royal decree. . . .

---

nished jaws, and hands and feet stained with leprous spots. . . . His subjects declare him to be a centagenarian, and he is certainly dying of age
and decay—the worst of diseases" (*Zanzibar*, 2:219). Kimweri died five
years later, in 1862 (for details, see Chapter 6). The third set of facts is
the history of the subchiefdom of Mponde. Krapf observed in 1852 that
the chief of Mponde was a woman. We know from the oral traditions
that quite a long time elapsed from the time Kimweri succeeded to the
kingship until a woman became chief of Mponde. Kimweri married a
woman from Mponde, had a son by her, and, when that son was old
enough to be responsible, made him chief over his mother's kinsmen.
When the young chief's mother died, he blamed his maternal uncle. The
chief killed his uncle, and was sent by Kimweri to a different territory.
Kimweri then married another woman from Mponde, and waited until
her daughter was old enough to take over the subchiefdom. (For the
complete history of Mponde, see the Appendix.) All of this happened
before 1852. The events could not have been compressed in time because
each of the two chiefs was born and grew to maturity (successively) during Kimweri's own mature years. Unless Kimweri was married to his first
Mponde wife before he became king, 1815 seems a rather late estimate.
The fourth piece of evidence for the chronology of Kimweri's reign is the
report of Thomas Boteler, based on a visit made in 1824, that "a short
day's journey above the [Pangani] fall there is an archipelago of islands,
thickly inhabited; and at some distance beyond them, is situated the town
of Vooga, where dwells the Kiniuere or chief of all the Wannekah tribe."
See Boteler, *Narrative of a Voyage of Discovery to Africa and Arabia
Performed in His Majesty's Ships Leven and Barracouta from 1821 to
1826 under the Command of Capt. F. W. Owen*, 2 vols. (London, 1835),
2: 176.

No. People would come from each corner of the land. People came from Mlalo, saying, "Your highness, Ye Nyumbai, Simba Mwene, Mlalo is distant. We are unable to come all the way to Vugha to argue cases. Give us a chief." And Kimweri sent out his son Dafa to be chief of Mlalo.[13]

. . .

Kimweri ye Nyumbai ruled for many years. . . . He sent out his children to rule, and he was greatly respected. He ruled the whole country, all the way to Pangani and Vanga. He governed all the Digo. All the people he treated as his children. The whole country obeyed the Kilindi. . . . Those were peaceful days. Not all kings had peaceful reigns, but peace was the characteristic of Kimweri's years. If a person was about to lose his wife because he had no livestock to pay as bridewealth, he would go to the king and say, "Your highness, my wife is being taken." Or an elder would say, "My lord, my son is about to lose his wife." Kimweri would say, "Go to such and such a place. I have a cow being kept there. Take it." Ye Nyumbai did not like to be told, "This man is of a lineage you know well." He would say, "All of them are my people." When Kimweri sent a son to rule an area he would say, "Build a village with your fellow men, and listen to them. If you come across an evil man, bring him to trial for his evil. But if you see a man who means no harm, don't persecute him. Because you and your subjects are all my children.[14]

One of the most surprising elements in the golden age view of Kimweri ye Nyumbai's reign is the idea that there were not Kilindi in the Shambaa chiefdoms until Kimweri's reign—that the real expansion of the kingdom from southern Shambaai took place at this time. The analysis given above, of the expansion of the kingdom during the reign of Kimweri's father Kinyashi, is based on local traditions of very narrow distribution, which were collected in order to test the popular view. The local traditions for much of Shambaai are summarized, chiefdom by chiefdom, in the Appendix to this chapter.

13. Historical traditions: Kimweri Magogo, 24 March 1967.
14. Historical traditions: Boaz Mjata, 15 July 1967.

What the popular tale seems to mean, when it says that Kimweri ye Nyumbai's sons were the first chiefs of the greater kingdom, is that with the coming of Kimweri's sons, all previous
chiefs became irrelevant. Take Mlalo as an example. We know
from local traditions collected at Mlalo, some of which are given
as explanations of the history of a chiefly grave site, that Kinyashi's son Mahimbo was the first Kilindi chief there, and that
he was replaced by Kimweri's son Dafa. Mahimbo had to step
down to make way for Kimweri's son. In establishing the legitimacy of his rule, Dafa could point to his father's importance as
king of Vugha. But Dafa had no significant relationship with the
previous chief of Mlalo. Thus most of Dafa's descendants, when
asked about the history of Mlalo, would describe the following
scheme:

Mbegha
|
Bughe
|
Kinyashi
|
Kimweri ye Nyumbai
|
Dafa

That is, it would be in their interests to ignore the existence of
an earlier chief of Mlalo who had at one time been a rival claim-
ant to the chiefdom. They emphasize the importance of Kimweri
ye Nyumbai, who is their source of legitimacy. While the traditional history of Vugha is continuous, from Mbegha to the present, the history of each chiefdom is discontinuous, since any
powerful king removed the children of his predecessor. Kimweri
ye Nyumbai was the most recent king to make a clean sweep of
the chiefdoms, and it is therefore in the interests of every chiefly
line to emphasize his importance, and to ignore the existence of
earlier local Kilindi rulers.

The reasons for Kimweri ye Nyumbai's success, after his father's failure, are to be found in the history of relations between
Vugha and the rival kingdom of Mshihwi. To honor his father's
memory, Kimweri made a great assault on Mshihwi, where

Kinyashi's enemy Limo had been succeeded by his son Mtoi. When Kimweri's attack failed, Mtoi took one last chance at unseating the king of Vugha and taking the kingdom for himself.

In the end, Kimweri and Mtoi saw that the advantages of peace were great, that war simply weakened each side. Kimweri knew that his father had been unable to take control of southern Shambaai because of the threat from Mshihwi. Finally the enemies made peace. Each agreed not to interfere in the affairs of the other. Kimweri would treat Mshihwi as an independent kingdom; Mtoi would give up any hope of overthrowing the king of Vugha. The peace gave Kimweri the freedom from outside pressure he needed to transform Kinyashi's great, sprawling, loose kingdom into a tightly knit state.[15]

| *Kings of Vugha* | | *Kings of Mshihwi* |
|---|---|---|
| | Bughe | |
| Kinyashi Muanga Ike | | Limo |
| Kimweri ye Nyumbai | | Mtoi |

Early in his reign Kimweri ye Nyumbai engaged in careful long-term planning for the consolidation of his rule: he took a wife from an important lineage in each of many subject areas with the hope of making each woman's son chief over his mother's home territory. He may even have begun his campaign of marriages before his father's death, while he was still merely the royal heir.

Once Kimweri ye Nyumbai's sons began to come of age the most difficult period of his reign began, for he had to remove the old chiefs from the major chiefdoms of Shambaai before he could rule through his sons. Kimweri was faced with two separate local patterns, one much more difficult to deal with than the other.

He had to act with the greatest caution in the territories where

15. The peace is described in Historical traditions: Mnkande Kimweri, 26 December 1966.

his father, Kinyashi, had not succeeded in removing earlier
chiefs. In these places the chiefs were entrenched, and had developed independent bases of power. In addition, the men were
the brothers of Kimweri's father, men of the older generation. It
would have been unseemly to treat them with insufficient respect. Ye Nyumbai dealt gently with the old men. He left the old
chief of Gare-Ubii undisturbed at his capital at Gare, for example, but installed a chief at Ubii. Kimweri was satisfied to control
half the area while he awaited the old chief's death.

In places where Kinyashi Muanga Ike had succeeded in establishing his own men, Kimweri ye Nyumbai was able to act with
more vigor, for the chiefs were merely his half brothers, and less
deserving of respect. At Mlalo, for example, one tradition maintains that Kimweri took over the chiefdom by threatening his
half brother with death, if he did not step down.

Kimweri ye Nyumbai, in establishing solid control over all of
his kingdom, did not meddle in the affairs of every minor village,
nor did he personally see to the removal of each insignificant
Kilindi functionary. He awarded a large chiefdom, like Mlalo, to
a "house," that is, to one of his wives with all her children and
grandchildren. The oldest male in the "house" was made chief,
and his territory was administered by a staff of other members of
the "house"—either his own children or his brothers and sisters.

Kimweri united all the far-flung territories of the kingdom by
sheer prolificacy of procreation. Virtually every minor subchiefdom in Shambaai was governed by a child or grandchild of Kimweri. In addition he sent his children to rule the eastern provinces. Abdallah bin Hemedi 'lAjjemy listed thirty-six children of
Kimweri who ruled in East Usambara and Bondei. Lowland territories near the ocean were left to govern themselves: the indigenous rulers were confirmed in their positions by Kimweri, and
they paid regular tribute to Vugha.[16]

Kimweri ye Nyumbai achieved the territorial integration of
the greater Shambaa kingdom more successfully than any king

16. *H.z.W.*, Sura 42. The list of Kimweri's children agrees in all overlapping details with the traditions. Krapf described government in the
lowlands (*Reisen*, part 2, pp. 117, 276).

before or after him. The installation of loyal chiefs throughout the kingdom was only one element in the achievement of integration. The greatness of Kimweri's accomplishment was in his success at binding the subjects of the kingdom to their chiefs, and at making himself the focus of the loyalty of his many subjects.

The key to Kimweri's achievement was the relationship of *utumba,* of the mother's brother. Kimweri made each chief's maternal uncle a deputy to represent the interests of the subjects. The maternal uncle was himself a commoner, and yet he commanded the chief's respect. If the people were unhappy with their chief, they would complain to his maternal uncle, who would then reason with his nephew. The more unpopular the chief, the greater the pressure on his uncle. And if the chief did not respect his uncle's opinion, if the uncle felt the pressure of the commoners was too great, the chief deaf to his admonitions, he could report the matter to Kimweri. The king could, if necessary, take away a chief's territory.

One man, whose father had been the maternal uncle of chief Kaaghe of Gare, described the relationship between his father and the young chief, as it was arranged by Kimweri ye Nyumbai:

> My father had a village at Vugha and a village at Shashui, several miles away. Chief Kaaghe was the son of my paternal aunt. When he was sent to Gare to rule, my father's father had already died. Then Kimweri ye Nyumbai said to my father, "Please follow the boy to Gare. I want you to follow him, for when he does cruel things to the people of Gare there will be no one to discipline him. Go to Gare together with your sister, and watch the lad. Keep track of the good things he does and the bad." Then Father came to this land . . . and if the people of Gare were angry at something they would come to Father and say, "Look at what your child has done." Father would tell him, "Son, the people of Gare are angry. They have been angered by such and such. If you keep on doing that I will go to tell Kimweri at Vugha."[17]

17. Historical traditions: Mdoe Zayumba, 8 June 1967.

It is clear why the power of the chief's maternal uncle is one of the things Shambaa, in their traditions, treasure most about the reign of Kimweri ye Nyumbai.

While the common people of Shambaai enjoyed protection from local tyranny as a result of Kimweri's ability to discipline his sons, the king's benign regard was not directed toward the eastern provinces. In this very important respect, as in many others, the subjects outside Shambaai did not enjoy the full benefits of royal rule. The incorrigible sons of the king were sent to the eastern territories, where their misdeeds would not be directed against Shambaa subjects, but against foreigners. In one case, when chief Ng'wa Kimungu of Shembekeza killed the royal heir, Kimweri removed him from Shambaai and sent him to East Usambara. He said, "This person killed my son. . . . Don't let him stay here in Shambaai. Send him somewhere far away. Make him go to Bondei."[18]

Kimweri's rule was more firm and more just than that of his father, but he shared the assumption of all Shambaa kings that the "aliens" within his realm did not deserve the full benefits of royal rule. Late in his reign Kimweri's military grip began to weaken, and there were minor rebellions in the east, while Shambaai remained firmly loyal until his death.[19]

APPENDIX: HISTORIES OF THE CHIEFDOMS OF SHAMBAAI

The interpretations presented in this chapter strain the sources to their limit. This is not so, to the same degree, in any other portion of this work. The reason is that the growth of the

18. Historical traditions: Ng'wa Paula s/o Ng'wa Kimungu, 12 July 1967.

19. Krapf came across one such rebellion in 1852 (CMS, CA5/016–177, Journal describing Dr. Krapf's proceedings from the 10th of February to the 14th of April 1852, 3 March 1852). Krapf's colleague Erhardt learned that a son of Kimweri ye Nyumbai had been killed by the son's Digo subjects, near the coast (CMS, CA5/09–15, Erhardt's journal, August 10, 1853).

kingdom was a gradual process, and therefore it is impossible to use great numbers of traditions to reconstruct a single event, as in the history of Mbegha. The elders of the chiefdom of Mlalo remember how Mlalo was brought into the kingdom, but are not interested in fitting this event into a broader history of the expansion of the kingdom. The same is true for the other territories.

Because of this, the history of the growth of the kingdom is twice removed from its sources, while the history of the founding of the kingdom is only once removed. In the history of the founding it was necessary to compare critically a number of sources in order to reconstruct the history of an event. In this chapter, it was necessary to reconstruct the history of each chiefdom of Shambaai separately, and then to build the broader interpretations upon these microhistories, and upon the rather sketchy royal histories for the period.

The histories of the separate chiefdoms are presented here, in abbreviated form, so that the reader who wishes to question the interpretations presented can do so on the basis of materials which are somewhat closer in content to the sources.

## Ubii-Gare

The chiefdoms of Ubii and Gare are at the eastern end of the southern chain of chiefdoms. These two lands were closely linked. They were both near to the land of the Mbugu, and had a common route to the plains. In the days of Bughe the two together probably formed a single chiefdom. Even after Kimweri ye Nyumbai made two separate chiefdoms of the areas, the chief of Ubii was the local rainmaker for both.

The traditions on early government in Ubii and Gare contradict one another in a number of details. But it is possible to reconstruct a probable series of events. The first Kilindi chief of the area governed Ubii and Gare together as a single chiefdom. He was Dafa, the son of Bughe.

Dafa's full sister went with him to help govern. She married a local notable named Mahanyu, of the village of Handei. She and her husband governed Handei, and after Mahanyu's death their son succeeded as subchief.

Dafa was still alive when Kimweri ye Nyumbai became king. Kimweri did not depose Dafa, but he took away the Ubii section of Dafa's chiefdom and made Mshuza, one of Kimweri's oldest sons, chief of Ubii.

As Mshuza grew older he made his own sons (Kimweri's grandsons) subchiefs within the chiefdom of Ubii. Ng'wa Kobe was made subchief of the village of Nguu, Kivo of what is now Lushoto, Mhaio of Mankunguu, and Kimweri of Mwagho.

The only subchief who was not Mshuza's son was Kiunguia, a son of Kimweri ye Nyumbai, whose mother died when he was young. He was raised at Ubii by Mshuza's mother. Ye Nyumbai wanted to make Kiunguia chief of Shembekeza (at Bumbuli), but Mshuza's mother refused to part with her adopted son. Mshuza gave Kiunguia part of his chiefdom at Ngulwi. It is interesting to note that while Mshuza divided with own chiefdom into units for his sons to rule under him, he had to cut off part of his land for Kiunguia to rule independently, for while his own sons were expected to be subordinate to Mshuza, his half brother Kiunguia was expected to be partially independent. In cases where subchiefs were of the chief's generation (as at Gare, below), they were full siblings—children of the same mother.

Once Mshuza was well established at Ubii, Dafa died at Gare. Dafa's son Kolowa succeeded him. But with the old man dead, Kimweri could act vigorously. Kolowa, faced with the choice of retiring voluntarily or being attacked from both Vugha and the neighboring chiefdom of Ubii, retired. Kimweri sent his son Semboja as chief. Semboja went to Gare as a young boy of about eight with his mother's brother (a Gare man) as guardian, educator, temporary judge, collector of tribute for immediate use and in trust, coordinator of rites for the welfare of the land. Semboja, whose career as a terrifying slave raider is described in later chapters, was even as a child a difficult person. It was reported that he shot poisoned arrows at the treasured hunting dogs of his subjects. When Semboja's guardian handed over control, the commoners waited for a suitable incident to complain to Kimweri. This came when some cows wandered into Semboja's maize garden, and he chopped with a bush knife at their legs.

After this and one further complaint, Kimweri removed Semboja as chief of Gare. The young chief was sent to Ngua, which was seen as a suitable position: it was a small and insignificant territory at the southwestern corner of Shambaai, overlooking the plains at a point where the Maasai and Iloikop, moving through, were forced to follow a path near Shambaai, between Ngua and the Zigula mountain of Mafi facing it. According to the traditions, Kimweri felt that Semboja's violent temperament would be usefully employed against the Maasai.

Kimweri then sent his son Kaaghe to Gare. Kaaghe was supported by his full brother and sister as subchiefs. His brother Chambi was subchief of Handei. The mother of Kaaghe and Chambi was not herself from Gare, although Kaaghe's mother's brother was sent by Kimweri to supervise the young chief's rule.[20]

## Vugha

If we move southeast from Ubii-Gare, the next chiefdom is Vugha itself. Vugha had an anomalous pattern of government because it stood in a special relationship to the king. There is a saying that Vugha has only one Kilindi—the king himself. This is more a statement of principle than a description of reality. But it is true that near the center of the chiefdom there were no Kilindi chiefs. Possibly there was the threat that other Kilindi might challenge the authority of the king. Perhaps it was also an enactment of the image in the Mbegha myth of a solitary male Kilindi ruling a country of Shambaa "women."

It is true, at any rate, that in the central part of the chiefdom there were no Kilindi except for the king. At Kihitu and Baghai, for example, appointive officers who were members of subject lineages ruled, and they were directly responsible to the royal

20. Historical traditions: Athumani Mdoe, 5 February 1968; Hasani Magogo, 25 December 1967; Jaha Mtoi, 22 April 1967; Lihani Shemnkande, 12 June 1967; Mdoe Zayumba, 8 June 1967; Mpira Sanju, 31 January 1968. See also, A. Karasek, "Beiträge zur Kenntnis der Waschambaa," ed. A. Eichhorn, *Baessler-Archiv* 8 (1923–24): 46–47.

court. These officials were called *wadoe*. At Nkolongo, near the plains, Kimweri ye Nyumbai placed a man who had many sons to guard the path which was used by Maasai-speaking raiders as they climbed up into the mountains. The war drum beaten at Nkolongo gave warning to the people at Vugha.[21]

There were three towns near Vugha that no Kilindi could enter: Ziai, Kighuunde, and Kidundai. The history of Ziai was given in Chapter 3. At Kidundai a Kilindi killed the indigenous leader of the village. In anger the leader's kinsmen drove the Kilindi out. The traditions do not agree on the name of the royal aggressor.[22]

Kilindi were prohibited from entering Kighuunde, although the reasons for the prohibition are unclear. The ruling Kika lineage has occupied Kighuunde only since the days of Kimweri ye Nyumbai. It had been a Nango village, and the Kikas were moved in to defend against raiders from the plains.[23]

While the villages near the capital were ruled by non-Kilindi, there were subchiefdoms at the edges of the Vugha territory which were ruled by Kilindi. Mponde, to the east of the capital, provides a vivid example of the statecraft of Kimweri ye Nyumbai. When Kimweri came to the throne, Mponde had never had a Kilindi ruler. The lineage of the Washu Waja Nkobo had always controlled its own local affairs. The lineage head was Shemdoa, and when Kimweri ye Nyumbai decided to put a Kilindi in Mponde he married Shemdoa's sister. The first male child of this union, Mkanka Mghanga, became subchief in the village of his mother's brother.

Shemdoa and his sister (the chief's mother) had a violent argument, and then the woman broke a cooking pot and pronounced a curse. This is a form of suicide. Some time afterwards she died. In a rage over his mother's death, Mkanka Mghanga killed his uncle.

21. Historical traditions: Salehe Mwambashi, 29 March 1967.
22. Historical traditions: Mbwana Mkanka Mghanga, 7 May 1967; Shemaeze, 9 May 1967.
23. Historical traditions: Mbwana Mkanka Mghanga, 7 May 1967; Mhammadi Kika, 20 April 1967.

Kimweri ye Nyumbai sent his Kaoneka (one of the court officials) to investigate the case. Kimweri decided on two measures, once he had heard the facts of the case. First, he moved Mkanka Mghanga to another chiefdom. Second, he married a daughter of the murdered man. According to normal Shambaa standards this was a completely shocking marriage (to Kimweri's wife's brother's daughter), but it was acceptable because Kimweri's purpose was clearly political. He wanted to father another chief of the same descent as Mkanka Mghanga. The first child of this union was a girl named Mahombwe. The second was a boy named Kibanga. Mahombwe was subchief at Mponde until Kibanga grew up and took over. When Krapf passed through Mponde in 1852, the subchief was a woman. This must have been Mahombwe.[24]

The subchiefdom of Bagha, to the northeast of Vugha, did not have a Kilindi chief until the time of Kimweri ye Nyumbai. It was a border area between the Shambaa and the Mbugu. Mbegha met an Mbugu leader at Mke Jumbe near Bagha, which was then no-man's-land. They agreed at the meeting to keep their spheres of influence separate.

Bagha was probably of strategic importance to Kimweri ye Nyumbai, for it sat astride the most convenient route for invading Vugha from Mshihwi. The first subchief of Bagha was a woman named Ombago, who served while her younger full brother Zuakuu was growing up. Zuakuu failed as subchief and had to leave Bagha. The next chief was Kihedu, son of Kimweri by a different mother. Neither Kihedu's mother, nor Zuakuu's, was a Bagha woman. We can see that while Kimweri often married women from a particular chiefdom so that their children might serve in that chiefdom (as in the case of Mponde), this was not universally the case. Indeed it could not be, for some wives came from outside the kingdom. Kihedu's mother, for example, was from Zigula.[25]

Some of the other sons of Kimweri ye Nyumbai who occupied

24. Krapf, *Reisen,* part 2, p. 297.
25. Historical traditions: Abdallah Mweta, 13 June and 15 June 1968; Kasimu Kimweri, 1 February 1968; Mahimbo Kihedu, 1 February 1968; Mbwana Mkanka Mghanga, 13 November 1967.

subchiefdoms of Vugha were: Bira at Mkumbaa, Mshaghasho at Mbuzii, Mazima at Mpangai, Tunguu at Mamba, Mdengeezi at Kwa Doe.

## Bumbuli and the Surrounding Area

Bumbuli lies to the east of Vugha. In this land there was a correlation between traditional subservience to the king and the relatively powerful position of the subject lineages. The chief of Bumbuli was the heir apparent to the kingdom. The heir was the son of the king's great wife, who was selected when the king acceded to the throne. The great wife might be a wife he had married before accession, or she could also be a woman taken as wife after the king entered Vugha. Often the great wife was a Nango of Bumbuli, so that when the young heir went to occupy the seat of his chiefdom, he lived near his mother's lineage. Bumbuli was the ideal place for the training and the protection of the heir. The Nango had every interest in protecting the young prince, for after his accession they would have great influence as the mother's brothers of the king. Since the chief threat of war in the early kingdom was from Pare, to the west, the position of the heir in the eastern portion of the mountains was relatively secure.[26]

Bumbuli was the only chiefdom in Shambaai where a new king did not face any resistance to the installation of a loyal chief, for the king himself had given up the chiefdom of Bumbuli in order to move to Vugha.

The subject lineages at Bumbuli were in a very strong position, for it was their job to educate a young and inexperienced chief in the ways of government. The young man was trained at Bumbuli for the responsibilities he would ultimately assume at Vugha. The young chief's minister, his *mdoe,* was his tutor in affairs of state. This is the way the son of one *mdoe,* glorifying his father's influence a bit excessively, described the education of a chief of Bumbuli:

26. Krapf, *Reisen,* part 2, pp. 124–25.

When Mnkande came to Bumbuli he was a young lad. Kimweri sent him, saying "Take care of the boy." It was the *mdoe* who raised him, and showed him the art of government. "My friend, there's a drought developing. What shall we do?" They would go to find a magician, to hire him. People would say, "The chief has the gift of rain. We have gotten food to eat." As the chief grew up, he bought different kinds of rain magic. But in Bumbuli the chief does not yet have his hereditary magic. . . . If the chief wants to make a raid, the *mdoe* says, "What's wrong there? Why do you want to attack?" The battle plan will be put aside. The chief proposed, but the *mdoe* disposed. There was no chiefly medicine. If the chief saw that a man was shot at, but the bullet did not enter his body, he would purchase the man's charms. As the chief grew up he would judge cases himself, but the *mdoe* would review the decision. The chief could not judge cases if the *mdoe* did not agree to it.[27]

Since each chief of Bumbuli is expected to move on to Vugha, the list of the chiefs of Bumbuli is thought to be the same as the list of the kings of Vugha, each man being chief of Bumbuli early in his career and king of Vugha later. There is a tendency in this setting for elders to describe the most recent ruler of the chiefdom as the first one, for all the previous ones achieved renown as kings of Vugha, and are not remembered as past chiefs of Bumbuli. And when there was no suitable heir to the king at Vugha, the *mdoe* (the local minister) governed Bumbuli.[28]

Because of the relative weakness of the chief, Bumbuli itself was decentralized. It was really a congeries of chiefdoms, all of them directly responsible to Vugha. One of the most important was Shembekeza, where Kimweri ye Nyumbai placed his son Kihamia Ng'wa Kimungu. The Kilindi of Shembekeza no longer remember the details of rule before the accession of Kimweri ye Nyumbai, although we know of the importance of this district in the Mshihwi wars. The local Kilindi elder said, "The Kilindi had already been spread across the land. The Kilindi who had come to rule Vugha, Kimweri, fathered children, and then the previ-

27. Historical traditions: Mdoe Saudimwe, 7 August 1967.
28. Historical traditions: Boaz Mjata, 15 July 1967.

ous chief would leave. People would say, 'Those are the old Kilindi, the powerless Kilindi.' . . . I don't know anything about the
old Kilindi of Shembekeza. Right near the village there is a
grave site, and people say that a woman named Okwaho is buried
there."[29] When Ng'wa Kimungu was placed in Shembekeza,
Kimweri's son Mnkande was already chief of Bumbuli.
Mnkande was the royal heir. A rivalry between the two brothers
(*wandughu*) developed, with very important results:

> [Mnkande and Ng'wa Kimungu] played at sending one an-
> other evil charms. That fellow at Bumbuli would send ter-
> rible things. When they got here this one would think up
> something good to send back. Well, this went on for a
> while, and then Mnkande died. The Kimweri said, "This
> man killed my son." So he was removed from Shembekeza.
> He said, "He shouldn't stay there. Let him go somewhere
> very far away." Ng'wa Kimungu went to Bondei, and
> Mnkande's sister Chamvigha became chief of Shembekeza.[30]

Near Tamota, another of the towns of Bumbuli, chief Choghoghwe, a son of Kimweri Mbegha (probably Bughe's brother
Maua) was the earliest known Kilindi. His capital was at Mkaie.
Kimweri ye Nyumbai replaced the old chief through subtle indi-
rection. Instead of removing Choghoghwe, he sent his son Ng'wa
Butu to live in Tamota, which was then a minor village in the
old chief's realm. As Kimweri's influence grew, and with it
Ng'wa Butu's, Tamota became the local capital and Mkaie declined until it was a minor village. There is a great similarity between Kimweri's action here and at Gare, another place where
the chief was of the older generation.[31]

At Mahezanguu, another of the lands of Bumbuli, the Kilindi
have no knowledge of a chief who ruled their land before Kimweri ye Nyumbai, although it is probable that there had been an
"old Kilindi." The first chief was Mboghoo, son of Kimweri.
When he died of smallpox, his full brother Kunguu entered Ma-

29. Historical traditions: Ng'wa Paula s/o Ng'wa Kimungu, 12 July
1967.
30. Ibid.
31. Historical traditions: Mandia Ntuue, 23 July 1967.

hezanguu, which is near the Luengera Valley. Kunguu's son explains that when his father became a grown man Kimweri sent him to Mahezanguu to take up the dangerous position, which was under pressure from the "Maasai," who passed through the valley. Kunguu left the more placid chiefdoms to inexperienced men. Whether or not this was the case, it is an example of the practice of giving a district to a "house."[32]

There are three towns in the land of Bumbuli that the Kilindi may not enter: Tekwa, Wena, and Nkelei. Each is ruled by a subject lineage. Tekwa and Wena are ruled by the Nango. In Nkelei the people of the town explain that there is a certain kind of magic which is important for the defense of the realm and with which the Kilindi may not come into contact. But this is a common kind of explanation after the fact, and the actual historical origin of the prohibition is unclear. The town has always been governed by the Washu Waja Nkobo, the only descent group I have ever come across that claims to have lived in Shambaai since time immemorial.[33] In Mlungui, the chiefdom adjoining Bumbuli, the chiefs before Kimweri ye Nyumbai are not remembered, the first known chief being Mdolwa Magogo son of Kimweri ye Nyumbai.[34]

## The Northern Chiefdoms

The keystone of the northern group of chiefdoms was Mlalo. There are fascinating fragments of traditions on the pre-Kilindi government of Mlalo. The Kilindi admit that before they arrived the Kijelwa and Taita lineages were politically dominant. In fact, when the ancestors are invoked at the chiefly grave site at Mlalo, the first name mentioned is that of Saguruma, a Kijelwa chief. The first Kilindi ruler of Mlalo was Mahimbo, the son of Kinyashi Muanga Ike. There is a superficial discrepancy between the

32. Historical traditions: Asumani Msagati, 5 August 1967; Jani Kunguu, 4 August 1967.

33. Historical traditions: Bakari Shekwaho, 17 July 1967; Mdoe Saudimwe, 7 August 1967; Mwejuma Ngoda, 5 August 1967; Saguti Shekiondo, 30 July 1967.

34. Historical traditions: Barua s/o Makange, 22 February 1968.

information in the oral traditions, that Kinyashi's son was the first Kilindi, and the contention in *Habari za Wakilindi* that Mlalo was among the lands which accepted Mbegha as ruler and judge (Sura 14). It is probable that at the very latest Mlalo accepted Kilindi dominance during the reign of Bughe. In this case it would appear that Saguruma was a tributary chief under Bughe, and that he became much more powerful than an ordinary lineage head as a result of his integration into the Kilindi political structure. This would explain why the Kilindi acknowledge his importance, and invoke him at the grave site.[35]

When Kimweri ye Nyumbai acceded to the throne he began to put pressure on Mahimbo to relinquish his chiefdom. According to one tradition, Kimweri did this with great delicacy:

> Kimweri's kinsman was at Mlalo. But then the king thought to himself, "What should I do about this? Mlalo would be a beautiful land to possess." He took his son Dafa, and said to Mahimbo, "Friend, live together with your child. You will keep one another company." Mahimbo said, "What is my kinsman doing? Why has he brought a person here?" Then Mahimbo drank poison and died.[36]

According to another version Kimweri threatened Mahimbo, who then retired.[37]

When Dafa became chief of Mlalo he was still a young man, and so he went with some of his full siblings who ruled the subchiefdoms until he could procreate a group of subordinates. But it seems that Dafa did not have many children, or that they were young through most of his reign, for in a number of places the collateral lines persisted. For instance, in the subchiefdom of Handei, Dafa's sister (*umbuje*) Kighenda ruled. She married a son of a local notable, a Bondei named Makumba. She was replaced for a while by her brother Shegao, but then her son Ma-

35. Historical traditions: Ali Mashina, 18 July 1968; Hassani Kinyashi, 17 July 1968; Nasoro Maghembe, 18 July 1968; Yosua Hermasi, 19 July 1968.

36. Historical traditions: Boaz Mjata, 15 July 1967.

37. Historical traditions: Ali Mashina, 18 July 1968. The Dafa mentioned in this quotation was not the same as the Dafa of Gare.

gili became chief. Dafa's son Shewai became chief only much later, after the death of Kimweri ye Nyumbai. At Ng'wangoi, Dafa's brother Shekimweri was the first subchief. The most prominent group there at that time was the Kwizu lineage, and a Kwizu was the first *mdoe* of Shekimweri. But it soon became obvious that the Kwizu was powerful and that he did not wish to cooperate with the Kilindi, and Shekimweri chose another lineage from which to take his *mdoe;* in addition the Kilindi have ever since been prohibited from entering the Kwizu village. Dafa's sons who did occupy subchiefdoms fairly early were Chambo who governed Baghai, Maghembe at Ngulu, Ng'wa Siafu at Kifuiyo, Kimweri at Bungoi and later at Dule.[38]

The three minor chiefdoms of the northern group are Mlola, Mtii, and Mbalu. At Mtii the first known Kilindi was Gao, son of Shebughe. When Kimweri ye Nyumbai acceded he replaced his kinsman with his son, Fovo ya Nyiao. Fovo ya Nyiao died during his father's lifetime and was replaced by Kimweri's son Jang'andu. The first known chief at Mbaramu was Makaamangi, son of Kimweri. At Mbalu, Ng'wa Nyoka, son of Kimweri, was the first Kilindi in an area which had been dominated by the Nango, Wavina Nkaa. The first known Kilindi at Mlola was Msangazi, son of Kimweri.[39]

38. Historical traditions: Ali Mashina, 18 July 1968; Hassani Kinyashi, 17 July 1968.

39. Historical traditions: Kasimu Kimweri, 1 February 1968; Mbwana Mkanka Mghanga, 7 May 1967; Mzimbii Mpemba, 20 July 1968.

# 5 · SHAMBAA POLITICAL ECONOMY FROM TRIBUTE TO TRADE

The political economy of the Shambaa kingdom changed, in the nineteenth century, from one based primarily on tribute and territorial control to one based primarily on trade. It is possible to see the implications of this change in every period, indeed every major event, in Shambaa history after 1840. This chapter is about the beginning of the process during the reign of Kimweri ye Nyumbai. Kimweri ruled through the end of one era and the start of another: he took power in about 1815; the years of rapid economic change began in the mid-1830s; he survived until 1862.[1]

## Tribute and Trade before 1835

There was a strong continuity in the economic needs of the state from the time of Mbegha through the early years of Kimweri ye Nyumbai. As the history of the growth of the kingdom showed, from the earliest days new groups drawn into the state showed their submission by paying tribute in livestock, staples, and service. The kings, from Mbegha on, supplied their loyal followers with great quantities of meat.

1. Evidence for 1862 as the date of Kimweri's death is given in Chapter 6, note 5.

The kinds of goods needed by the king (or by the chiefs) were the same as those needed by any ordinary villager. The king needed to supply his courtiers and guests with the staple and livestock, and to provide starch, meat, and beer for public ceremonials. Only the magical charms were unique to the court: no ordinary citizen would have ones like them.

Tribute was collected from the entire population. The agricultural skills of the Shambaa were equally accessible to all men, although the older men of any village were expected to have the greatest expertise. The tools, too, were in the possession of all men. Specialization of production based on intense capital investment or special skills did not, for the most part, exist. Each homestead produced food and then consumed it. As a result, the tribute which came to the court was the product of thousands of men, each tending his own garden.[2]

The amount of goods which came to the court was not related to the quantity of excess production at any given time and place, but to the quality of the relationship between a subject and his chief, and to the services which the chief provided. A lineage involved in constant litigation paid a much higher proportion of its wealth to the political establishment than one which was never involved in cases. There was actually an inverse relationship between production and tribute levels in time of famine, when people brought gifts to the chief so that he would be encouraged to restore the fertility of the land.[3]

From the point of view of the king or chief, the only way to increase the amount of tribute significantly was to increase the number of subjects. If the level of taxation of the subjects who

2. For the major sources on the nature of tribute, see Chapter 4, note 10. For a full discussion, see Feierman, "Concepts of Sovereignty," Chapter 7.

3. The historical traditions are full of discussions of how, in time of famine, people brought gifts to the chief. One extended discussion is that of Mandughu Chai, 15 June 1968. A late nineteenth-century case is described in F. Gleiss, "Magili, der Herr der Heuschrecken," *Nachrichten* (August 1898): 128–30. While it is no longer tribute to an established political authority, large gifts are given to important rain magicians to this day.

were in the king's territories was increased intolerably they would rebel or, if they could, move away. Since the goods taken as tribute were grown by all the men of the kingdom, each on his own plot, there was no way to rationalize production in order to increase the surplus available to the state. The only way to increase the supply of tribute was to increase the number of subjects on the land, or to control a larger area of populated land.

Shambaai was a highly favored kingdom because there was a relatively high density of population in the fertile mountains. Since the king's messengers traveled on foot, great sparsely settled areas were not as desirable as small dense ones.

Tribute was collected for each local chief within his own chiefdom. The king got the tribute of the chiefdom of Vugha; he also was sent a portion of the tribute collected by other chiefs, and he could send his own collectors to any part of the kingdom. The collectors, in each case, lived at the court: they were not spread evenly over the territory. In fact, there was no specialized corps of collectors. When the court was running short of livestock, the chief would send out his courtiers, or the local hangers-on, to collect some tribute. At times men of the court would go out collecting on their own initiative. This was legitimate so long as they gave the chief a portion of what they collected. A tribute-payer who wished to protect his own interests would go along with the collectors to the chief's court, to be sure that his tribute got there, and to get credit for having paid, since it was accepted that no homestead could be repeatedly required to pay. While it is clear that there was tension between the men who lived constantly at court and those who spent most of their time in small villages, it was recognized both at the court and by the cultivators that no chief could remain in power unless large numbers of cultivators chose to live in his chiefdom.

Small, compact, densely populated chiefdoms were preferred not only for ease of tribute collection, but also because the subjects were expected to work on the plantations of the chief (or of the king), which were near the court. The more spread out the population, the harder it was to require the labor of the subjects.

For military purposes, too, density of population was important. Here again, there was no great technological specialization: the weapons of the king's men were not better in any way than the weapons of the ordinary cultivators. Each man had his spear, his shield, his bow and arrows. A system of war drums could bring thousands of soldiers together at very short notice in southern Shambaai.[4] The wealth captured in successful wars was an important supplement to tribute.

The argument here, that the political economy of the early kingdom relied heavily on the mountain farmers, depends on an important assumption: that Kimweri ye Nyumbai and his predecessors did not derive their wealth and power, to any significant extent, from trade. The early kings did receive as tribute, and they traded, one tusk of every elephant killed by a Shambaa hunter. There were no elephants in the mountains, however; few Shambaa men ever spent much of their time hunting in the plains. The early kings also occasionally sold war captives. The kings used their small quantities of trade goods mainly for the purchase of magical charms to control rain and to protect their armies. It was thought in Shambaai, and still is, that the most exotic charms are the most certain to be effective; since the charms are unfamiliar, counter-magic is unknown. The kings also purchased cloth for the royal household. But trade was peripheral to the political economy of the early kingdom, and tribute central. The kings used tribute wealth to acquire the trade goods they needed, rather than using trade to acquire political followings. The negative hypothesis, that trade had not been important, is very difficult to demonstrate. The evidence is necessarily indirect and circumstantial.

First, there is the fact that at the very time Kimweri ye Nyumbai was consolidating his power, the two ports which served Shambaai and the surrounding region were in severe decline. Pangani and Tanga were at their lowest points as trading towns in the mid-1820s.[5]

4. F. LangHeinrich, in "Die Entwickelung des Verkehrs in Westusambara," *Nachrichten* 27 (January 1913): 7–12, reported that southern Shambaai could, by the use of drums, assemble a force of 6,000 men.

5. Part of a British naval expedition, led by Captain Owen, passed the Pangani coast in 1824 and reported the area very little frequented. Some

By the 1840s and 1850s the coastal towns had recovered. While they were under Kimweri's sovereignty, however, they were at the same time trading colonies of the Sultan of Zanzibar. Kimweri was recognized as king, but he was not permitted to trade (for details, see below).

The most important evidence on the relative significance of trade and tribute in the early years of the kingdom is the pattern of expansion from Mbegha's original base in southern Shambaai. The kingdom expanded to the populated areas of northern Shambaai, then to East Usambara, and then to the fertile hills of Bondei, leaving independent those barren and sparsely populated areas which would have been most important for trade.

The villages which lay in the plains just below the northern and southern rims of Shambaai were the natural trading centers of the area under royal control. They were strung together to become stopping places on the caravan routes of the nineteenth century. But they had existed even a hundred years before. They were natural collecting points for ivory, and if trade had been important to Kimweri ye Nyumbai's predecessors they would have been careful to control the plains villages. But while the villages, because of their location, were clearly at the mercy of Shambaa rulers, they were never conquered. They were in the hands of small colonies of outsiders—Kamba, Segeju, Kwavi (Iloikop Maasai).

The villages along the northern edge of Shambaai were served in the nineteenth century by the port of Tanga. Traveling westward from the coast, the most important were Buiti, at the northern tip of East Usambara, then Dongo Kundu, and on to Kitivo and Mbaramu, in the plains below the northern rim of

members of the expedition visited Tanga and saw that "The population does not exceed three hundred; but some time back it was considerably more, for, previously to the harassing attacks of the Imaun's forces, Tanga was a greater mart for ivory than Mombas or any other place in the vicinity. It is now reduced to the utmost poverty, the inhabitants living solely on fish and a sparing supply of Kaffer corn, or millet, from the interior" (Captain W. F. W. Owen, *Narrative of Voyages to Explore the Shores of Africa, Arabia, and Madagascar,* ed. Heaton Bowstead Robinson, 2 vols. [London 1833], 1: 427).

Shambaai. Buiti was occupied by a small colony of Segeju, Dongo Kundu by Kwavi, while Kitivo and Mbaramu were Kamba colonies.

The other route led from Pangani, which served as the port of southern Shambaai, as well as Ngulu, Irangi, and Maasai country. The caravan stops on this route, as it passed Shambaai, were Tarawanda, Makuyuni, and Mazinde. The first of these was a Kwavi colony, the second a Zigula village, the third a Zigula village which was also a regular Kwavi stopping place. Tarawanda and Mazinde were taken over by Shambaa chiefs after the nineteenth-century trade transformation.[6]

The Kamba, the main inhabitants of the northern villages, have a great reputation in Shambaai as elephant hunters. Their colonies were not isolated from one another: each maintained contact not only with its sister colonies, but also with Ukambani. The evidence, then, points to the Kamba as the area's early ivory traders. The Segeju probably traded also. They manned the nineteenth-century caravan station at Buiti, and had a reputation near the coast as the slave hunters of an earlier period.[7]

Once the members of a hunting colony collected a quantity of ivory, they brought it to coastal markets themselves. Burton reported that Tanga's ivory, which in 1857 was purchased by car-

6. T. Wakefield, "Routes of Native Caravans from the Coast to the Interior of Eastern Africa, Chiefly from Information Given by Sadi Bin Ahédi, a Native of a District Near Gazi, in Udigo, a Little North of Zanzibar," *Journal of the Royal Geographical Society* 40(1870): 303f; O. Baumann, *Usambara und seine Nachbargebiete* (Berlin, 1891), pp. 10f, 114; Burton, *Zanzibar,* 2: 116f, 143ff; Krapf, *Reisen,* part 2, p. 273. Another bit of evidence is a song, from the *gao* ritual, about a Kamba who controlled Mbaramu:

> There is a Kamba named Kongomeo,
> No one goes down to the Mbaramu plains.

The song has an obscene, untranslatable, double meaning.

7. Baumann, *Usambara,* p. 10; Bethel MS, H. Dupré, "Land und Volk in Usambara," p. 10; Burton, *Zanzibar,* 2: 119; J. P. Farler, "The Usambara Country in East Africa," *Proceedings of the Royal Geographical Society,* n.s. 1 (1879): 85. In the 1860s, Kimweri ye Nyumbai's son, Semboja, the trading chief at Mazinde, sent a Kamba caravan to bring ivory from Ngulu (*H.z.W.*, Sura 88).

avans to the interior, had previously been brought by the people
of the interior to Amboni market.[8] One advantage which may
have led the members of the hunting villages to locate their colonies so near to the densely populated areas of Shambaai was the
potential for trade of meat in exchange for plant foods.

The point here is that ivory hunting and trade were carried on
in the eighteenth century, even though they were not particularly
important in the political economy of the kingdom. Colonies of
alien traders were dotted around the edges of Shambaai throughout the eighteenth century. Among these, the Kamba colonies
appear to have been the most significant. Although the kingdom
expanded enormously through the closing decades of the eighteenth century, and the turn of the nineteenth, the early kings of
Shambaai never conquered the Kamba, and never set up trading
posts of their own in the plains, as Shambaa chiefs were to do in
the second half of the nineteenth century. It is the opinion of the
present author that the willingness of Shambaa kings to keep
their hands off the Kamba colonies is a sign that the kings were
uninterested in carrying on extensive trade. Quite possibly, the
alien traders in their colonies were useful middlemen. Their
small colonies were vulnerable to attack, and one would imagine
that they were less likely to become deeply involved in the politics of the kingdom than Shambaa traders would have been.

The difficulty with casting the Kamba in the role of the main
ivory hunters and traders of the eighteenth century, is that scholars who have studied Kamba history carefully, agree that the
hunters and traders did not begin to move out from their homeland in what is now Kenya until the closing years of the eighteenth century.[9] According to oral traditions collected at the
northeastern tip of Shambaai, however, Kamba hunters had
been present well before the founding of the Mshihwi kingdom
in the late eighteenth century. Pare traditions say that Kamba

8. Burton, *Zanzibar*, 2: 130f.

9. See John Lamphear, "The Kamba and the Northern Mrima Coast,"
in *Pre-Colonial African Trade*, ed. Richard Gray and David Birmingham
(London, 1970), pp. 75–101; Kennell Ardoway Jackson, "An Ethnohistorical Study of the Oral Traditions of the Akamba of Kenya" (Ph.D.
diss., University of California, Los Angeles, 1972), Chapter 6.

hunters were present eleven generations ago, which must have been earlier than the beginning of the nineteenth century.[10] There are, then, two views of the dispersal of Kamba hunters and traders. To one who sees history through the eyes of today's Kenya Kamba, it appears that extensive trade began no earlier than 1780. To the historian standing further south, looking at history from the vantage point of the Pangani Valley, it seems clear that the Kamba were active throughout the eighteenth century.

Two major pieces of additional evidence have been found which support the Pangani Valley view of history, that Kamba hunters and traders were already spread through the northeastern quarter of what is now mainland Tanzania by the early years of the eighteenth century, and quite possibly earlier. First, many of the peoples of the coast around Bagamoyo, opposite the southern half of Zanzibar, have traditions about an early Kamba entry into the area. An examination of the chronological clues in the traditions suggests that the Kamba arrived by the first quarter of the eighteenth century. The traditions assert that these early migrants were the same as the Kenya Kamba. Indeed, in the years of the nineteenth century for which we have documentation, and up to the present day, Kamba traders and hunters have been present in Bagamoyo's distant hinterland.[11]

The second piece of evidence is an oral tradition which Krapf

10. Kimambo, *Political History of the Pare*, p. 119. For the Shambaa traditions, see Historical traditions: Mika Kimweri, 13 July 1966; Mngano Mahimbo, 5 November 1966. Krapf reported in 1848 that there had formerly been Kamba living in the Luengera Valley, below Mshihwi (CMS, CA5/016–173, Journal of a Journey to Usambara, July–December 1848, 1 August 1848).

11. According to the traditions of the Doe, the Zaramo, and the historic coastal Muslims, the Kamba conquered the coast around what is now Bagamoyo. Their presence is remembered as an oppressive one against which the peoples of the coast and its hinterland united. The coastal Muslims asked for, and received, the assistance of the Zaramo and the Doe, who at that time, according to the traditions, lived further inland than they now do. The armies of the interior drove out the Kamba, and remained near the coast where they now had allies. For the traditions on the war see H. Krelle, *Habari za Wazaramo* (Lushoto, 1935); Carl

heard in 1849. According to this tradition, as told by an important Kamba trader (Kivui Mwenda), the Kamba originated in the area around Mt. Kilimanjaro, in what is now northern Tanzania. They had migrated to their home further north, but they had never given up trade with their former neighbors, from the time they had first entered their new homeland. Since we know that the trader with whom Krapf spoke was born between 1785 and 1800, and that he would have had the opportunity during his childhood to hear older men speak of the beginning of trade, it is probable that the institutions of trade had not been created in the eighteenth century.[12]

---

Velten, *Schilderungen der Suaheli* (Göttingen, 1901), pp. 153–57; Franz Stuhlmann, *Mit Emin Pascha ins Herz von Afrika* (Berlin, 1894), pp. 34–35; Charles Sacleux, *Dictionnaire Swahili-Français* (Paris, 1939), entries for *Kanda*, and *mDibuli;* Walter Thaddeus Brown, "A Pre-Colonial History of Bagamoyo" (Ph.D. diss., Boston University, 1971), Chapter 4; G. S. P. Freeman-Grenville, *The East African Coast* (Oxford, 1962), pp. 233–40; E. C. Baker, "A Note on the History of the Washomvi of Dar es Salaam," *Tanganyika Notes and Records,* no. 23 (1947), pp. 47–48; A. B. M. Mtawa, "How the Wadoe got their Name," *Tanganyika Notes and Records,* no. 31 (1951), pp. 79–80. The Kamba of Kilosa, inland from Bagamoyo, are described in T. O. Beidelman, "Some notes on the Kamba in Kilosa District," *Tanganyika Notes and Records,* no. 57 (1961), pp. 181–94. Several bits of evidence have been used for determining the chronology. According to Baker's tradition, one of the main actors in the war was Muhammad bin Shale El Hatimi. Brown ("Pre-Colonial History of Bagamoyo," pp. 71 and 83) reports that this individual lived between 1670 and 1735. Brown (ibid., p. 81) examined one tradition which dated the event to 1704. He emphasized, however, that a tradition collected in the twentieth century cannot be reliable for dating events in the eighteenth. According to the traditions collected by Sacleux, the events occurred either during or shortly after the era of the Debuli on Zanzibar, in other words no later than the fifteenth century. These traditions should not be taken at their face value, but they do indicate that Sacleux's informants thought of the Kamba period as being in the distant, mythical past. Sacleux left Zanzibar in 1898; it is unlikely that his informants, speaking before that date, would have described a nineteenth-century event in mythical terms.

12. CMS, CA5/016–174, Journal descriptive of a journey made to Ukambani in November and December 1849 by J. L. Krapf, 3 December 1849. Kivui Mwenda was known to Krapf simply as Kivoi. The identifi-

It is important to ask why, in view of the evidence given here, excellent scholars working carefully from their sources believe that the dispersal of Kamba hunters and traders began in the final decades of the eighteenth century. To a certain extent, the chronological obscurity is a result of the characteristics of Kenya Kamba oral traditions. Much of Kamba precolonial chronology is based on the dates of named famines. No famines are remembered before the late eighteenth century, although famines must have occurred before that time. Generalized descriptions of the development of trading institutions are undatable; they describe the order of events, but do not give evidence for duration. The exploits of individual traders are remembered. Most traders mentioned, however, were leaders of trading parties from Ukambani to the coast. This form of trade began much later than that of the dispersed colonies. The traders who left their homeland to trade in strange lands, who had no significant activities in Ukambani and left no progeny there, are the least likely to be remembered in oral traditions.[13]

All the documentary evidence on the precolonial Kamba was written in the nineteenth century: it describes a Kamba dispersal which undoubtedly took place in the nineteenth century, and it is unclear on whether the movements were merely the most recent in a centuries-old history of dispersal, or whether the movements were unique to the nineteenth century. That traditions of recent migration can mask a long history, is shown by a twentieth-century tradition collected in East Usambara, and presented in the official district book as part of the definitive history of the local Kamba: "The Wakamba of Daluni left their own country in Kenya in the time of the Germans. My grandfather, Makumi was the leader, and 36 of his family came away with him be-

cation, and the year of Kivui Mwenda's birth, are given by Jackson, "Ethnohistorical Study of the . . . Akamba," p. 251. Kivui also told Krapf that the long history of Kamba trade with peoples to the south preceded Kamba trade to Mombasa.

13. This paragraph is intended only as a summary of the difficulties of constructing a chronology from Kamba traditions. For an excellent full study of the characteristics of the traditions, see Jackson, "Ethnohistorical Study of the . . . Akamba."

cause there was a great famine in the land." Irrefutable evidence
exists, however, that the Kamba colony in question was well established by 1853, at least forty years before the reported migration. A distinction must be made, then, between the history of a
colony, into which fresh migrants may come with each new famine, and the history of the recent migrants themselves.[14]

While much of royal trade was left in the hands of aliens, for
Shambaa subjects trade was essential to the household economy.
The ordinary cultivators of the eighteenth century traded constantly in subsistence goods. The goods, in other words, were for
the most part the same ones paid as tribute. The chiefs already
had access to them. There was no need for the requirements of
the rulers to impinge on the functioning of the markets.

The oral traditions maintain that markets have existed "since
the beginning of time."[15] These statements do not, by themselves, demonstrate the antiquity of Shambaa markets. But they
are strongly supported by the great complexity of local trading
patterns, which must have taken a long time to evolve. In addition, there is evidence that markets did not spread from the
coast, for in the coastal towns the Muslim week was used to determine market days, while in Shambaai a market repeated itself
every fifth day.[16]

Makuyuni, just west of the southern tip of Shambaai, was a
typical large market. It was located between the two ecological
zones of Shambaai and *nyika,* between the Shambaa and the Zigula. The location of the market enabled people to trade for
seed, since their harvest seasons differed, and to trade for food
when only one of the two zones was experiencing famine. In ad-

14. The tradition quoted is from TNA, Lushoto District Book. J. Erhardt, the missionary explorer, reported seeing the Kamba at Daluni in
1853 (CMS, CA5/09–15, Journal containing an account of my journey
to Usambara and back, 22 August 1853).

15. Historical traditions: Mntangi Saidi and Mandia Nguzo, 28 February 1968. The claim here is made for Makuyuni market.

16. *Nachrichten,* May 1894, p. 75, April 1897, p. 63; Historical traditions: Shechonge Kishasha, 28 June 1968; Farler, "Usambara Country,"
p. 87.

dition, there was trade in local specialties. The Zigula brought metal implements, game meat, and salt, while the Shambaa came with bananas and tobacco.

Coastal traders were not unknown at a place like Makuyuni. They came with cowrie shell beads which they exchanged for either samli (butter with the solids skimmed off) or tobacco. The coastal people came in small groups rather than caravans, and went no farther than Makuyuni.[17]

Markets depended on political order for their success, but they were not normally used for the collection of tribute. In one late nineteenth-century case where people at a market were made to pay tribute it was a cause for bitter resentment.[18] People who came to a market paid, as an entrance fee, a small bit of whatever they had brought to trade (*ngeu*), but this was the property of the destitute man who swept and cared for the marketplace.[19]

One did not have to wait for market day to trade. Trade took place anywhere people gathered. In a village it was quite natural for a man with a surplus of seed to sell some to a neighbor who did not have enough. Men also went on longer trips, to trade in villages outside Shambaai. Shambaa men would go to trade their livestock for iron implements at the villages of Pare smiths. Trade with the Kwavi was possible only if one had a Kwavi blood partner. Otherwise it was considered too dangerous. The Kwavi sold livestock and bought Shambaa tobacco. At times five or six men banded together to make the three-day journey to Pangani, at the coast, to sell samli or tobacco for cowrie beads. Once at the coast they could either visit traders privately, or wait for the market day.[20]

17. Historical traditions: Semnguu Koplo, 27 November 1967. Dr. Kimambo has informed me that the salt in question was *magaddi,* a kind of soda. I have used the word *salt* because the traditions speak of *munyu,* and that word is used today for salt.

18. Farler to W. H. Penney, October 1887 (USPG-UMCA, Box A 1 VI).

19. Historical traditions: Mdoembazi Guga, 29 November 1967.

20. Historical traditions: Mdoembazi Guga, 29 November 1967; Semnguu Koplo, 27 November 1967. The journey to Pangani was three days, starting from Vugha.

No one trader traveled a great distance, yet products could go quite far by progressing from trader to trader or from market to market. In 1848 the Shambaa sold their tobacco to the Digo, who then took it to the Mberria market, northwest of Mombasa, where Mombasa traders met with the Galla. There is no way of knowing whether the Galla resold the tobacco at some more distant point.[21] Shambaa entrepreneurs sold goat skins in Pare to get samli, and then sold the samli at Pangani.[22]

Even within Shambaai goods progressed from market to market. Salt, which was extracted on the plains near Mombo, was sold by Zigula to Shambaa at the Mombo market, resold to other traders at the Mishegheshe market near Vugha, continued on to the Kikuyu market west of Bumbuli, and was carried for sale at other markets farther to the east.[23]

All over Shambaai there were fixed rates of exchange for some goods. The smallest unit was the round, hard cake of tobacco. Forty of these packed together in banana leaves were called an *mzungu* (pl. *mizungu*). The following relationships of value were unchanging:

$$6 \; mizungu = 1 \; \text{billy goat}$$
$$12 \; mizungu = 1 \; \text{nanny goat}$$
$$3 \; \text{billy goats} = 1 \; \text{bull}$$
$$6 \; \text{billy goats} = 1 \; \text{cow}$$

In this way, while there was no general-purpose money which could serve as a standard of valuation and a means of payment for all goods and services, several kinds of wealth could be exchanged at regular rates. The standardization of these particular rates of exchange was useful, for livestock was used as bridewealth, and was consumed in ritual feasts. A man who owed a cow for bridewealth could pay one goat at a time. And a group of men joining together to make a feast would contribute cakes of tobacco to share the cost of a goat.[24]

21. Krapf, *Reisen,* part 2, pp. 94, 113.
22. Historical traditions: Semnguu Koplo, 27 November 1967.
23. Historical traditions: Mzaia Shekumkai, 13 July 1967.
24. Historical traditions: Leo Hasani, June 1967; Mzaia Shekumkai, 13 July 1967. LangHeinrich, *Schambala-Wörterbuch,* p. 356; Dupré, "Land und Volk," p. 82.

Because of the great variations in the availability of food crops from year to year and from season to season, there were no fixed, customary rates for the exchange of livestock for grain. In time of grave famine a goat brought very little maize indeed. In a time of plenty, young men sold surplus produce for goats in order to save up for bridewealth.

People traded, in other words, not only in order to acquire products that were scarce locally, such as iron or salt or cowrie beads, but also for the conversion of one form of wealth to another. Bridewealth could be paid in goats but not in maize; yet a successful farmer could sell maize for goats in order to marry.[25]

This reconstruction of eighteenth-century Shambaa trade, incomplete though it may be, provides a part of the answer to one of the most puzzling questions of East African history—the question of the sources of wealth in the coastal towns before the nineteenth century. The problem is that for many centuries towns have flourished all up and down the East African coast. While Kilwa, and the towns to the south of it, quite clearly had intense trade relationships with vast sections of the interior, the towns north of Kilwa, up to what is now northern Kenya, did not, so far as we know, send caravans into the interior until the late eighteenth century at the earliest. Not only are there no records of caravans, but there appears in many cases to have been a self-conscious avoidance by coastal Muslims of extensive trading trips into the interior. Before the nineteenth century, in the coast around what is now Bagamoyo and Dar es Salaam, the Zaramo chief of the hinterland was known as 'the chief who does not see the water,' while the Shomvi coastal Muslim leader was called 'the Shomvi who does not see the [setting] sun.'[26] Relationships of avoidance were common between leaders of hinterland peoples, and leaders of the coastal towns on the central Tanzanian coast.

It is dangerous, and undoubtedly incorrect, to generalize from the eighteenth-century Shambaa experience to the history of all parts of the coast in all centuries. Nevertheless, the record of early Shambaa trade tells us about one possible set of institu-

25. Paul Wohlrab, "Einzelheiten," *Nachrichten* 6 (January 1892): 10.
26. Brown, "Pre-Colonial History of Bagamoyo," p. 105.

tions for the organization of trade. The record is illuminated because the Shambaa, while not themselves coastal people, lived
near enough to the coast to have direct trading relations before
the days of the caravan trade. Early Shambaa trade with the
ports was, as we have seen, not part of a long-distance caravan
network, but was local trade. It was similar to the early trade of
the Nyamwezi of the interior with their neighbors the Gogo, who
were also people of the interior.

From the evidence of the Shambaa and their neighbors it appears that the coastal towns were supplied with provisions and
trade goods in three ways. First, and most obviously, there were
close ties between the coastal towns and their immediate neighbors. Constant interchange took place, for example, between
Mombasa and the Nyika peoples, and between Tanga and the
Digo. The peoples of the immediate hinterland were especially
important as suppliers of provisions, because of the difficulty of
transporting bulky crops from more distant regions. Second,
goods filtered to the coast from market to market, as they were
passed on from one trader to the next. We have seen how Shambaa tobacco was resold several times on its way to the Galla,
and how salt passed through many hands even within Shambaai
itself. In this way samli from Pare reached the coast even when
the Pare people and the coastal people all remained at home.
Third, some men went directly to the coast from the interior, or
to the interior from the coast. They traveled in small groups
rather than large caravans, and they rarely ventured farther than
three days' march, or about a hundred miles. Some Shambaa
took their samli or tobacco to the coast themselves, and some
Digo from the coast went as far inland as Shambaai to trade
their shell beads. The Kamba who live around the edges of
Shambaai made a specialty of hunting ivory, which they carried
themselves the two or three days' walk to the coast.

In these ways Tanga and Pangani were supplied with goods
which filtered to the coast from the interior, even though direct
contact with the distant interior was nonexistent, and direct contact with the near interior was limited.

Coasting trade in small locally-built vessels concentrated

goods from many small ports in the few towns where larger long-distance vessels called more frequently.[27] Quite probably, the towns on the Kenya coast, with their poor and narrow hinterland, relied more heavily on the coasting trade than did Tanga and Pangani. This trade, however, could not have sustained the entrepots without the substantial quantities of goods which came from many small ports, each tapping its own hinterland.

## The Intrusion of Trade on Politics, 1836–1862

From the 1830s, demand for the products of the Pangani Valley, including slaves, increased rapidly in intensity, and new products from the world beyond East Africa, including firearms, became more easily available than they had been. Trade was now possible on a much greater scale than before. With the introduction of firearms and the increasing importance of the sale of slaves, trade came to affect the balance of power in the Pangani Valley.

Because Kimweri ye Nyumbai's old style of politics had been so successful, and because that style depended on the careful control of foreign influences in his kingdom, Kimweri never took full advantage of the new political possibilities. As a result, from 1836, when trade expanded rapidly, to 1862, when Kimweri died, the eager entrepreneurs from among the neighbors of the Shambaa increased their power and their territory at Kimweri's expense.

Growing European demand for East African ivory stimulated trade, and made Omani involvement in the region profitable. Seyyid Said, who had assumed complete power as ruler of Oman, in the Persian Gulf, in 1806, became more and more deeply involved in the affairs of Zanzibar until he moved there permanently in 1840.

As Seyyid Said's interest in Zanzibar grew, increasing num-

27. C. S. Nicholls, *The Swahili Coast: Politics, Diplomacy and Trade on the East African Littoral,* 1798–1856 (London, 1971), pp. 77.

bers of immigrants from Oman and other Arabian ports settled there. These new immigrants soon outnumbered the earlier Arab settlers in Zanzibar and Pemba.[28] With the Sultan's encouragement the new settlers began to produce cloves and other plantation crops. The resulting demand for labor led to a great expansion of the slave trade on the mainland.[29] The Pangani Valley, in the hinterland opposite Pemba, was ideally located as a source of plantation slaves.

At the same time, the intensification of communications of East Africa with the northern Indian Ocean and the Red Sea led to an increase of the trade in slaves in that direction. The export of slaves to the north from East Africa increased steadily from 1811 to 1842. The number dropped after the Treaty of 1845, between Seyyid Said and the British, prohibiting the export of slaves from East Africa, but then increased again after Seyyid Said's death in 1856.[30]

The final source of the demand for slaves, a demand which had such a profound effect on the history of the Pangani Valley, was within East Africa. Once new sources had been developed, the supply itself created a demand. When the price of slaves declined, as a result of the Treaty of 1845, the peoples of Mombasa's interior, who had never used domestic slaves, began to find new uses for slaves in order to take advantage of the depressed price.[31]

While the great increase in demand was a generalized stimulus to political and economic change, it was the Zigula who actually pioneered the trade in the Pangani Valley region. The Zigula, immediately south of Shambaai, were the first to get fire-

28. Sir John Gray, *History of Zanzibar from the Middle Ages to 1856* (London, 1962), p. 136.

29. Sir John Gray, "Zanzibar and the Coastal Belt, 1840–1884," in *History of East Africa,* vol. 1, ed. Roland Oliver and Gervase Mathew (Oxford, 1963), pp. 216ff.

30. J. B. Kelly, *Britain and the Persian Gulf,* 1795–1880 (Oxford, 1968), pp. 414–16, 616, 622–23.

31. J. L. Krapf, Memoir on the East African Slave-trade, etc. CMS, CA5/016–179, p. 27; Krapf, *Reisen,* part 1, pp. 249f, 318.

arms, and the first to engage in the large-scale sale of slaves. As a result, the nineteenth century was a period of rapid Zigula expansion in both territory and power.

The shock which set Zigula changes in motion was a great and devastating famine, which occurred about 1836.[32] Many Zigula sold themselves as slaves during the famine, in return for the assurance of being fed. Those who returned to their homeland afterwards brought with them a knowledge of conditions in a wider area of East Africa, and they became traders.

Some of the Zigula who sold themselves were taken to Somalia by Barawa traders. There they continued to speak their language and to think of themselves as Zigula into the twentieth century.[33] A great number, however, merely crossed the narrow channel to Zanzibar. Once in captivity so near to home they conspired to escape: "According to a well-concerted plan a large party of the conspirators assembled one moonlight night on one of the plantations. They made their way thence to the seashore to the north of Zanzibar roadstead. Arriving there in the early hours of the morning, they boarded a number of Arab dhows, surprised and killed or overpowered the members of the crew, raised anchor, made sail and crossed over to the mainland."[34]

The process of famine, enslavement, escape, provided those who went through it with an education in spite of themselves. These were men who had grown up in Zigula, who had Zigula interests at heart, and yet who understood all the new developments that were taking place on Zanzibar. They were able to

32. Burton wrote in 1860 that the famine happened "about twenty years ago" (Sir Richard F. Burton, *The Lake Regions of Central Africa*, 2 vols. [New York, 1961], 1: 125). Krapf reported a similar famine around Mombasa in 1836 (*Reisen*, part 1, pp. 208f, 314).

33. For a general description of Bantu speakers in Somalia, see V. L. Grottanelli, "I Bantu del Giuba nelle tradizioni dei Wazegua," *Geographica Helvetica* 8 (1953): 249–60. I am grateful to Lee Cassanelli for notes in English on this article.

34. Gray, *History of Zanzibar*, p. 141. The escape is also described in Père Picarda, "Autour de Mandéra: Notes sur l'Ouzigoua, l'Oukwere et l'Oudoé (Zanguebar)," *Les Missions Catholiques* 18 (1886):227.

mediate between two cultures and to provide leadership in grasping new opportunities, just as mission men of a later generation provided leadership as cultural brokers. Kisabengo, who founded the great town of Simba Mwene, at the western foot of the Luguru mountains, and who was infamous over a great territory as a slave raider, was typical of the new leaders. He built his political power on the trade in slaves, which he learned as a slave himself before the great escape.

Under the leadership of Kisabengo, and men like him, the Zigula expanded, in the north, at the expense of the Shambaa, and in the south, at the expense of the Doe, Kami, and Kwere. Stanley wrote, in 1872, that "thirty years ago the Waseguhha [Zigula] were limited to a narrow belt of country between the Wasambara [Shambaa] and the Wadoe [Doe]."[35] Burton, in 1857, came upon the Doe in the process of moving south. And a French missionary, writing from Mandera in 1886, said that the area had formerly been the land of the Doe, but was now on the Zigula side of the Kwere-Doe-Zigula border.[36]

In contrast with the education of Zigula leaders as slaves on Zanzibar, Kimweri ye Nyumbai had undergone his training as future king of Shambaai, learning magical rites and the subtleties of Kilindi dynastic politics. This education, which had served him well for consolidating his rule within the kingdom, left him unprepared to take advantage of new opportunities which presented themselves. At some time between the end of 1843 and the beginning of 1845, Seyyid Said allied himself with Kimweri. It would presumably have been useful to the Sultan, recently settled at Zanzibar, to work closely with the most powerful ruler of the coastal hinterland. Seyyid Said sent a number of soldiers, Krapf says 600, to make war against the Kwavi (Iloikop Maasai) on the borders of Shambaai. According to Krapf, Seyyid Said expected a handsome present from Kimweri, but received only thirty-five pounds of ivory. Seyyid Said, angry at the insult,

35. Henry M. Stanley, *How I Found Livingstone: Travels, Adventures and Discoveries in Central Africa* (New York, 1872), p. 243.
36. Burton, *Lake Regions,* 1: 123f; Picarda, "Autour de Mandéra," pp. 185, 297.

came near to making war against the Shambaa, and in the end allied himself with some of the Zigula chiefs.[37]

In the face of the Zigula challenge, Kimweri sold slaves and began to acquire flintlocks, but he never mastered the diplomacy of trade. From 1836 to his death in 1862 Kimweri ye Nyumbai was constantly losing ground to the Zigula. He never acquired as many guns as the Zigula chiefs, nor did he raid intensively for slaves.

The contrast between Kimweri's strength at trading and that of the Zigula is especially striking if one considers their relative positions, during this period, at the coast itself. Kimweri ye Nyumbai, "ruler of the coast," was not allowed to trade directly with Zanzibar. He had to leave trading in the hands of the coastal Muslims. Krapf earned the hatred of the coastal people by smuggling one of Kimweri's courtiers to Zanzibar with some ivory, to trade directly with the European companies. During the same period, the Zigula were in direct communication with Zanzibar. They sold their ivory, grain, and cattle themselves on the island, without having to pay coastal middlemen.[38]

Because of the ability of the Shambaa soldiers to raid the coast at will, Kimweri ye Nyumbai was left in political control there, while Seyyid Said, Sultan of Zanzibar, controlled trade. When a dignitary of Tanga, Pangani, or Tangata wanted to assume the title of *Diwani* (local chief), he would go to Vugha to present Kimweri with trade goods, and then he would seek confirmation of his appointment from the Sultan of Zanzibar, who presented the *Diwani* with a gift so that he would guard the Seyyid's interests. Kimweri's courtiers and soldiers collected tribute in the coastal towns, while Seyyid Said's representatives collected duty on ivory passing through the ports. The only overlap in their spheres of authority came when Kimweri tried to develop his own contacts with the world beyond East Africa. In March of 1852 Kimweri offered Krapf Mt. Tongwe, inland from

37. CMS, CA5/016–177, Krapf's Usambara Journal 1852, 20 March 1852.

38. CMS, CA5/016–179, Krapf's Memoir on the . . . Slave-trade," p. 36. Krapf, *Reisen,* part 2, pp. 279, 316f.

Pangani, as a mission station. Within a year, Seyyid Said had garrisoned Tongwe and neighboring Chogwe. Kimweri tried to convince the missionaries that he could give them the spot if only he were supplied with powder and guns.[39]

Kimweri ye Nyumbai was slow to take up the slave trade not only because of his poor relations with the Sultan of Zanzibar, but also because Shambaa political values insisted on the importance of subjects as payers of tribute. Kimweri did not feel free to sell his subjects; the only large scale source of legitimate slaves was from the subjects of Kimweri's enemies. Zigula political leaders governed small chiefdoms, and were therefore free to raid neighbors. For these reasons, other rulers in the Pangani Valley were selling whole villages at a time when Kimweri was disposing of an occasional criminal.[40] In other words, while the economic forces at work in the region favored slave trade, Kimweri's success in consolidating power within a large kingdom and his predisposition to the old politics led to a lag in Shambaa participation. In the wars after Kimweri's death there was a spectacular spurt in the number of slaves coming from Shambaai.[41] Kimweri ye Nyumbai was also slow at purchasing guns. When his father, Kinyashi Muanga Ike, died, guns of any kind

39. The joint government of the coast is described in some detail by Krapf, *Reisen,* part 1, p. 284, part 2, pp. 105, 127, 177f. Krapf himself observed the collection of tribute by Kimweri's soldiers at Pangani, and the visit by the *Diwani* of Pangani at Vugha to pay the king's dues (part 2, pp. 130, 276). The offer of Tongwe is described in part 2, p. 300. Subsequent developments were reported by Erhardt, CMS, CA5/09–15, Erhardt's Usambara journal, September 1, 1853.

40. Krapf, *Reisen,* part 1, pp. 184f, part 2, pp. 129, 279; Burton, *Zanzibar,* 2: 194.

41. J. Kirk, "Visit to the Coast of Somali-land," *Proceedings of the Royal Geographical Society* 17 (1873): 340–41. While this spurt was a result of the dynastic war well after Kimweri's death, the slave trade continued greater than during his lifetime until German colonization. The traditions maintain that Kimweri ye Nyumbai did not trade in slaves at all, but Krapf saw that indeed he did. I have examined this in the light of all the other evidence on nineteenth-century history and have taken it to mean that Kimweri ye Nyumbai did not raid for slaves in the predatory manner of his successors. Also, according to the traditions, the first Arabs

were unknown in the Pangani Valley region. After the Zigula began to use guns with devastating effect, Kimweri bought them too, but he never caught up. In 1852, according to Krapf, Kimweri had only 400 guns, while one of the important Zigula chiefs had 600.[42]

The guns themselves were flintlocks which were dangerous to the users; they would have been effective only if the Shambaa had known about volley firing. One informant insisted that only if you first rubbed your nose, and then rubbed the oil onto the flint, would the gun go off.[43] Earlier weapons were retained, and men with guns fought alongside men with spears. In spite of their poor quality, firearms seem to have been very important for Shambaa warfare. Perhaps this was because of the frightening noise guns made. Perhaps, inefficient as they were, the guns were still more effective than earlier weapons.

Kimweri ye Nyumbai's backwardness at trade led to the gradual diminution of his domains at the hands of Zigula chiefs. It is possible, using successive reports of explorers, to document the changes in Kimweri's receding border. In 1844 Kimweri was on the offensive. When Krapf visited the coast in that year he found that Zigula villages at Bweni, just south of Pangani, had just been destroyed by Kimweri's soldiers. By 1848, when Krapf passed through Bondei, he reported that Kimweri's rule of the Bondei had softened out of fear that they would ally with the

---

came to Shambaai during Kimweri ye Nyumbai's reign. Historical traditions: Jaha Mtoi, 28 November 1967; Kimweri Magogo, 1 December 1967; Mdoembazi Guga, 29 November 1967.

42. This is one of those marvelous subjects where the oral traditions agree with the written documents in every detail. Krapf reported that the Zigula took greater advantage of the coming of firearms (*Reisen,* part 1, pp. 184f, part 2, p. 307), and so did the testimony of an elder who lived in a Zigula-Shambaa border area (Historical traditions: Chamhingo, 25 December 1967). Both the historical traditions which I collected and Abdallah bin Hemedi 'lAjjemy's precolonial report of traditions agree that at Kinyashi's death guns were unknown, and that they were introduced during the reign of Kimweri ye Nyumbai (*H.z.W.,* Sura 39). Historical traditions: Boaz Mjata, 15 July 1967; Jaha Mtoi, 28 November 1967).

43. Historical traditions: Mdoembazi Guga, 29 November 1967.

Zigula. At that time the Kamba, who had been living in the Luengera Valley with Kimweri's permission, had been driven out by the Zigula.[44]

Four years later, in 1852, Krapf visited again. Near the coast he saw the devastation which the wars had caused.

> Although naturally very fertile the greater portion of these lowlands is a perfect wilderness, partly in consequence of the incursions of the Wasegua [Zigula], partly from the indolence of the inhabitants. The mountain which lies nearest the coast and to the northern bank of Pangani, is Tongue, the district round which is said to be extremely fertile. Twelve years ago, it seems there were about and on this mountain numerous villages and plantations, which, however, were destroyed by the Wasegua, and the inhabitants consequently retreated to the north, to the mountains of Mringa and Pambire. The Wasegua appear to have procured fire-arms in Zanzibar, where newly opened European and American commerce had introduced them in large numbers, and to have surprised the Wasambara [Shambaa], ignorant until then of such weapons. Abandoned, this district of Tongue soon became a forest and the abode of elephants and buffaloes; but its old inhabitants meanwhile have not forgotten their fertile plains, and abide their time when they may with safety return again to Tongue.[45]

Burton and Speke visited Kimweri in 1857, and by that time the route Krapf had taken from Pangani was closed because of Zigula raids. The people of Pangani recommended a circuitous route starting from Tangata on the coast farther north.[46]

Kimweri ye Nyumbai's preference for the usages of traditional leadership was a definite hindrance in his protracted war with the Zigula. The northern Zigula he was fighting against were new men, men who rose to positions of leadership because of their ability to master new techniques of warfare, as well as new

44. Krapf, *Reisen*, part 1, p. 284; part 2, pp. 115, 122.

45. Ibid., part 2, p. 280; the English version is in *Travels, Researches, and Missionary Labours, during an Eighteen Years' Residence in Eastern Africa* (London, 1860), p. 374f.

46. Burton, *Zanzibar*, 2: 149.

forms of political organization. The enemy Kimweri took most seriously was Kivuma, who had his headquarters on Mafi Mountain, which faces Mazinde.[47] Kivuma was a soldier of fortune who fought his way to power; his original home was not at Mafi.

At another village not far from Korogwe, Sultan Mamba—a Zigula who had been to Zanzibar—supplied Burton and Speke with beef and milk and then jerked his thumb toward the blue hills of Shambaai and declared that the explorers had already become Kimweri's guests. The chief explained that "his people had but three wants—powder, ball, and brandy, and that they could supply in return three things—men, women, and children."[48]

According to the historical traditions, Kimweri ye Nyumbai's most important weapon in fighting back was control of the rain. Kimweri hurled famine at his enemies.[49] No doubt the Zigula took the threat seriously. One of the earliest missionary visitors to Shambaai came across a Zigula war party heading up into the mountains to avenge a drought.[50]

It should not be thought that the kingdom's losses were a special local case, peculiar to the Pangani Valley. At many places in East Africa, in the same period, the great polities of an earlier period, built around areas of high fertility and dense population, were declining, while trade-based polities, sometimes located in relatively barren areas, were gaining in strength. The Nyamwezi of what is now western Tanzania were building their power on trade, while their neighbors in Buha were becoming less powerful than they once had been. On Kilimanjaro, Kibosho, with its great population, was struggling to maintain its position in the face of the rising power of Moshi, which had strong ties with the peoples of the plains. Even the kingdom of Buganda, while ex-

47. Kimweri kept a Muslim magician, Bwana Osman, at his court, mainly to make magic against the chief of Mafi (Krapf, *Reisen,* part 2, pp. 299f).

48. Burton, *Zanzibar,* 2: 193f.

49. Historical traditions: Mdoembazi Guga, 15 June 1967.

50. Universities Mission to Central Africa, *Bluebook, 1868* (London, 1868), pp. 9f. This occurred after Kimweri ye Nyumbai's death.

tremely fertile, got much of the impetus for its nineteenth century expansion from its domination of trade routes.

In the Pangani Valley, the shift in the balance of power between the Shambaa and the Zigula was merely the most dramatic hint of the changes to come. At the same time there was a hidden shift in the balance of power within Shambaai itself, which was even more of a threat to the survival of the kingdom. By the time Kimweri ye Nyumbai died, in 1862, Vugha was no longer the real center of power. One of Kimweri's sons, Semboja, had understood that power now depended on trade, and he had created a commercial center at Mazinde, ideally located for the trade in slaves, guns, and ivory. Semboja did not attack Vugha during his father's lifetime; he remained a veiled threat. Yet any political settlement after the old king's death would have to take account of Mazinde.

Semboja was born to a relatively unimportant "house" of the capital, but he was the great innovator among the Kilindi of his generation. Semboja ruled first at Gare (see pp. 110–11), then moved to Ngua, in the mountains overlooking the Zigula plains, and finally moved his headquarters down to the Zigula town of Mazinde. He was thus the first major Shambaa chief ever to have his capital in *nyika*—the lowlands—rather than Shambaai. By 1852, when Krapf visited, Semboja was well established at Mazinde.

Because he was the first of the Kilindi to understand the importance of trade, Semboja was destined to be the most important single actor in the succession dispute which would follow ye Nyumbai's death. But during the 1850s his power was tangential to Shambaa politics. Kimweri remained in control. He lived to such a great old age that he was, in a way, a museum piece at his death. The change in the nature of political power which had long been manifest among the Zigula was latent in Shambaai, as Semboja awaited his father's death.

# 6 · REBELLION AND REVOLUTION

Power relations between the king and chiefs in the Shambaa kingdom depended on two factors. The first was the behavior associated with particular kinship relations between the king and each of his chiefs. The influence of kinship relations clearly did not result from the broad social forces which affected society, which changed through time, and which made one century or generation different in unpredictable ways from the next. Some configurations of kinship relations were characterized by the subordination of the chiefs to the king, others by resistance to royal authority. The forces leading to competition among half brothers, for example, were not much different in the eighteenth century than they were at the end of the nineteenth. Given the existence of recurrent patterns of competition within the Kilindi lineage, it was possible for competing chiefs to seek support outside the lineage in different ways in every generation. Sources of support, then, are the second major factor in Kilindi power relations. Important chiefs might have been allied with Kamba hunters in one generation, and with coastal traders in the next. Dependence on particular nonroyal descent groups for support could shift with changes in the relative size and power of individual groups. Changing political conditions beyond the borders of the Shambaa kingdom also affected patterns of support. The rebellion and revolution which broke the kingdom apart in the late 1860s can be seen as a result of the coincidence of an extremely difficult dynastic situation and drastic change in the sources of support.

If one ignores sources of support and considers only the realm of Kilindi descent, then power relations between king and chiefs depended on the overlap between ideals of proper behavior in an intimate family setting and ideals appropriate to the offices. When the chiefs were sons of the king, the authority of a father over his sons reinforced that of a king over chiefs. At such times the king's position of strength was supported not only by ideas about the father-son relationship, but also by the self-interest of the sons. Any son who challenged the king's authority was at the same time attempting to raise himself to a position of preeminence over his brothers. They could be relied on by the king to provide an army for the enforcement of his will against a refractory chief. When the chiefs were half brothers of the king, the competitive quality of sibling relations undermined the king's authority over his chiefs. In addition, the interests of the chiefs as a group were opposed to those of the king, for he was expected to attempt to remove them, so that he could put his sons in their places. The usual response of chiefs was to band together to resist the king's initiative. The moment of crisis in the development of royal power relations would come at the death of a powerful king, who had installed his sons in the chiefdoms, and had therefore left his successor with a thriving sibling group of competitors.

Kimweri ye Nyumbai in the nineteenth century, like Bughe in the eighteenth, had used the father-son relationship to govern the whole of the Shambaa kingdom. The kingdom in Bughe's time, however, had included only southern Shambaai. Kimweri had made his sons chiefs through the whole of Shambaai, East Usambara, and Bondei. He had removed all earlier chiefs who, by the time of Kimweri's old age, had reverted to the status of commoners. At this time virtually all the Kilindi in the Shambaa kingdom were descendants of Kimweri ye Nyumbai. The moment Kimweri died, the network of descent relations he had created to increase his authority would work to weaken any possible successor. All the chiefs of Kimweri's kingdom could be expected to band together in order to resist the attempts of a new kin to replace them with his own sons. Only the new king's full siblings, who expected to share the fruits of their brother's success, could be expected to support him.

The succession would be made doubly difficult by the fact that Kimweri's son Mnkande, the heir to Vugha, had died some years before, and so Mnkande's son, Shekulwavu, became heir. This meant that every effort by the new king to dominate his chiefs, or to replace them with his own men, would be seen as an act of disrespect by the king to men of his father's generation. The family ideals, in this case, would be in direct conflict with the ideals of office. The chief with the greatest authority over the future king, for whom the conflict of roles would be greatest, was Mshuza of Ubii. At the death of the royal heir (Mnkande), Mshuza had inherited the heir's great wife, mother of the future king. He therefore had the authority of a father over the king. In addition, Mshuza had been given some of the most important rain medicines by Kimweri ye Nyumbai.

Change in the sources of chiefly support had come with the increasing importance of trade in the Pangani Valley region. Semboja, son of Kimweri ye Nyumbai, was chief of Mazinde, in the plains. He had a relatively minor position in descent terms, but he controlled the greatest portion of the trade of southern Shambaai in the 1860s. He was a violent man, an ambitious man, and he wanted to be king himself.

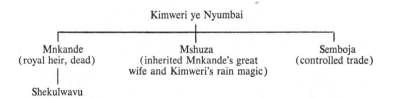

In Shambaai, where trade had not yet had much impact, the common people of each chiefdom could be expected to support their own chiefs against the new king. Kimweri ye Nyumbai had carefully supervised the chiefs of Shambaai, had heard appeals against the judgments of his sons, and the sons themselves had married locally. The effect of intermarriage over a period was to blur the lines which separated Kilindi and commoners, and to integrate Kilindi into the local community.

The future king's only possible sources of support, in his initial efforts to dominate the chiefs, would be from the chief and people of Bumbuli, from the people of Vugha, and from the people of Bondei. Bumbuli was the heir's own chiefdom, the one over which he could place a full brother without having to remove an earlier chief. The elders of Vugha lived off tribute; they would tolerate any king so long as he was strong enough to collect tribute from all of Kimweri's territories. But if the king proved too weak to retain for them their wealth and power, they would shift their support to the king's enemies.

In Bondei the majority of the common people were willing to assist a new king in any actions which promised to rid them of their Kilindi chiefs. The full story of Bondei actions in the period awaits the collection of Bondei oral traditions, but it is certain that the relations between chiefs and commoners were very much worse in Bondei than they were in Shambaai. Kimweri ye Nyumbai's supervision had been loose in the eastern portions of the kingdom. He had sent there some of the chiefs who had failed in Shambaai. Because of this, and because the areas near the coast were affected most severely by the onset of the slave trade, the effects of Shambaa rule were more harsh the further east one went, with the exception of the coastal towns. There is evidence that, perhaps as early as the 1840s, a son of Kimweri had traded great numbers of Digo slaves, from the immediate coastal hinterland, and was ultimately killed by them. Erhardt, the missionary explorer, saw in 1853 that Kilindi chiefs were unable to provide their Bondei subjects with protection from Zigula attacks. In 1854 chiefs who ruled territories in Bondei were seen selling Bondei slaves at the coast. Bondei acts of armed resistance to Kimweri's rule were taking place as early as 1852. By the middle 1860s, after more than a full decade of Zigula slave raiding, many Bondei were eager to rid themselves of the harsh and uncertain rule of their chiefs.[1]

The first act of the drama of succession did not await Kimweri's death. It took place in the late 1850s or early 1860s, when Kimweri was too old to care for himself, let alone the kingdom. Kimweri ye Nyumbai realized that some transfer of authority would have to take place. He was too old to hear cases, too old to leave his house. In his dotage his control of the affairs of the kingdom began to slip. Toward the end Semboja at Mazinde began to sell his Shambaa subjects into slavery, and the old king found himself unable to do anything about it.[2]

Kimweri was still alert enough, however, to worry about the problems caused by his age. He knew that he was losing control. He knew, also, that too many of his sons had strong personalities and devoted followings, and that after his death they would destroy the kingdom fighting one another to control it. Kimweri ye Nyumbai decided that while he was still alive he would install his grandson Shekulwavu, son of the dead Mnkande, of the great house. Kimweri hoped that Shekulwavu's appointment would result in the return of vigorous rule to Vugha, even though the young king would not be greeted *Simba Mwene* until after his grandfather's death.

If one reflects on Shekulwavu's disastrous end, the burning of his capital, his death, one may well wonder whether Kimweri's decision was merely a silly senile judgment. Shekulwavu was thrust into an unusually difficult position, for he had to establish

1. CMS, CA5/09–15, Erhardt's Usambara journal; Erhardt reported what he had heard about the trading of Digo slaves and the murder of Kimweri's son in the journal entry for 10 August 1853. For reports on the lack of security in Bondei see the journal entries for 13 November and 20–22 November 1853. Erhardt reported in his Extract of a Journal Kept at Tanga from March to October 1854, that when he had criticized a Kilindi chief for selling slaves, the chief "indifferently excused himself that his were offenders. Muigni Hattibu his brother [a son of Kimweri] was the man who ate up all the Wasinsi [Bondei]" (1 April 1854). Krapf described armed resistance against Kimweri ye Nyumbai's tribute collectors in his Usambara journal, 3 March 1852 (CA5/016–177).

2. Historical traditions: Jaha Mtoi, 28 November 1967.

his authority over the territorial chiefs, men he called "father" (*ishe*), men who were old and powerful. When ye Nyumbai announced his decision to the courtiers at Vugha, they doubted that the young king could make his will felt. They said, "How are you going to make Shekulwavu king? After all, you have your own children. Won't they make trouble?" Simba Mwene Kimweri ye Nyumbai responded immediately: "No they won't. They are my own children and I am their father."[3] Kimweri, in other words, believed, like all Shambaa, that the father's will affects the affairs of his sons even after his death. This is a belief, however, that old men take somewhat more seriously than their sons.

After discussing the matter with his most respected courtiers, Kimweri ye Nyumbai sent out runners to bring the important chiefs from among his sons to Vugha. Ye Nyumbai explained his decision to them, and while they were not happy they saw no way of making their aged father change his mind.

Mshuza of Ubii, the son Kimweri considered most likely to defeat Shekulwavu if a succession dispute developed, was made to swear a solemn oath, and then to drink water mixed with fragments of a broken clay pot. Mshuza swore that neither he nor his sons would ever enter Vugha as rulers. (I knew one descendant of Mshuza's, a man of some influence locally, who, no matter how urgent his business there, would never enter Vugha. The oath, in other words, is taken seriously to this day).[4] Mshuza's oath ensured that he would be kingmaker, but not king.

Shekulwavu became acting ruler of Vugha while his grandfather was still alive. The people of Vugha, who for a long time had known nothing more lively at the royal court than ye Nyumbai's request for live coals to light his pipe, now had a young virile king. Shekulwavu "ate" the fines that came to Vugha with-

---

3. Historical traditions: Kimweri Magogo, 3 April 1967.
4. Kimweri's decision to make his grandson king is described in a number of Historical traditions. These include: Ali Sabago, 20 February 1968; Boaz Mjata, 15 July 1967; Jaha Mtoi, 22 April 1967; Kimweri Magogo, 3 April 1967; Mdoembazi Guga, 29 November 1967; Salehe Ali, 11 November 1967.

out consulting his grandfather. He made himself at home in the secluded private quarters of Kimweri's wives. Vugha was alive with scandal.[5]

The tellers of traditions usually argue that Shekulwavu's licentious behavior during this period was the first step in his downfall. But another interpretation is possible. Shekulwavu was laying claim, while he could, to fines from the whole kingdom which would be his when he established control over the whole kingdom. By "eating" the fines, or using the wealth, he must have been trying to attract a personal following. The women also would be Shekulwavu's at Kimweri's death, for in Shambaai grandsons may inherit wives from grandfathers. Here again, the young king was trying to establish his claim while he could.

Any attempt by the young king to establish real control would have been thought shocking by Kimweri ye Nyumbai's sons. Shekulwavu is not censured in the traditions because he was forceful or because he offended Shambaa sensibilities. The real reason for censure is that he ultimately failed.

Finally, early in 1862, an entire era of Shambaa history ended with the death of Kimweri ye Nyumbai.[6] At first Kimweri's

5. Historical traditions: Kwavi Senkunde, 28 May 1968, text 2; Mahimbo Kihedu, 1 February 1968; Mdoembazi Guga, 29 November 1967.

6. Farler gives the date of Kimweri's death as 1868 (Farler, "Usambara Country," p. 84). Baumann gives it as 1869 (Baumann, *Usambara*, p. 186). Since neither Baumann nor Farler was a witness to the events, it is difficult to understand where either found the date of Kimweri's death. 1868 is clearly too late, for Abdallah bin Hemedi 'lAjjemy tells us that Shekulwavu caught smallpox a considerable time after ye Nyumbai's death, and we know that the illness occurred in 1868 (*H.z.W.*, Sura 106; UMCA, *Bluebook, 1868*, p. 10).

The 1862 date is given in two sources, although both use Krapf's information. Richard Thornton wrote in February 1862 that he had heard from Krapf that "the old chief of Usambara, who was one of the most powerful chiefs on the coast is dead and I am afraid his kingdom will now be split up" (Richard Thornton to Miss Helen Thornton, 12 February 1862, Rhodes House, MSS Afr. s. 27).

Krapf himself procured his information during a trip to Pangani, where he went as one of a party which intended to found a mission station in the Shambaa kingdom. He wrote, "In the meantime I went up to Mombas, whilst my friends ascended the river Pangany to the distance of death was kept secret. In accordance with the custom, the kingdom had to suffer the profound disorder that was the meaning of kinglessness. Men of the court were sent to a point where the high road from Bumbuli passed beneath the cragged face of Mount Kwa Mongo, which rose over the capital. At the lonely spot where the roads split to pass above and below a boulder, a great wooden club was used to bash in the head of a passer-by, as a sign that the mourning of Kimweri was everyone's mourning.

Then there came a period when people feared to use the pathways which were, by analogy with Shambaa physiology, at once the arteries and the nerve paths of the kingdom. Weeds overran the paths, and because the subjects were forbidden to tend their farms, weeds overran the gardens. The Shambaa were to remember that without their sovereign there was no orderly growth but only the growth of rank weeds, no fertility, no order, no movement, no communication, no unity, no society.

Finally, the Kilindi met to distribute the dead king's property, and the mourning was ended. The Bondei Kilindi, who could not tolerate the diminution of the *Simba Mwene*'s authority, convinced their fellows to pass the undivided wealth of Kimweri ye Nyumbai on to his grandson.[7]

Shekulwavu began his reign with great strengths and great weaknesses. He had taken complete control of the resources of Vugha before his grandfather's death, and now the Kilindi had legitimized his control. But while he was strong at the capital, he faced great difficulties in dominating the chiefdoms. Each of the great territorial chiefs was, by this time, a man of considerable prestige and experience, and in addition the chiefs were all brothers of Shekulwavu's dead father, Mnkande. The king was expected to honor the chiefs as he would any of his "fathers"

---

20 or 24 miles, where they convinced themselves, that for the present no mission-station can be taken up, owing to the distracted state of the country in consequence of the death of old King Kimeri, who died a few weeks ago" (CMS, CA5/016–96, letter no. 34, Krapf to H. Venn, 17 April 1862).

7. *H.z.W.*, Sura 72.

(*ishe*), yet the power of the king depended on his ability to re-move them and replace them with his own men.

Faced with this dynastic problem, Shekulwavu increased his power and expanded his base very slowly indeed. The elders of Vugha became more and more impatient with the weakness of the king and with the lack of tribute. They tried to push Sheku-lwavu to more vigorous action. But in the six years between the death of Kimweri ye Nyumbai and the death of Shekulwavu, the young king managed to take control of only a few chiefdoms. He gave his brother Kibanga, son of Mnkande, the minor chiefdom of Manka. At Ngulwi, a marginal chiefdom which Mshuza's mother had insisted on creating for her favorite stepson, Sheku-lwavu put in Mlekwa Nyuma, son of Mnkande.[8]

Each time Shekulwavu succeeded in taking over a chiefdom the Kilindi of Shambaai strengthened their defenses. If the mo-mentum of political events worked for the king, the chiefs would all, sooner or later, be made into *Wakiindi wa kaya*—into com-moners, or Kilindi of the common hearth, rather than Kilindi of the court.

Mshuza, Shekulwavu's stepfather, had the pivotal position in the politics of the period. The Kilindi of Shambaai looked to him for leadership as their elder brother, heir to some of Kimweri's most potent charms, and heir to Shekulwavu's mother. While the people of Vugha exerted pressure on Shekulwavu to be harsh with his father's brothers, the chiefs of Shambaai were exerting pressure on Mshuza to restrain his "son."

Finally, Shekulwavu's break with his stepfather came, and from there the loss of his kingdom was only a step. Mshuza and Shekulwavu quarreled first about the removal of the sons of Kimweri ye Nyumbai from their chiefdoms, then about Sheku-lwavu's mother, who had gone to live with her son and would not

8. For the history of Ngulwi see the Ubii history in the Appendix to Chapter 4. The tentative moves towards the removal of territorial chiefs are described in Historical traditions: Boaz Mjata, 15 July 1967; Mbwana Mkanka Mghanga, 10 April 1968; Mpira Sanju, 31 January 1968; Ng'wa Mnkande, 3 August 1967. Abdallah bin Hemedi 'lAjjemy disagrees in minor details while telling much the same story (*H.z.W.*, Sura 75).

return to Ubii. Mshuza returned home in a suppressed rage, and the mood in the small court of Ubii was like the mood of mourning, quiet and solemn, as men adjusted to the impact of great but inevitable events, and faced an uncertain future.

Then Mshuza took the irreversible step of having his son Mtoi swear blood partnership with Semboja's son Kimweri. The two greatest chiefs of Shambaai were now bound in an alliance to overthrow their king.[9]

When Shekulwavu learned that the chiefs were plotting against him, he made a trip to East Usambara, to marshal the support of the Bondei and of the Shambaa of East Usambara, across the Luengera Valley. Shekulwavu swore an oath with the elders of the eastern territories, giving them permission to drive out their Kilindi chiefs, his father's brothers.[10] It is difficult to know the motives of the Bondei, and of the Shambaa of East Usambara, without local traditions. It seems most likely that the Shambaa of East Usambara, who appear to have been the most important group present, accepted the legitimacy of Kilindi rule, but wished to get rid of the set of oppressive chiefs who were then governing. While there were undoubtedly some Bondei whose motives were the same, there were others who wished to be rid of Kilindi rule altogether. They accepted an alliance with Shekulwavu because it promised to bring about the removal of the chiefs, which would have been much more difficult without the cooperation of the king. A short time later, once the chiefs had been driven out of the region, the people of East Usambara

9. The relations between Shekulwavu and Mshuza are well described in the Historical traditions. See especially the tradition of the son of Mtoi; it was his father who swore the comradeship which made the alliance: Jaha Mtoi, 22 April 1967. Another tradition which is especially interesting is that of Kwavi Senkunde, 28 May 1968, text 2. Kwavi's father, Senkunde, was one of the most important courtiers under Shekulwavu and later became chief minister of Shekulwavu's enemy and successor—he was the Fouché of the period, whose chief virtue was his ability to survive. See also the tradition of Semboja's great-grandson, the most recent king, Kimweri Magogo, 3 April 1967.

10. *H.z.W.*, Suras 79–80.

accepted continued rule by Shekulwavu's Kilindi, at the same time that the Bondei refused to accept any chiefs.

The actual cause of war was a dispute between Semboja, Shekulwavu, and the people of Vugha over the principle of refuge. In Shambaa politics the court of the king serves as a refuge for criminals, and for all those who offend against lesser chiefs. The acceptance of refugees is a declaration of strength, for a chief may be willing to make war to recover a particularly important, or a particularly offensive, prisoner.

Tests of the relative strength of the king and his territorial chiefs were of two kinds. In the first, the chiefs made the initial move—the declaration of fealty or of independence. Each chief, for example, decided whether the king was so weak that tribute payments to the royal capital could be withheld. Each chief decided whether his own power was so great that he could condemn a criminal to death without transferring the case to the king's court.

In the second kind of test the king himself had to take the initiative—he had to declare the greatness of his own power. This occurred when a refugee from the court of a territorial chief appeared before the king to plead for protection. By bestowing his protection the king declared that his own power was greater than that of the fugitive's pursuer. By refusing his protection the king conceded his own weakness.

The crisis came when a wife of Semboja's, an Mbugu woman, could tolerate her husband no longer and fled from Mazinde. She knew that if she returned to her family they would be punished and Mbuguland devastated, so she fled to Vugha, invoking the right of any Shambaa subject to take refuge at the court of the king.

The people of Vugha tried desperately to persuade Shekulwavu not to take this last step in his decline to the level of a minor territorial chief. They argued with the king, citing the maxim, *Cheingia Vugha hachiwa*—"Vugha is a stronghold, a refuge for any man." When the king showed signs of weakening, they argued, "If you send back a refugee then we will know that

we ourselves are not completely subject to your discipline, for if
we offend you we can always flee to another chiefdom."[11]

Shekulwavu admitted his weakness by returning Semboja's
wife. With a weak king in office, the people of Vugha were divided. Some felt, at this point, that only desperate measures
could save the situation—that the Bondei, who were eager to rid
themselves of the Kilindi, should be unleashed and allowed to kill
all the territorial chiefs. In this way Shekulwavu, who wanted to
do away with his father's brothers so that he could put his own
men in, would use the force of the Bondei commoners, many of
whom wanted to eliminate Kilindi rule altogether. The danger of
this tactic, of course, was that Shekulwavu, by using the Bondei
for his own purposes, might in the end become the tool of the
Bondei.

Other officials of Vugha, including the Mdoembazi of the
eastern section of town and the Kaoneka of the west, were play-
ing a more subtle game. They ostensibly remained with Shekulwavu, but secretly went over to Semboja. With their help the
situation degenerated:

> One of the men of Vugha called Senkunde told a story to
> Shekulwavu. You are the son of Mnkande . . . your uncles
> want to treat you like a doormat. What are you afraid of?
> The Sultan of Vugha cannot be removed whether war comes
> from the sky or underground. Kimweri [Shekulwavu] be-
> lieved what he was told and never considered that they were
> deceiving him. His arrogance increased and he looked down
> on his uncles.[12]

Senkunde was later to marry Semboja's sister and become chief
minister of Vugha (Mlughu) under Semboja's son Kimweri
Maguvu.[13]

Semboja provoked Shekulwavu's first act of open defiance in

11. Historical traditions. The quotation is from Zumbe Barua wa
Ngulu, 22 February 1968; see also Hassani Magogo, 25 December 1968;
Mahimbo Kihedu, 1 February 1968. *H.z.W.*, Sura 81.

12. *H.z.W.*, Sura 82.

13. I am using the name Maguvu, even though it is an anachronism at
this date, to avoid ambiguity, since Kimweri was the name of a generation, and therefore of half of all Kilindi. Shekulwavu was a member of

a characteristic manner. The king had returned Semboja's wife with an admonition that the woman should not be punished. The woman tried to escape again, was caught, and, by Semboja's order, had her ears cut off. Then some slaves took refuge at Vugha. When Semboja sent a message asking for their release, Shekulwavu had no choice. He said, These slaves "come from Vugha, and they have returned home."

Semboja and Mshuza called a great meeting of all the sons of Kimweri ye Nyumbai to make plans for assembling an army. The attack had to be planned so that the real attackers would never be identified, for a Shambaa chief could never attack his own king, nor were Shambaa subjects expected to fight one another. Foreigners would be called in, and if the attack failed it would be explained as an ordinary cattle raid, completely unrelated to the affairs of Shambaai.

The Kilindi sent to Taita for the main body of troops. The men who went included Mshuza's son Mtoi and a Swahili of Pangani. Mashombo, ruler of Mshewa, in Pare, was instrumental in recruitment, for he had trade and political connections with both Semboja and the Taita. The Taita came in the hope of winning great booty. Men near marriageable age fought in the hope of procuring bridewealth. Older men expected to augment their herds or to increase their lineages by capturing women and children.[14]

The Kilindi of the eastern territories were driven into Semboja's camp by the alliance between their subjects and Sheku-

the same generation, and so he could legitimately be called Kimweri, just as Kimweri could be called Shekulwavu. Senkunde's career is described in Historical traditions: Kwavi Senkunde, 28 May 1968, text 2.

14. The fullest description of the meeting is in the Historical traditions: Mhammadi Kika, 20 April 1967. It took place at Fumbai, the present Soni market. For other descriptions of the politics of the event, see Jaha Mtoi, 28 November 1967, and Kwavi Senkunde, 28 May 1968, text 2. Abdallah bin Hemedi 'lAjjemy knew the Swahili who was sent to Taita (*H.z.W.*, Sura 102). His book *Habari za Wakilindi* is a primary source for the period beginning with the escape of Semboja's wife to Vugha (1867?), until the end of the narrative, about 1873. The role of Mashombo is described by Kimambo, *Political History of the Pare*, pp. 153–54. For Taita motivation see Charles New, *Life, Wanderings, and Labours in Eastern Africa* (London, 1873), pp. 334f.

Iwavu. Semboja, because of his importance as a trader, was able to mobilize the support of forces outside Shambaai. In addition to the Taita, Semboja sent a caravan to his friend Jetha, the Banyan of Pangani. He received sixty porter-loads of gunpowder alone, in addition to guns and bullets and flints. Shekulwavu, in turn, made blood partnership with Abdallah bin Hemedi 'lAjjemy, who was useful for his contacts at the coast. While Semboja relied on the Kilindi of Bondei, Shekulwavu sent to get help from the Bondei commoners.[15] Semboja did not get the full support of the Kilindi of Shambaai. The role of the chief of Mlalo, a son of Kimweri ye Nyumbai, is unclear.

The Taita, when they finally came, were given a plan of attack by Semboja. They were divided into two groups: one which feinted towards the capital, and the other which attacked. The first group came across the mountains from the north, climbing at Mlola and passing through Gare to Kighuunde, immediately north of Vugha.

It was a time when clouds hung heavy on the peaks and clung to the mountainsides. When the defenders of Vugha headed north to defend their capital they did not see the second group of attackers climbing the steep escarpment from the plains in the west. The Taita, mountain people themselves, easily climbed the escarpment at Kidundai and burned the poorly defended capital. The king's soldiers, who had gone out to meet the first group of invaders, saw smoke rising from the town behind them.[16]

Shekulwavu barely escaped with the regalia, and fled to the plains at the foot of the escarpment, where he built a stockade at Vuruni, at a place called Kwe Tango.

While Shekulwavu was fleeing from Vugha, his allies were on the offensive in Bondei. The common people of Bondei rose up, with Shekulwavu's connivance, and seized the wives of their Kilindi lords. The action was the result of resentment unleashed and it was also a signal of a political position which had been taken by the Bondei. It is useful to distinguish between the broad

15. *H.z.W.*, Suras 86, 88, 104–6. UMCA, *Bluebook, 1868*, p. 13.
16. Historical traditions: Ali Sabago, 20 February 1968; Kimweri Magogo, 3 April 1967; Kwavi Senkunde, 28 May 1968, text 2; Mdoe Zayumba, 8 June 1967; Mhammadi Kika, 20 April 1967.

feeling that the Kilindi were (or were not) legitimate rulers, and the narrow alliances between particular groups of Bondei and particular groups of Kilindi. There were those who questioned Kilindi legitimacy and resented the fact that chiefs had been taking wives without paying bridewealth. There were others who had given their daughters in order to seal alliances with the chiefs. These latter were the people who had prospered through Kilindi rule. Those who seized women out of resentment questioned the legitimacy of Kilindi rule (for marriage without bridewealth was a chiefly prerogative, even in Shambaai). Those who merely terminated their alliances understood that the time had come for the removal of one group of Kilindi, although there was a possibility that new alliances would be formed some day if Shekulwavu sent his sons to Bondei.

With the burning of Vugha and the flight of Shekulwavu there was a thoroughgoing realignment of political forces, for now the question was no longer whether Shekulwavu would be a weak or a strong king, but whether Semboja would succeed in taking the kingdom for himself. If he did, there was no doubt that he would be ruthless in destroying the power of the Kilindi of Shambaai, and in subduing the Bondei.

The first consequence of the burning of Vugha, therefore, was that the chiefs of Shambaai refused to continue fighting. They had achieved their goal by destroying Shekulwavu's power. The subject lineages of Bondei, understanding that their own position was desperate, sent fighters to help Shekulwavu at Kwe Tango. When Alington, of the Universities Mission to Central Africa (UMCA), was at Magila in 1868, many of the villagers were away at Kwe Tango.[17]

Semboja, deprived of the help of his fellow chiefs in Shambaai, had two main sources of support. First, the Kilindi of Bondei knew that their power would be destroyed by rebellion unless Semboja took Vugha. They joined the forces at Mazinde. Second, Semboja appealed to all his trading partners; he called in all his political debts and sent messages to the important trading chiefdoms of Zigula. He sent for Muhammad Sowa of Ki-

---

17. UMCA, *Bluebook, 1868*, p. 15; *H.z.W.*, Suras 128, 131–41, 145.

wanda, won over Maulwi, Geleza, and Kilindi. His blood partner, chief of Mkalamo, came to help.[18]

The pattern of alliances which emerged during the fighting at
Kwe Tango was to survive, with minor changes, for the years
which remained up to the German conquest. In the fighting
which continued for twenty years, Semboja relied on mercenar-
ies and trading allies, together with the Kilindi of Bondei, while
the sons of Mnkande were supported by the people of East
Usambara, by the Bondei, and by those people of Shambaai who
found Semboja's rule intolerable and fled eastward to join his
enemies.

Bitter but indecisive fighting began at Kwe Tango, and continued for over a week. Then Semboja, according to all the Shambaa traditions, cast a black spell over Shekulwavu's gun. When
the king fired, the gun exploded in his hands, and he died shortly
afterwards.

After the king's death, the claims of legitimacy belonged to
Shekulwavu's son Kinyashi, who was then only a child. The
dead king's brother Chanyeghea inherited custody of the child,
as well as leadership of the sons of Mnkande.

Then all the Kilindi met to decide the succession. Semboja
wanted to become king, but did not have sufficient support, and
the meeting ended indecisively.

After the public meeting there was a secret meeting between
the two principals, Chanyeghea and Semboja, the proceedings of
which are one of the murkiest occurrences in Shambaa history.
Semboja's great-grandson insists that the chief of Mazinde gave
Chanyeghea permission to accede as regent, but then Chanyeghea went mad and began killing Kilindi. Other informants insist
that Semboja instructed Chanyeghea to kill all the Kilindi of
Bondei, and that he—Semboja—would murder the chiefs of
Shambaai. This was a ruse. Semboja had no intention of killing
the chiefs. But he knew that once Chanyeghea had begun his
work, the Kilindi would have to turn to him for his military
strength. Mazinde would become the place of refuge.[19]

18. *H.z.W.*, Suras 129, 131–41, 145.

19. Historical traditions: Ali Sabago, 20 February 1968; Barua Makange, 22 February 1968; Kimweri Magogo, 3 April 1967. *H.z.W.*, Suras
152–54.

At this time in the dispute the Bondei who wished to break all ties with the Kilindi, and with the Shambaa kingdom, gained the upper hand. Up to this time the groups of Bondei which wanted to end Kilindi rule, and those which had benefited from Kilindi rule, joined together in support of Shekulwavu and against the local chiefs. Shekulwavu's death, however, had freed the Bondei of the oath they had made with him, which they had regarded as binding. Now the consensus was the royal rule had to be ended altogether. The Bondei who rejected Kilindi rule won over even those who had gained from alliances with the chiefs. Only those Bondei who had been detached from their own lineages to become chiefs' men were expected to oppose the revolutionary forces. This was the point made by Chanyeghea's messenger, when he said, "There are many of the Bondei who are of Kilindi blood, who are accustomed to robbing people of poultry and goats. If they have orders from the Kilindi, Arrest your father, they go and do it without shame. They have no names, they are simply chiefs' soldiers and slaves, and they are slaves because they have stolen. If he meets someone on the road, even if it's his mother's brother's child, or his brother's child, or his father's sister's child, he strikes him and takes all he has. Will you be able to persuade them to join you in the business of the Kilindi? But it is not your business but mine. I will make my arrangements to get them, I do not trust you."[20]

The Bondei decided as a group to ignore the men who had been allied with chiefs, to risk all, and to rid their land of Kilindi rule altogether. They did not trust the Kilindi—any Kilindi—to deal fairly with them once the Bondei had taken the lives of their Kilindi chiefs. They thought that, if they remained within the kingdom, they would have the reputation of killers of chiefs, and they would be punished for their resentment of authority. If Chanyeghea became king at Vugha, he would also become head of the Kilindi lineage, whose members the Bondei proposed to

20. *H.z.W.*, Sura 155. My translation varies from the published one in two respects. It is a bit more literal, in the listing of relations met on the road, and *wapuna*, a Shambaa word, is translated as "soldiers and slaves" rather than "robbers and highwaymen." For the meaning of this word, see LangHeinrich, *Schambala-Wörterbuch,* and Steere, *Collections for a Handbook of the Shambala Language,* p. 11.

murder. The Bondei thought any Kilindi deceitful enough to connive at the murder of chiefs, and then to punish the murders. One of the Bondei elders explained this to the messenger of the sons of Mnkande:

> "The Kilindi are born liars. Do not rely on the word of any of them, it will not be true. A Kilindi will take two stones and hit you with one, and if you ask him why he hit you with a stone, he will show you the other and say, with what did I hit you? A stone? but here is my stone. That is the way they act. Now we agree to do as [Chanyeghea] asks; but when he is in power and has the dominion he will turn on us and say Pay me your dead. You have killed my uncles, you have taken their property, you have sold my brothers, you have given my uncles' wives in marriage, now hand over the adulterers. . . . Now we have driven out the Kilindi, we have taken their property and given their wives to others. We have become their enemies and even if we accept this matter we will never make with them any agreement whatever. That is our decision."[21]

It would be much too simple, then, to state that the kingdom was split by a succession dispute—by a rebellion which accepted the legitimacy of Kilindi rule but disputed the right of a single individual or faction to assume control. Semboja was a rebel in this sense, for he himself wanted to be heir to the legitimacy. But the Bondei position was transformed through action into a revolutionary one. By the time of Chanyeghea, the Bondei consensus was that Kilindi rule should be destroyed altogether; the war was one of rebellion at the center augmented by revolution at the edges of the kingdom.

The Bondei had been exploited and they knew it. Under the Kilindi their tribute had gone to Vugha, but they had received little in return. They could not, like the commoners of Shambaai, appeal to the kin against the injustices of the chiefs. Each chief took what he wanted from his subjects. Even in the days of Kimweri ye Nyumbai there had been minor revolts.[22]

21. *H.z.W.*, Sura 156.
22. For the position of the Bondei in Kimweri ye Nyumbai's kingdom, see Chapter 4.

Here are some of the grievances of the Bondei at the time of Chanyeghea's war:

> The capture of our children and their being given in marriage by force without our receiving dues or cattle.
> Their slaves and guards robbing people whom they meet in the road.
> If a man is accused of witchcraft no evidence is called but he is killed and his children are taken and sold.
> If they want food they send men into our towns to take goats and chickens and if the owner says a word he is beaten.
> If one of their wives has parents they do not allow her to visit her father or mother.[23]

The Bondei had been plundered for many years by minor Kilindi chiefs and now they were making a revolution. There is nothing unusual, in world history, about action by an oppressed group starting with modest goals and developing into a revolutionary movement as violent action continues.

Chanyeghea's role in the planning of Kiva, as the war was called, was to arrange for cooperation between the Wakiva, the Bondei rebels, and Mwaiko, slave of Sultan Majid of Zanzibar, who was Wali of Fort Tongwe, the Sultan's establishment in the immediate coastal hinterland. Mwaiko supplied arms to the Wakiva, profited from the enormous export trade in slaves that resulted, and helped to plan a conspiracy for the death of the Bondei Kilindi.[24]

The plan was a simple one. The Bondei were to accept the return of their rulers, and then to murder them. Mwaiko met with the Kilindi of Bondei. He explained that the Sultan of Zanzibar wished a return to monarchical order, and that the Bondei would accept a return to stable rule if they were assured that the worst abuses of Kilindi rule would be corrected.

The Kilindi accepted. They returned with their subjects to their original districts. The wives were brought to court, and there was an outward appearance of calm. But the Bondei had fixed a date for a general uprising. The leaders tied a series of knots in banana fiber. Each man had the same number of knots,

23. *H.z.W.*, Sura 169.
24. Farler, "Usambara Country," p. 85.

and each cut one off with the passing of each day. The day of destruction would come when there were no knots left.[25]

Before that day ever came, the plan of rebellion began to break down. The slaves of Tumba, the strongest of the Kilindi, refused to murder him. Mwaiko decided that the killing must begin immediately or the entire plan would break down. Several days of wild confusion followed. Subjects sitting in quiet conversation with their chief would suddenly slash at him with their machetes. Some Kilindi were shot, others stabbed. Their children were seized on the paths and sold into slavery. Grievances decades old were avenged. The Kilindi survivors, with Tumba among them, fled for Mazinde.[26]

Once Kiva had returned the government of Bondei to the hands of the Bondei leaders, its forces pushed up into East Usambara and then into Shambaai in an attempt to destroy the kingdom altogether. The most important attack came directly across the Luengera Valley, through Bumbuli. The Bondei forces streamed into each successive Shambaa chiefdom, making appeals for a general revolt of all subjects against all chiefs. If the Shambaa would only divulge the hiding place of their chief he could be eliminated, Shambaai freed.

The closer they got to the heartland of the Shambaa kingdom, the less support the Bondei received. And at the fringes, the Shambaa who betrayed their chiefs were those not related by marriage to the Kilindi. Many of the Kilindi of the Bumbuli region were forced to flee. At Mlola, chief Shekinyashi was killed by Kiva.

By the time the forces of Kiva reached Dindia, just north of Mlungui, Semboja had managed to get reinforcements from Taita. Together with the Kilindi of the occupied zone they pushed the Bondei north from Dindia to Mpaau, then back to Shembekeza, which overlooks the Luengera Valley from the Shambaa side. Finally, when they discovered that Shembekeza did not have enough water to support a besieged garrison, the Bondei retreated across the valley.[27]

25. *H.z.W.*, Suras 156–76.
26. Ibid., Suras 176–81.
27. Historical traditions: Juma Shekumkai, 18 July 1968; Kasimu Kimweri, 1 February 1968; Mahimbo Kihedu, 1 February 1968; Ng'wa

Chanyeghea fortified the town of Mghambo, which looked down on the valley from the east. But with the defeat of Kiva came a brief period of total disorder, known in Shambaa tradition as the time of Pato. This can best be translated as "rapacity" in both its senses. It was a time when men were given over to inordinate greed, to taking for themselves. It was also a time when men subsisted by the capture of living prey.

The irony of Kiva is that the Bondei had risen up to stop being exploited, but their revolution led to a period of intense slaving, when chief sold commoner, and when the stronger of two neighbors sold the weaker. Since Chanyeghea had no wealth, his war effort was financed largely through the sale of slaves.[28] In the period of Pato, selling slaves became the activity of every man of strength. One informant explained that in this period "people simply seized and sold one another. If someone came across you and you weren't very strong he would just grab hold of you. Off to be sold you go."[29]

Thousands of slaves were sold at Pangani. John Kirk, the British Consul at Zanzibar, visited Pangani in 1873 and reported,

> Two years ago the valleys between the Ushambala hills and the highlands themselves were peopled with very industrious races. This was the old kingdom of Kimwere. . . . The tribes commenced fighting with each other. Captives were sold—slaves brought in thousands into Pangani, which suddenly became a great place of export, from having imported slaves from Quiloa [Kilwa] the year before. This slave war did not last long.[30]

There was an enormous increase in the export of slaves during Pato, and then relative order was reimposed.

The violence of Pato led to major shifts of population, as people tried to find safe places to live. The Luengera Valley, which was relatively unprotected, had once been populated. People had

Paula s/o Ng'wa Kimungu, 12 July 1967; Shekulwavu Kinyashi (Mlalo), 17 July 1968; Zumbe Barua wa Ngulu, 22 February 1968.

28. Edward Steere, *Central Africa Mission* (London, 1873), p. 9.

29. Historical traditions: Kimweri Magogo and Mbwana Mkanka Mghanga, 19 May 1967. See also Barua Makange, 22 February 1968.

30. Kirk, "Visit to the Coast of Somali-land," pp. 340–41.

begun moving up the mountainsides during ye Nyumbai's reign in defense against increasing Zigula and Kwavi raids. During Pato the last of the valley's population left, and this rich area was unoccupied during the 1870s.[31]

Many Mbugu, who were now at the mercy of their old enemy Semboja, moved eastward to Bondei. Places like Magila, which were relatively secure and distant from the areas of active fighting, grew in population.[32]

Both the new population pattern and the new political situation were ultimately stabilized, and so the outcome of the period of warfare was a complete victory for the forces of decentralization. The chiefs of Shambaai chose not to be governed by Vugha. They selected Semboja's son, Kimweri Maguvu, as next king of Shambaai. Maguvu, like Shekulwavu, was a generation younger than most of the territorial chiefs, and therefore found it difficult to establish centralized control, for which he would have had to dominate his father's brothers. The sons of Mnkande created a small kingdom in East Usambara. The Bondei freed themselves from Kilindi overrule and returned to an earlier pattern of rule by village elders. The villages maintained only a loose relationship with Kilindi rain magicians. One of the central tenets of Shambaa political ideology was that the most important rain magician should control the instruments of political power. The Bondei villages made payments to the leader of the sons of Mnkande for his services in bringing rain, but they refused to recognize his right to demand their services in war, to demand regular tribute, or to hear their cases. The way in which all this happened, and the characteristics of the regional pattern of political action, will be discussed in detail in Chapter 8. Here it is important to note only that the division of the Shambaa kingdom into a chiefless Bondei, a small kingdom in East Usambara, and a divided Shambaai, represented a complete triumph for the forces of decentralization.

31. Keith Johnston, "Notes of a Trip from Zanzibar to Usambara in February and March 1879," *Proceedings of the Royal Geographical Society,* n.s., 1 (1879): 553.

32. Steere, *Central Africa Mission,* pp. 9f; Baumann, *Usambara,* pp. 121, 185; Farler, "Usambara Country," p. 84.

That victory should provide an instructive example, for it supports the inadequately accepted contention that just as African societies often progress from statelessness to kingship, they also may progress, under other circumstances, from kingship to statelessness, or from centralization to decentralization.[33] In other words, centralization and decentralization are merely two adaptive processes. Large-scale polities are neither higher nor more evolved forms than those small in scale. In addition, the revolution in Bondei provides a useful corrective to the idea found in *African Political Systems* and in the work of Max Gluckman that, in the words of Fortes and Evans-Pritchard: "In these [African] states there is only one theory of government. In the event of rebellion, the aim, and result, is only to change the personnel of office and never to abolish it or to substitute for it some new form of government."[34] This notion may have seemed persuasive to those who observed indigenous polities at the height of the colonial era. But the Bondei, in the precolonial situation of the late 1860s, wanted to be rid of the entire *system* of kingship—they wanted neither to capture the legitimate office nor to split it into two similar offices.

It is clear that we must speak of rebellion, not revolution, when we analyze a court culture and the conflict within it. But the Shambaa kingdom had a core of men who accepted the court culture at the center, and were rebels. In addition, the kingdom had subject peoples around its fringes who did not accept its legitimacy.

In another, more strictly local, sense, Kimweri ye Nyumbai had been able to bring the benefits of royal rule to the people of Shambaai, but the Bondei had been too distant and too foreign to be offered the advantages of centralization. Because of this, the Bondei helped to destroy the kingdom from within.

33. This point was made by John Omer-Cooper, "Kingdoms and Villages, a Possible New Perspective in Africa History" (Paper delivered at the University of East Africa Social Science Conference, Dar es Salaam, January 1968).

34. M. Fortes and E. E. Evans-Pritchard, *African Political Systems* (London, 1940), p. 13. See also Max Gluckman, *Order and Rebellion in Tribal Africa* (New York, 1963), p. 9.

# 7 · THE PRELUDE TO COLONIAL RULE

The 1870s and 1880s were years of violent slave-trading unequaled in the history of the Pangani Valley region, and of Shambaai. Yet these were the years of the victory of the campaign for the abolition of the slave trade. Coupland, mistaking the medicine for the cure, wrote that during this time the East African slave trade was dead, because the humanitarian people of England had wished its death.[1] As more of the indigenous history of East Africa has become known, it has become apparent that the abolition campaign was only a small part of the total European influence on East Africa during the period. There was a great European demand for "legitimate commerce." It was not regarded as significant that some of the goods of this commerce, especially cloves, were produced by slave labor, while others, including ivory and wild rubber, were collected by freemen whose subsistence needs often were provided by slaves. Nor was it regarded as significant that European firearms, with which Africans could enslave one another, were among the goods traded.

There are striking similarities between the period immediately before colonial rule and the postcolonial period. Then, as now,

1. Sir Reginald Coupland, *The Exploitation of East Africa*, 2d ed. (London, 1968), p. 229. For an extreme statement of the success of abolition, see Peter Collister, *The Last Days of Slavery* (Dar es Salaam, 1961).

characteristics of international trade had a profound effect on African society—an effect which, to a great extent, could not be controlled from within the African continent. Then, as now, the forces which affected East Africa did not originate in any one nation. Once it is argued that the demand for products was a driving historical force, it becomes impossible to point to any one nation or continent which was ultimately responsible. The culprit was a system of action. In the 1870s and 1880s, the demand for East African products originated in India and America, as well as Europe. Within the trade system of the period, even the effects of the abolition campaign, which had been created in response to humanitarian impulses, became twisted. But the analogy between the two periods must not be carried too far. The internal structure of African society today is to some extent a legacy of decades of colonial rule. In the late precolonial period most societies of the interior of East Africa had not been in intimate contact with the west.

During the 1870s and 1880s in Shambaai, increased local conflict fed the trade in slaves. It was a time when chiefs indulged in raid and counterraid, when they financed wars by selling their own subjects, when, for a fee, they permitted kidnapping on the paths of their own territories. In Pare the 1880s are remembered as *Kibonda,* the period of violence. Political leaders no longer cared for the welfare of common people in their own territories. In this period Pare women could go to market only if they had armed escorts. In Bondei and Digo, nearer the coast, the records of UMCA missionaries are filled with reports of village headmen raiding neighboring villages for slaves, while commoners kidnapped one another's children.[2]

The increase in the slave trade of the Pangani Valley was partly a result of the effectiveness of the British navy in slowing the supply of slaves from Kilwa, in the south, to Zanzibar, Pemba, and the hinterland of Tanga and Pangani. This does not mean, however, that the southern slave trade stopped at this

2. The situation in Pare is described in I. N. Kimambo, "Enlargement of Scale among the Pare" (Paper delivered at the University of East Africa Social Science Conference, Dar es Salaam, January 1968), p. 7.

time. The relationship between the abolition campaign and the slave trade was a complex one. It is worth examining briefly, as it relates to Shambaa history.

In 1873 the Sultan of Zanzibar outlawed the export of slaves from the mainland of East Africa, and in 1876 he forbade the arrival of slaves at the coast from the interior and the fitting out of slave caravans by his subjects, and at the same time instructed his governors to seize and imprison those found disobeying his order. But the Sultan's governors were not vigorous in their prosecution of slave traders, and British sea power had no effect on the overland trade.

The southern interior, which before abolition had supplied many of Zanzibar's slaves, increased its "legitimate commerce." The Makonde, for example, collected wild rubber and exchanged it for brass wire, cloth, and gunpowder at the small ports between Lindi and the Ruvuma River. With the cloth they bought slaves from passing Yao dealers. The slaves worked the fields of the Makonde, while their masters traded and collected rubber. According to Suzanne Miers, "Missionaries at Masasi reported that they had never seen so many slave caravans on their way from Yao country to the coast."[3] Most of the traders disposed of their slaves while still a few days' march in the interior. The missionaries' observations were made in the early 1880s.

While new uses were being found for slaves in the southern interior, the trade to the north continued after abolition, with overland routes supplanting transport by sea. After 1873 the demand on Pemba was met by Kilwa merchants who marched slaves overland to Pangani and then smuggled them across the narrow channel. The abolition of the trade on land in 1876 was directed against this overland traffic. But in 1877 the trade was still going on.[4]

3. The description of the use of slaves by the Makonde is taken from Suzanne Miers, "Great Britain and the Brussels Anti-Slave Trade Act of 1890" (Ph.D. diss., University of London, 1969), p. 185.
4. J. P. Farler to British Anti-Slavery Society, 13 March 1877 (Rhodes House, MSS Brit. Emp. s. 22). Farler to Allchin, 23 February 1877 (USPG-UMCA, Box A 1 VI).

The campaign to interrupt the flow of slaves from the south slowly succeeded, however. In addition, the trip from Kilwa to Pangani was expensive in mortality, and the price of slaves was higher the farther north one went. At the same time that southern slaves were becoming more scarce and expensive, demand for slaves was at its height at Pemba, the plantation island across the channel from the Pangani Valley. Pemba's clove plantations had been spared the worst effects of the hurricane which had devastated Zanzibar in 1872, and the planters on Pemba were expanding their plantations.[5]

The need for slaves on Pemba could much more easily be satisfied in the Pangani Valley than in the distant South. Bondei, Shambaai, Pare, and the interior of Zigula became the most convenient sources of plantation slaves. The only groups which escaped enslavement were those on the coast itself, for they had mastered sea travel and could easily escape from the island, while landsmen who lived just a few hours' march into the interior had no way of leaving. The slaves who came up from the South were put to work on farms on the coastal strip, for it was impossible to hold Pangani Valley slaves so near to home.[6]

The involvement of political leaders in the intensive trade in slaves led to a transformation of the political culture of the Pangani Valley in general, and of Shambaai in particular. During the two decades before colonial conquest the community of interest between chiefs and subjects within Shambaai was destroyed. In its place there developed a sharp conflict of interest between the chief as slave trader and his subjects as exploitable commodities. The world demand for East African products led to a series of destructive innovations in social organization.

The slave trade had a similar effect in many parts of Africa, but the pattern of change was unusual in the Pangani Valley for two reasons. First, intensive trading in slaves came to this region very late, and therefore it is possible to study the effects of trade on political organization in some detail. Second, the effects of

5. Gray, "Zanzibar and the Coastal Belt," pp. 238f; Coupland, *Exploitation,* pp. 221f.

6. Baumann, *Usambara,* pp. 61, 107, 153; Historical traditions: Semnguu Koplo, 16 November 1967.

intensive trade were felt only in the last two decades before conquest; the shock of the slave trade was soon followed by the
shock of conquest, and therefore the period of trade was a pre-
conquest. The erosion of trust between leaders and their followers in this period made it impossible for the Shambaa to unite in
resistance to conquest. It is true that during Bushiri's rebellion
against German domination Semboja's soldiers plundered the
expedition of Baumann and Meyer. But these soldiers had for
more than twenty years been plundering the villages of ordinary
Shambaa cultivators, and so it is hard to cast them in the role of
freedom fighters. The real resisters were those Shambaa, Mbugu,
and Bondei who fought Semboja and the traders in the 1870s
and 1880s, and who fled to palisaded villages where they could
farm in peace and not be enslaved.

The pervasive forces at work in the Pangani Valley were
those of the world market, but the historical actors were indigenous people working in their own self-interest to change local
political usages. The chiefs of Shambaai became involved in the
trade in slaves and ivory because through it they were able to
acquire guns, powder, and other exotic trade goods. At the heart
of the political transformation was a shift from livestock to trade
goods as the most important form of chiefly wealth.

In the days of Kinyashi Muanga Ike and Kimweri ye Nyumbai, courtiers and loyal subjects at the capital had been rewarded
with meat which had come to the capital as tribute in livestock.
On days of public ceremonial great quantities of meat had been
consumed. And Kimweri ye Nyumbai had given away goats or
cows to help with the bridewealth of his loyal subjects. (See
Chapters 4 and 5.)

Livestock remained important in the 1870s and 1880s, but in
addition guns, powder, and cloth in unprecedented quantities became necessities of court life, and trade became essential to the
maintenance of a court. European observers maintained that the
guns in common use were of such inferior quality that they had
no practical value. But if the firearms were ineffective, the
Shambaa themselves seem to have been unaware of their short-
comings. Semboja schemed to make sure that his rivals and po-

tential enemies did not get guns or powder. Any plans for a major battle included the dispatch of a caravan to the coast for the purchase of powder. In fact a number of elders have maintained that Semboja decided to go to war against the town of Kihurio in the late 1880s simply because he had stolen a weapon from some European explorers (Baumann and Meyer) that was much more advanced than the guns then in use. When the town of Mazinde was searched by the Germans after Semboja's death, they found 170 pounds of powder and 20,000 percussion caps.[7]

The shift from authority based on control over the disposal of livestock and of the subjects' tribute labor to authority based on a monopoly of some kinds of imported goods had a profound effect on the political organization of the Shambaa. In the earlier period the chiefs and the king had drawn on the resources of the subjects within their territory. Every political leader therefore had had an interest in expanding his tribute base—a chief by attracting people to his chiefdom, and the king by expanding his territory. Kinyashi Muanga Ike had fought his wars in the late eighteenth or early nineteenth century in order to expand his tribute-paying territory.

Rainfall had been of the greatest importance for the kingdom in the earlier period. The areas which could support the heaviest population were the mountain areas of the highest rainfall. And subjects were happiest living in the chiefdom of the greatest rain magician. So long as the success of a leader had been directly related to the number of his subjects, chiefs and their subjects had had interests in common. In the new environment the most

7. Paul Döring described the ineffectiveness of Shambaa firearms in *Morgendämmerung in Deutsch-Ostafrika* (Berlin, 1901), p. 88. For a description of how Semboja withheld firearms from potential rivals, see Historical traditions: Kimweri Magogo, 1 December 1967. For another example of the selective sale of firearms see Farler to British Anti-Slavery Society, 27 April 1877 (Rhodes House, MSS Brit. Emp. s. 22), which describes how the coastal traders would not sell arms to the Bondei. The search of Mazinde is described in Lieutenant E. Storch, "Über das Strafverfahren gegen den Jumben Mputa von Wuga und über die Einsetzung des Jumben Kipanga von Handei in Wuga," *Nachrichten* 9 (September 1895): 138–40.

important political towns were in the plains, where the rainfall was not high, no great population could be supported, but the major trade routes were accessible.

The community of interest between the king and his subjects was destroyed by the rising importance of foreign goods. The unfortunate effects of the trade in slaves and guns were made more extreme by the continuation of the dynastic dispute which had begun with the burning of Vugha and the rising of the Bondei. All during the 1870s and 1880s intermittent but bitter warfare continued between Shekulwavu's heirs, who had settled in East Usambara, and Semboja's forces, which were usually led by his son Kimweri Maguvu, king of Vugha. It will be shown in Chapter 8 that there were a number of points at which Semboja's forces believed they could gain final victory through a decisive battle. At other times Shekulwavu's heirs believed they could decisively improve their position. There was also competition between the king and the chiefs of Shambaai for control of the chiefdoms. As each crucial battle was planned, the important leaders sold slaves to buy arms for the final victory. If King Kimweri Maguvu had succeeded in defeating the eastern Kilindi and dominating the chiefs, he might have been able to protect the Shambaa and to procure slaves by raiding against all of their neighbors, although even in this case he would not have had the same interest in territorial expansion as his predecessors. With Maguvu's political failure, however, it was the Shambaa people themselves who became the exportable commodity.

In traditional Shambaa society, long before the era of the large-scale selling of human beings, there was a status which may, for want of a better word, be called that of a slave. A slave, or *mtung'wa,* was a person who, for one of several possible reasons, had his ties to his own lineage broken and was attached instead to the court of a Kilindi. In Shambaa jurisprudence crimes were usually punished by requiring the offender to pay an indemnity to the lineage of his victim. If the offender's father was alive, he was liable, too. If the father was dead, then all the dead man's sons usually kept some wealth as a fund from which to pay indemnities, in which case the entire group was liable. Quite

often the members of the lineage at its largest extent would contribute toward an indemnity, although the largest group which
could be forced to pay was the group which held a fund of inherited wealth in common. If an individual or a fund-holding
group was unable to pay an indemnity, the chief would pay and
one member (or more) would become a slave. Or if one dangerous member threatened the welfare of a large group, his father
could take him to the chief and hand him over as a slave, legally
detaching him from the lineage, which was no longer liable for
his actions. Prisoners of war were in a similar position, as people
without local descent ties.

Slaves could be redeemed from their position; they could possess farms and livestock, marry, and they had time to work their
own farms. They strengthened the position of the ruler by filling
his capital with men personally dependent on him. Since the
criminal elements lived under the eye of the chief, everyone in
the countryside felt a bit more secure. The royal capital is often,
in everyday conversation, called Shambaa society's garbage
dump.

Even in the days of traditional servitude a slave could be
killed. The *Gao* initiation, when performed for the young Kilindi, involved the murder of a slave.[8] Slaves also could be sold.
But what was new in the third quarter of the nineteenth century
was the rate of turnover resulting from the constant sale of
slaves to keep the court supplied with arms. This, in turn, meant
that the traditional sources of supply from litigation, warfare,
and people selling themselves in time of famine were inadequate;
new sources had to be developed.

Legal procedures were revised to increase the supply of
slaves. At Vugha in many cases where criminals in the old days
would have been killed, they now were sold instead. In Mshihwi,
Shatu (the chief) stopped killing witches and used them in his
slave army instead. In the case of very serious crimes in Shambaai, the criminal himself was killed and the whole of the responsible group sold into slavery. The offenses for which people

8. Historical traditions: Mbwana Mkanka Mghanga, 24 January 1968.

could be enslaved became more and more trivial. In the atmosphere generated by the quest for slaves, a man at Vugha might steal a distinctive piece of his enemy's clothing and place it in the women's quarter of the court, so that his enemy would be sold. A UMCA missionary in Bondei reported the case of a woman who was sold for stealing two vegetables.[9]

At the same time that judicial enslavement increased, there was a dramatic rise in the level of violence. Kilindi made war not only to gain political objectives, but also as a way to keep up the supply of slaves. The son of one Kilindi chief of the period has described the process: "At this time [in the late 1870s and the 1880s] every Kilindi needed to make war so that he could capture slaves to sell for gunpowder."[10] There was a capital investment involved in each war: a chief had to sell slaves to purchase powder so that he could make war to capture slaves.

In the Shambaa view only enemies or strangers were supposed to be attacked, and so it was relatively defenseless non-Shambaa people living near the Shambaa who were hardest hit. Mbugu traditions are virtually universal in describing this period as one of great hardship, especially at the hands of Semboja, for Mazinde was near the Mbugu heartland. Many Mbugu moved to East Usambara, where Semboja's enemies had settled at the end of the wars of rebellion and revolution.[11] The Bondei also were vulnerable; they suffered intermittent attacks by Semboja's forces.[12]

9. The change from killing to selling criminals at Vugha is described in the Historical traditions: Mbwana Mkanka Mghanga, 17 May 1967. The Mshihwi case is described in Kimea Abdallah, 12 October 1966. The practice of selling a criminal's lineage is described in Mbwana Mkanka Mghanga, 13 November 1967. The description of how clothing would be placed in the women's quarters is from Salehe Ali, 20 December 1967, text 2. The case of the Bondei woman is from J. P. Farler, *The Work of Christ in Central Africa* (London, 1878), p. 22.

10. Historical traditions: Mahimbo Kihedu, 1 February 1968.

11. Baumann, *Usambara,* pp. 184 f.

12. There are numerous examples. For two incidents, see Umba Logbook, 1886–1894 (TNA, UMCA-CPEA), p. 34, July 12, 1888; H. W. Woodward, "Misozwe News," *Central Africa* 7 (August 1889): 122.

Because of the continual warfare, vast areas of Shambaai and Bondei which previously had been heavily populated were deserted, as people fled to areas which, because of their natural defenses, were more secure.[13]

Even the rule that war should be made only against enemies or foreigners was often violated. Semboja had his Maasai-speaking allies make raids on all parts of Shambaai, even on Vugha itself; on their return they would split the spoils.[14] Once, after the people of Bumbuli had all gone to fight Semboja's enemies in East Usambara, the chiefs of Shembekeza and of Bumbuli decided that the spoils of war had been much too poor, and they proceeded to make war against their own people, of the small area called Mavumbi, who were rich in cattle and women. They acquired at the expense of their allies what they could not wrest from the hands of their enemies.[15]

The supply of slaves was augmented through the introduction of a method which lacked any legitimacy—kidnapping. Roving kidnappers were a constant threat, and women would go to the field during this period only when they had an escort. A chief did not normally track down a kidnapper so long as the criminal gave the court a portion of the trade goods he had received. While the criminals were left unmolested by the political authority—at Mazinde they were usually Semboja's soldiers—they were not permitted to amass large quantities of gunpowder, but instead had to take cloth.[16]

The chiefs themselves sometimes acted as kidnappers. One man of the chiefdom of Mazinde, remembering those days, said: "If you had a lot of goats and a village full of children, off you

13. Letter from J. P. Farler in *Central Africa* 5 (July 1887): 103; Baumann, *Usambara*, pp. 188f.

14. Historical traditions: Jaha Mtoi, 28 November 1967; Jawa Samahoza, 25 December 1967, text 3; Hasani Magogo, 25 December 1967; Semnguu Koplo, 7 November 1967.

15. Historical traditions: Mhammadi Mshaka Ngoto, 7 August 1967.

16. Historical traditions: Jaha Mtoi, 28 November 1967; Mdoe Barua 14 November 1967; Mzimbii Mpemba, 20 July 1968; Semnguu Koplo, 16 November 1967; Shechonge Kishasha, 11 March 1967. H. W. Woodward, "A Story of Woman's Wrongs," *Central Africa* 2 (August 1884): 131.

all went."[17] Mtoi, the chief of Ubii, sold his mother-in-law into slavery.[18]

The unprecedented exploitation of the Shambaa population in the two decades before German conquest was accompanied by the reorganization of the courts and armies of the most important Kilindi. Shambaa courtiers and mass citizens' armies had until this time been the sources of Kilindi strength, but now they were not completely adequate for the job of procuring slaves. Since soldiers had to prey on the Shambaa population within a chiefdom, they would not have been able to do the job if they had been Shambaa themselves, attached by links of descent and affinity to most of their fellow subjects. Semboja's soldiers were mostly Zigula. Semboja's son, who was king of Vugha, had among his warriors Ng'indo, Maasai-speakers, Zigula.[19] Semboja allowed Maasai-speaking people to raid Shambaai in return for a share of the booty. In the earlier history of the Shambaa kingdom, the tactic of inviting foreign warriors had been used, but there is no evidence that it had ever been used against a chief's own subjects.[20]

Not only did foreigners become more important as warriors, but Shambaa who were known for their skill at fighting were moved from their original homes to distant chiefdoms, becoming, in effect, Shambaa-speaking foreigners, unconnected to the descent politics of their new homes. There were considerable rewards for the leading warriors, including a payment for each captive brought in. Some men spent their lives following the action from one battlefield to another. In the collection of the oral traditions of subject lineages, one of the questions normally put to an informant was, where did your ancestors come from and why? The overwhelming majority of lineages had come to their

17. Historical traditions: Chamhingo wa Mkumbaa, 25 December 1967.

18. Historical traditions: Jaha Mtoi, 28 November 1967.

19. Historical traditions: Chamhingo wa Mkumbaa, 25 December 1967; Juma Shekumkai, 18 July 1968.

20. Historical traditions: Bakai Kimweri, 18 July 1968; Hasani Kinyashi, 17 July 1968; Mnkande Kimweri, 2 December 1966.

present places of residence before the middle of the nineteenth century, and informants said that they had moved to escape famine or to escape war. Only for the late nineteenth-century movements were there respondents who said that their fathers or grandfathers had moved *to be nearer to the war.*[21]

The Kilindi brought in outsiders not only to serve as warriors, but also, at times, to rule subordinate territorial units. The king of Vugha made a Yao slave the chief of Bumbuli; this would have been impossible in earlier days. At least one of Semboja's subchiefs at Mazinde was a Zigula.[22] This period saw, in other words, a complete reversal of the policy of Kimweri ye Nyumbai, who had been careful to give to the people of a district a chief whose mother was a woman of that district. The ties of kinship had restrained the chief in his behavior toward his subjects, and they had promoted feelings of loyalty among the subjects. Now feelings of loyalty were beside the point; chiefly feelings of restraint were unproductive. In the new politics the head of the most important chiefdom in Shambaai was a Yao slave, and the warriors of the most powerful Kilindi leader were Zigula.

Not all common people allowed themselves to be taken as passive prey. There were a number of small but significant battles fought in the Pangani Valley through the late 1870s and the 1880s by ordinary cultivators against slave traders. Sometimes there was merely the action of a lineage going out to fight kidnappers. At other times a chief was attacked by the common people on whom he preyed. These conflicts took place both within single ethnic groups and across ethnic lines. They were fought between traders and traded: ethnicity was largely irrelevant.

In Pare, for example, there was a reaction by the mountain cultivators against the expanding influence of the traders in the plains towns in the early 1880s. There were a number of trading

21. Historical traditions: Ali Shechonge, 11 March 1967; Ghoda ja Kae, 12 July 1967; Mhammadi Mshaka Ngoto, 7 August 1967; Shemueta Shembilu, 2 August 1967.

22. Baumann, *Usambara,* p. 173. Historical traditions: Chamhingo wa Mkumbaa, 25 December 1967.

towns in the plains below Pare, mostly in the hands of Zigula traders or of Semboja's agents. In 1880 or 1881 Semboja took over Gonja, one of the towns on Pare's eastern trade route. At the same time raids by all the traders pushed deeper into Pare itself. The expansion and intensification of trade contracts led to a popular movement against the trading towns. The Pare saw the movement as a fight against "Shambaa" influence, but while those who fought the traders came from the territory of Mbaga, the rulers of Mbaga were completely excluded from the movement. Isaria Kimambo argues that there was a serious split between the ordinary cultivators and their chiefs—a new conflict of interest. "To the . . . rulers and wealthy people," Kimambo writes, "an alliance with the [trade] colonists was useful since this gave them a channel through which they could sell others as slaves." It was the ordinary Pare who feared and disliked the traders.[23]

In the East, at about the same time, a large number of ordinary Bondei cultivators looked to the UMCA mission for protection. When the mission began construction of a great stone church, which seemed to the local people like a fort, the most important trading chief, Segao of Mkuzi, led an attack on the construction site. In this case Segao, who was himself a Bondei, fought the potential protectors of his fellow Bondei.[24]

Even among the Mbugu, who lived far from the trade routes, there were some who collaborated in the attacks on their own people. Mavoa of the Gonja lineage made an alliance with Sem-

23. Kimambo, *Political History of the Pare,* pp. 175–76.

24. There are several reasons for accepting Farler's contention that Segao was a slave trader. The town of Mkuzi was on the trade route. In the later war between the Mazrui and the forces of the Sultan, Segao was the leader of the local supporters of the Sultan. This shows that he cultivated extensive contacts outside Bondei. Finally, he died the death of a slave dealer—his thumb became gangrened after he was bitten by a man he was trying to capture (Farler to [W. H.] Penney, 30 May 1881; Farler to Penney, 4 October 1881; Farler to Penney, St. Bartholomew's Day, 1881; Farler to Bishop Steere, 16 October 1881; Farler to Penney, All Souls Day, 1881; Farler to Bishop Steere, 19 November 1881; Farler to Bishop Steere, 23 November 1881; Farler to Penney, 26 October 1885, USPG-UMCA Box A 1 VI).

boja after he had lost his entire lineage in raids. When he was left with only three of his many dependents, he went to Mazinde and begged Semboja to make blood partnership. Semboja agreed. After that Mavoa would periodically visit Vugha and Mazinde, bringing small gifts each time, and no doubt bringing useful information. Now raids on the Mbugu would strike at other areas, but they never came to Mavoa's village. Mavoa became wealthier, and finally he was able to ransom two of his wives who had been enslaved in earlier attacks.[25]

The Mbugu of the area near Gare made a dramatic defensive attack on the Kilindi who victimized them. Chief Kikei of the Yamba subchiefdom at Gare is remembered by the Mbugu as the worst of the Kilindi. The final provocation came when Kikei entered the territory of the Mbugu, seized a child, and gouged his eyes. A number of Mbugu elders went to Yamba and respectfully requested an audience with the chief. One of the Mbugu asked Kikei if they might talk in private, and when the chief stepped outside the men clubbed the Kilindi to death. The Mbugu insist that this action led to a temporary reduction of Kilindi attacks.[26]

The Shambaa themselves sometimes attacked non-Kilindi kidnappers and slave traders. In one case the wives of a man named Kishasha were kidnapped near Vugha. Kishasha organized a counterraid, entered the trading town of Tarawanda in the plains, fought the traders, and recaptured his wives. On his return he gave a gift to the king to be certain of protection, since he had incurred the enmity of powerful traders.[27]

But while the Shambaa made individual attacks on kidnappers, they never rose up against their chiefs. There was a much safer way of resisting a tyrannical ruler. A subject who felt that

25. Historical traditions: Salehe Mbaruku, 11 June 1968.
26. Historical traditions: Ishika Kibabu, 19 June 1968; Nyaki Sempombe, 21 June 1968; Rere Komba, 15 June 1968; Singo Kumoso, 11 June 1968; Zahabu Mrindoko, 19 June 1968. I have been unable to establish Kikei's place within the Kilindi genealogy, but I suspect that the incident happened at about this time.
27. Historical traditions: Shechonge Kishasha, 11 March and 27 November 1967.

life in Shambaai was intolerable could flee to East Usambara to join the army of the sons of Mnkande, who were carrying on the fight to recover the kingdom from Semboja's son Kimweri Maguvu. In this way a subject could resist and be protected. Since the army of the eastern Kilindi was made up largely of those who had fled from Semboja and Kimweri, refugees were encouraged and were treated well. Refugees would fight to the bitter end, for they knew the terrible punishments that awaited them if they were defeated and captured.

I must emphasize that the argument concerning the importance of the trade in this chapter and Chapter 5 is my own, and that it does violence to the view of history which is generally accepted in Shambaai. It has been shown in the study of the myth of Mbegha that Mbegha's power, and indeed the power of any king, was ambivalent. It could be used to bring life or to bring death. Mbegha was transformed from one who brought death to one who brought fertility or life when he changed from a dispossessed person in his original homeland to the owner of the country in Shambaai. Shambaa explicitly say that famine and death are the result of *nguvu kwa nguvu,* "force against force," that is, political competition. When there is competition, leaders use their magical charms to assault one another, and not to bring fertility to the land. Fertility and life are the result of unchallenged domination by a single ruler who collects tribute from the entire land. When a ruler is unchallenged, he is able to use his magical charms for the welfare of his subjects. At the same time, there is peace rather than war. This is the reason Kimweri ye Nyumbai is remembered by all the people of Shambaai as a great and benevolent king. His rule was unchallenged, therefore he must have brought fertility to the land.

These ideas have been studied at length in another work.[28] Here it is necessary only to point out that most Shambaa attribute the slave-trading and general violence of the 1870s and 1880s to the divisions within the Kilindi lineage. Intermittent warfare between Semboja and Kimweri Maguvu on the one side,

28. Feierman, "Concepts of Sovereignty," Chapter 8.

and the eastern Kilindi on the other, continued throughout the 1870s and 1880s (see Chapter 8). Most Shambaa who know the history of the period refer to the dynastic competition as a cause, and the trade in slaves as an effect. According to a former court official:

> The Arabs traded with Semboja. Their merchandise was people. That is why the Arabs found a way of entering the affairs of the Shambaa. The Arabs were not involved in our affairs in the days of Kimweri ye Nyumbai. Their merchandise was people. In the days of ye Nyumbai there were no enemies.[29]

In other words, if there had been dynastic conflict earlier, then there would have been a slave trade earlier. Shambaa historical thought is based on the assumption that it is in the ruler's interests to increase the number of his subjects, and it is therefore in his interests to bring them fertility and peace. It is for this reason that one subject is reported to have remonstrated with Semboja in the following way: "Once you have finished killing all the people of the country, who will your subjects be?" Because Semboja seemed willing to see Shambaa killed and sold, there is a minority view, in Shambaai, that Semboja was a completely deviant kind of political leader: "The one who broke the ritual prohibitions (*miiko*) of the Kilindi is Semboja, when he sold people and made war."[30]

In support of the Shambaa interpretation, it can be argued that the increase in trade which had taken place before the death of Kimweri ye Nyumbai had not led to a change in conditions within Shambaai. Violence increased only after a dynastic dispute had torn the kingdom apart. The indigenous historical view thus integrates the Shambaa experience of events and Shambaa political ideas in a convincing way. The historian, however, examines events which are wider in scale than the experiences of any one individual, or any one chiefdom, and wider even than the whole of the Shambaa kingdom. Any interpretation which intends to satisfy historians viewing events from a distance must

29. Ibid., p. 391.
30. Ibid.; the argument is taken from pp. 390–92.

explain why people all over the Pangani Valley region, even beyond the limits of the area affected by the dynastic dispute, had similar experiences. In addition, according to accepted conventions of twentieth-century historians, explanations in which changing economic conditions lead to changing political conditions are more satisfying than those in which dynastic disputes lead to broad changes in political economy. Another way of putting this argument would be to say that although dynastic disputes were indeed a recurrent feature of Shambaa political life, the possible sources of support for competing chiefs changed in every generation. In the period under discussion the chiefs of Shambaai discovered a new kind of political economy in which the support of the mountain people was not nearly so important as the support of trading chiefs in the plains. Formerly, the people of the mountains had provided support in the form of tribute and services. Now chiefs had a choice. They could gather tribute from subjects, or they could sell subjects.

# 8 · THE DEVELOPMENT OF REGIONAL PATTERNS OF ACTION

## The War of Kimweri and Kibanga: A Regional Struggle

The struggle between the forces of Semboja and those of the sons of Mnkande continued through the 1870s and the 1880s, with each side searching for new sources of strength to end the war victoriously. Kimweri ye Nyumbai, and the rulers before him, had found their great strength among the common people of Shambaai. But under the new conditions, with trade far more important that it had been in the early kingdom, the significant battles were most often fought by foreigners—by non-Shambaa allies of Semboja, or of the sons of Mnkande. The key to victory was not how well one organized armies of Shambaa cultivators, but how well one organized a regional network of allies for trade and warfare.

There were two fundamental reasons for the increasing involvement of aliens in the affairs of the Shambaa kingdom. First, the economic resources which could be exploited for the export trade were not limited to any one locality: they were regional in their distribution, and needed to be exploited on a regional scale. The Maasai speakers and the Kamba had access to ivory, which was not available in Shambaai. Slaves were most easily gotten in Shambaai and Pare. Livestock came from a number of sources. Caravans could be controlled only if the chiefs on all the trade

185

routes cooperated. Thus it was necessary for Semboja, the greatest Kilindi trader, to become involved in the affairs of the
Kamba and the Maasai speakers, to deal with the Pare, and to
come to terms with the chief who controlled the trade route
which was an alternate to Mazinde's. The second reason for the
increased involvement of aliens in Shambaa affairs was the un-
easy relationship between Semboja and the commoners. As was
shown in Chapter 7, the cultivators of Shambaai could not be
expected to connive at their own enslavement. Under these circumstances, the best soldiers were foreigners seeking to enrich
themselves. Semboja's allies in the trading towns of the region
provided him with two services: they were trade partners who
regularly exchanged goods with him, and they were soldiers who
did not care about the internal affairs of Shambaai. Semboja's
trading partners, who were themselves enslaving the ordinary
people of their own localities, relied heavily on Semboja's soldiers to maintain order in their own spheres of influence.

In Pare, the trade routes in the plains ran past both the eastern and the western side of the mountains. Semboja had allies on
both sides. The East was more important in the internal affairs
of the Pare, the West for observation and control of the Maasai-
speaking peoples.

Semboja's two most important allies on the eastern side of
Pare were the chiefs of Kisiwani and of Kihurio. Kisiwani was a
plains town ruled by a Pare trader (Mashombo). The chief kept
a large group of Taita soldiers permanently at his court, and
they periodically raided into the mountains, capturing Pare
slaves who were then sold to Semboja. Semboja and the chief of
Kisiwani also helped one another in time of war. In fact it is
difficult to distinguish the armed aggression of politically in-
spired warfare from that of slave raiding. The chief of Kihurio
was Semboja's son-in-law, a Zigula who also had a trade-warfare
alliance with Semboja until the late 1880s.

Semboja established a colony at Hedaru on Pare's western
route; it was administered by a Kilindi "house" which had
moved from Shambaai. Hedaru was a key point for communication with the Maasai, who served Semboja as mercenary soldiers, and sold him ivory. The Maasai needed the permission of

Semboja's agent at Hedaru to proceed toward Mazinde in order to raid areas closer to the coast, including Shambaai itself. Semboja was always given a share of the booty.[1]

It is unclear whether the Maasai who passed Hedaru were members of the Sogonoi subgroup, or whether they were Iloikop Maasai. Both groups were allied with Semboja during the War of Kimweri and Kibanga. A group of Iloikop Maasai was camped permanently at Mazinde. Semboja made blood partnership with Maitei, father of the Iloikop Laibon, and was also a member of an Iloikop age-set. The Sogonoi Maasai attacked northern Shambaai as well as Bondei under Semboja's direction.

In addition to the Pare traders and the Maasai, Semboja's alliance network included a number of Zigula chiefs. The most important of these for the Mazinde trade system was Sadenga, the ruler of Mount Mafi, not far from Semboja's town. Caravans from the coast which followed the course of the Pangani River had only two possible routes from Maulwi to Pare: one went past Mazinde; the other passed Mafi. The Mazinde route was easier and the provisions better, but Semboja could not control movement through the area without the cooperation of Sadenga. Semboja took Sadenga's sister as his wife, and in addition made blood partnership with the Zigula chief.[2]

1. Semboja's relations with the Pare are described by Kimambo, *Political History of the Pare*, pp. 152–54, 169–71, 180–81. The description of Maasai relations is given in the Historical traditions: Jawa Samahoza, 25 December 1967; Salehe Ali, 11 November 1967; Shemzighua wa Mkumbaa, 25 December 1967. See also Justin Lemenye, *Maisha ya Sameni Ole Kivasis, yaani Justin Lemenye* (Nairobi, 1953), pp. 1–6, 33; H. H. Johnston, *The Kilima-Njaro Expedition* (London, 1886), pp. 312f; and Baumann, *Usambara*, pp. 193, 259ff.

2. The caravan route is described in G. A. Fischer, "Bericht über die im Auftrage der Geographischen Gesellschaft in Hamburg unternommene Reise in das Massai-Land," *Mitteilungen der Geographischen Gesellschaft in Hamburg* 5(1882–1883): 41. The alliances are described in Historical traditions: Barua Makange, 22 February 1968; Kimweri Magogo, 1 December 1967. The only other known ally of Semboja among the Zigula was Mgaya, the chief of Kwamkoro, whose forces joined in many of the battles in the dynastic dispute. This alliance is described in Zigula traditions in the Tanzania District Books, Tanga Provincial Book, Tribal History and Legends, Sheet No. 12.

The most important members of Semboja's military force
were the Zigula soldiers he maintained at Mazinde. Here again,
the men were slave raiders in time of peace, soldiers in time of
war. In addition, a group of Pare elephant hunters were maintained at Mpambei, a village in the chiefdom of Mazinde. The
chief, according to traditional law, was given one tusk of each
elephant killed. Semboja usually bought the other. The chief
kept the hunters supplied with powder.

Semboja and the other trading chiefs, by building regional
networks of trade and politics at the expense of the loyalty of
their own people, anticipated the work of the colonial and national governments by breaking down ethnic loyalties and inten-
sifying regional communications. In one significant respect the
nineteenth-century traders were more successful at regional integration than their colonial successors, for Semboja treated the
Maasai speakers as full partners in his regional enterprises. The
Germans did not consider that the Maasai speakers had a significant contribution to make toward the economy of the region.
Their prophecy was self-fulfilling.

The parallels between Semboja's use of traditional forms of
alliance, as he created his trade network, and Mbegha's, when
he had created the kingdom, are striking. The founder of the
Shambaa kingdom had initially met the need for new forms, for
a new scale of political activity, by making transitory alliances
which were so useful they developed into permanent institutions.
(see Chatper 3). Semboja used the same modes of alliance. He
was related to the chief of Kihurio by marriage, to a Maasai
leader by blood partnership, and to the chief of Mafi by both
marriage and blood partnership. The parallel between Semboja
and Mbegha is a significant one, for Semboja, like his ancestor,
was trying to establish a new relationship between territorial
scale and political action, by using transitory alliances in an attempt to build permanent authority.

Although Semboja succeeded in developing a firm power base
in the plains, among aliens, he was much less successful in
Shambaai. In the mountains he had no real services to perform,
no economic function to fulfill, that would lead either chiefs or
people to accept his leadership.

Semboja's first great failure in Shambaai came shortly after
the Bondei revolution, when he called a meeting of all the Ki-

lindi (excluding the sons of Mnkande) to name a new king of Vugha. Semboja intended to have himself made king, and if the Kilindi insisted on naming some other person, Semboja would kill that king as he had killed Shekulwavu.

The territorial chiefs would not tolerate Semboja as king. They knew that he was ruthless enough to kill them all and put his own men in their places.

The Kilindi chiefs worked out a brilliant tactic, and they maintained a united front. The problem was to find someone who would not be a strong king, but who would survive the threat of Semboja. The solution was to name Semboja's son, Kimweri Maguvu, to the position. The young man would be unable to dominate his uncles in their chiefdoms. And Semboja would probably not kill his son.

Semboja resisted, arguing that Kimweri was too young and weak, and would quickly be killed by his enemies. Ng'wa Kimungu, who had killed the royal heir in the days of Kimweri ye Nyumbai, and who in the disturbances had returned to his old chiefdom of Shembekeza, swore that he would be responsible for the safety of the new king, and he had his own son make blood partnership with Kimweri to seal the compact.[3]

The accession of Kimweri Maguvu was a setback to centralized rule in Shambaai. Vugha was rebuilt; Kimweri was called by the royal praise name, *Simba Mwene,* but many chiefdoms no longer paid tribute to Vugha, nor could the king place his own men in the chiefdoms. Each chiefdom became hereditary in the house of one of Semboja's brothers. When Semboja's brother Mshuza died at Ubii, for example, the chiefdom did not revert to the king: it was inherited instead by Mshuza's son.

Kimweri Maguvu never governed Shambaai, but he was able to depend on the chiefs of southern Shambaai for assistance in campaigns against the sons of Mnkande. The house of Ubii had been allied with Kimweri's father Semboja since the start of the dynastic dispute. Bumbuli had been left vacant during the long period of revolution and rebellion, and so Kimweri could make his own man chief there. And the chief of Shembekeza had sworn that he would support Kimweri.

While Semboja and his son had allies both in Shambaai and in

3. Historical traditions: Kimweri Magogo, 3 April 1967; Mdoe Zayumba, 8 June 1967; Mzimbii Mpemba, 20 July 1968.

the plains, the alliances in the plains were signs of victory, those in the mountains signs of defeat. In the plains they represented the fruits of a creative impulse—where once there had been nothing, Semboja created a network of alliances, and perhaps one day they might be more than just alliances. But in the mountains, Semboja had only alliances, where once there had been centralized rule.

The resources of the sons of Mnkande were much more meager than those of Semboja. Virtually all the important traders of the region had ties with Semboja, and none of them would trade with or fight for the sons of Mnkande. As a result, the forces of the eastern Kilindi dug in at positions that were off the trade routes, but magnificently placed for defense.

The main force of the sons of Mnkande was an army of the victims of Kimweri and Semboja: people who for a great variety of reasons fled eastward from their original homes in Shambaai. An ally of Kimweri Maguvu, arguing in the late 1880s that the war should be abandoned, told Kimweri he would never be able to defeat an army of his wives' ex-lovers. One tradition maintains that Kibanga, the leader of the sons of Mnkande, wore a bell on his leg in order not to surprise one of his wives with a lover.[4]

Each of the three main areas occupied by the eastern Kilindi was under the control of a different descendant of the "house" of Mnkande.

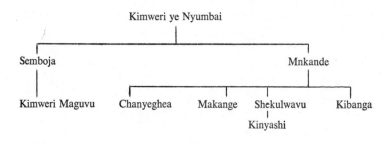

4. Historical traditions: Jaha Mtoi, 22 April 1967; Salehe Ali, 11 November 1967.

Two of the three areas were in East Usambara—the narrow chain of mountains across the Luengera Valley from Shambaai. The third was in the northeastern corner of Shambaai itself, near Mshihwi.

The southern half of East Usambara was the main center of the sons of Mnkande. It was there, at Mghambo, that Kibanga had his capital (after the death of Chanyeghea in the early 1870s). Mghambo was on a mountain peak overlooking the valley to the west. It was extremely difficult to reach, a useless position for trade, but easy to fortify and defend against invaders who would have to climb the mountain. The town was encircled by impenetrable brush, and outside this there was a second barrier of felled trees and deep trenches. The gateways were in walls of posts driven into the ground, so as to form a mass six feet thick. Each gate had two doors formed of heavy single slabs of timber.[5]

The other two major positions of the sons of Mnkande were the northern half of East Usambara, which is called Hundu, and Makanya, wedged between the independent pocket kingdom of Mshihwi and Kimweri Maguvu's Shambaai. As Kinyashi, the young royal heir of the eastern Kilindi, grew into adolescence, he was given Hundu. Makanya, which was the major threat to Vugha, was under the control of Makange, son of Mnkande.[6]

In addition to their three areas of control, the sons of Mnkande, led by Kibanga, could rely on most of Bondei for defensive support, for the Bondei did not wish to be made subjects of a triumphant Semboja. The people of Bondei, however, did not join in the attacks on Shambaai. They saw little reason to fight for Kibanga's total victory, and the greatest part of their combative energies was expended in defending their own homes.[7]

The sons of Mnkande never gave up hope of redressing the

5. Johnston, "Zanzibar to Usambara," pp. 550–51.

6. Historical traditions: Kasimu Kimweri, 1 February 1968; Mahimbo Kihedu, 1 February 1968; Mbwana Mkanka Mghanga and Kimweri Magogo, 19 May 1967; see also Farler, "Usambara Country," p. 84.

7. For an example of Bondei reluctance to join offensive operations, see the letter from C. S. B. Riddell, *Central Africa* 4 (February 1886): 20.

balance of power. They saw their first opportunity to gain important allies with the arrival of J. P. Farler, of the UMCA in April 1875. Here was a powerful foreigner who was not yet in Semboja's camp, and who chose to settle near the base of the eastern Kilindi. Farler settled permanently at Magila, in Bondei. Through 1876 there was a flurry of diplomatic activity. Kibanga asked Farler to arrange a truce between the two sides. During the course of the year Kibanga, acting for the sons of Mnkande, sent Farler gifts of a cow, three bulls, a calf, a goat, and a sheep. In addition he offered to send sixteen of his sons to Farler's school to be educated, although in the end there was not room for all of them. Semboja reacted by sending friendly messages to Magila.

The Bondei, too, tried to use Farler. The missionary was given half of the formerly great but now devastated town of Pambire to use for a mission station. The town had wasted away in the Kilindi wars, and as a result of Digo slave raids. The elder who made the offer suggested that if the missionary had guns the town would quickly thrive again. Farler wrote to Bishop Steere, "It would . . . be well if Dr. Kirk would ask Seyed Baghash [sic] to send a letter to the Wadigo through the governor of Tanga telling them that we had gone to live at Pambili and that they were not to molest us."[8]

The UMCA position in the War of Kimweri and Kibanga was dramatically determined in January and February of 1877, when a large force of Zigula attacked Bondei with the connivance of Semboja. The Bondei fled in defeat, and only the arrival of Kibanga and his men saved the mission. From this point Farler was a partisan: he was interested first in the protection of the Bondei, and then in the victory of the sons of Mnkande. A council of Bondei asked Farler to be their king, and a great many cases were brought to him for settlement.

Finally, in April 1877, Farler wrote to the British Anti-Slav-

8. Farler to Bishop Steere, 30 September 1876 (USPG-UMCA, Box A 1 VI). Materials used in the exposition of Farler's place in politics in this paragraph and as continued below include: Farler to Bishop Steere, 10 October 1876, and Farler to Allchin, 23 February 1877, ibid. See also, Farler, *The Work of Christ in Central Africa,* pp. 17–20.

ery Society offering to take up the fight against the slave trade if
he could be supplied with arms and ammunition: "The king of
Usambara [Kibanga] and my people the Wabondei hate the
beach people and the Arabs, and would be only too glad to do it
if they could get arms and powder. At present the beach people
refuse to let them buy powder."[9] Farler arranged for the English
Consul at Zanzibar to send a present of six rifles to Kibanga because, he maintained, it was Kibanga's opposition to the slave
trade which involved him in the war with Semboja.[10] The Magila
mission, with no single dominant indigenous ruler to rely on for
protection, and working in a time of frequent warfare, had no
choice but to become a political power itself—one of the many
powers which interacted to create the pattern of politics in the
Pangani Valley.

At the same time that Kibanga was sealing his alliance with
the missionaries and their followers, and learning that these new
allies could not send armed men to help attack Shambaai, Kimweri Maguvu was attempting to strengthen his position in northern Shambaai. Kimweri faced a serious threat in the north from
Makanya, the western outpost of the sons of Mnkande.

Kimweri strengthened his position in the two minor chiefdoms
immediately adjacent to the enemy's territory: Mlola, on the
northern rim of Shambaai, and Bagha, the land which was a
small buffer between Makange's outpost and Kimweri's capital.
Mlola had been without a chief since the time the ruler was
killed by the Bondei revolutionaries. Maguvu put his own man
over the chiefdom. Bagha, the buffer chiefdom, was already in
the hands of Kihedu, son of Kimweri ye Nyumbai, a man loyal
to the young king of Vugha. Kihedu moved his town to an im-
pregnable position in preparation for an attack that would surely
come.[11]

At this time Maguvu attempted to respond to the threat in

9. Farler to British Anti-Slavery Society, 27 April 1877 (Rhodes
House, MSS Brit. Emp. s. 22).

10. Farler to British Anti-Slavery Society, 28 December 1877, ibid.

11. Historical traditions: Kasimu Kimweri, 1 February 1968; Mahimbo Kihedu, 1 February 1968. The new chief of Mlola was Ng'wa
Nyoka, who was brought by Kimweri Maguvu from Mbalu, at the western edge of Shambaai. When Ng'wa Nyoka moved in he made a great

Shambaai at Makanya, and at the same time to establish his real
authority as *Simba Mwene,* ruler of Shambaai. He did this by
moving to take over Mlalo, the main northern chiefdom, which
was ruled at this time by a young and vulnerable generation
mate of Maguvu's (named Shekinyashi). But just as every attempt by the sons of Mnkande to win the help of armed foreigners was doomed to failure, so was Kimweri's attempt to rule
Shambaai doomed. There were several independent chiefdoms
which had a common interest in resisting Vugha, and which
found ready allies among the eastern Kilindi.

The young Mlalo chief's brother Shewai refused to allow the
patrimony of his "'house" pass to the king of Vugha. He joined
the forces of the sons of Mnkande at Makanya. He was joined
there by a subchief of Gare, who undoubtedly realized that if
Mlalo fell, Gare would be next.

While Kimweri at Vugha was still gathering his forces to attack Makanya, Shewai decided to take the offensive. He attacked the royal capital, sweeping aside the surprised soldiers of
Vugha. The forces of Shewai and the sons of Mnkande came to
within several miles of Vugha and then stopped. There are conflicting accounts of the battle, with each side claiming victory.
But the political outcome is clear: Shewai returned to Mlalo, and
Kimweri Maguvu was never to control the North. It was clear
that the power of the western Kilindi lay in the plains, with the
traders.[12]

The sons of Mnkande were ultimately driven, as a result of
their diplomatic isolation, to ally themselves with an equally iso-

---

show of force, leaving cloths and spears spread about the hillside that
faced Makanya, so that it looked from the distance as though he had a
great army. Because of this Makange did not attack Mlola during the
period of Ng'wa Nyoka's weakness, before he had built fortifications.

12. Historical tradition: Ayubu Nyeo, 31 January 1968; Hassani Kinyashi, 17 July 1968 (group testimony); Juma Shekumkai, 18 July 1968;
Lihani Shemnkande, 12 June 1967; Mdoe Barua, 5 November 1967;
Semnguu Koplo, 7 November 1967. At first Chambi, the subchief of
Gare, merely refused to fight in the army which Kimweri was assembling
for the attack on Makanya. But Chambi fled when he heard that Kimweri had decided to sell him into slavery, as punishment for insubordination.

lated force, the army of Mbaruk el Mazrui, who had rebelled against Zanzibari rule at Mombasa. The arrival of Mbaruk late in 1883 presented the sons of Mnkande with a seemingly superb opportunity, for the Mombasa rebel came into the area with a great army which had recently been augmented by 250 men from a runaway slave colony that had burnt to the ground. Mbaruk came into contact with the sons of Mnkande while moving about in the coastal hinterland in order to avoid the troops of the Sultan of Zanzibar.

Mbaruk agreed to join an attack on Vugha through Makanya, in an attempt to drive out Kimweri and take control of the kingdom. At a time when the rains were just breaking after a long dry season, the joint forces of the eastern Kilindi and Mbaruk attacked fiercely at Bagha, just northeast of the capital.

Kimweri Maguvu retreated, his forces in disarray, convinced that he was about to lose his capital. In despair he begged the chief of Ubii, heir to great rain magic, to help. Kimweri offered three cows: "The rain came down together with a violent wind, a wind that broke trees in half." In the wind, on the wet mountain paths, Mbaruk's men fell, slid, stumbled, and finally gave up in retreat.[13] In the counterattack the sons of Mnkande were driven out of Makanya, and many of their soldiers were taken captive.

At this point the real weakness of the sons of Mnkande in regional politics became evident. Having been driven, in the extremity of their isolation, to an alliance with the enemy of the Sultan, they were now attacked by the Sultan's forces.

Kimweri and Semboja sent a message to Zanzibar, informing Seyyid Barghash that the sons of Mnkande had joined forces with Mbaruk. Barghash ordered the Wali of Pangani to attack Hundu, the northern half of East Usambara. The Wali assembled a great force, calling on all his local allies to contribute men. The Wali's army, combined with the force of the western Kilindi, drove the sons of Mnkande out of Hundu.

The sons of Mnkande ended the War of Mbaruk with only one of their three major bases left—Handei, the southern part of

13. The quotation is from Historical traditions: Jaha Mtoi, 28 November 1967. The Ubii chief was Mtoi, son of Mshuza.

East Usambara. In June 1884, Kinyashi (the grandson of Mnkande) went to Zanzibar to restore relations with Seyyid Barghash. He was afraid that the Sultan would throw him in prison rather than make an agreement. But by July Kinyashi was back, the War of Mbaruk was over, and the sons of Mnkande had been reduced to governing a small rump state.[14]

Between November 1887 and March 1888 the western Kilindi, in their last major action as independent rulers, made a massed attack on the sons of Mnkande at Mghambo, in Handei. The attack failed because the eastern soldiers stayed in their own towns, while those who attacked slept on the ground and ate what food they could steal. It was a kind of warfare that was more debilitating for the besieger than for the besieged. The final battle has been described by an elder of Vugha: "When the Vugha forces had fought for a while, they became sleepy. After a while they would spend whole days sleeping. Yet the war would go on. Then they would become infested with lice. They spent

14. There is a remarkable combination of sources on the War of Mbaruk, for the UMCA missionaries recorded the Bondei side of it, while the descriptions in the oral traditions are rich, and agree with the mission sources. For the mission sources, see Magila Logbook 1884–1890 (TNA, UMCA-CPEA), pp. 13–27. This report gives an interesting picture of the relations between the mission, the Consul at Zanzibar, and the Sultan, for the Bondei of Magila refused to take part in the expedition against the sons of Mnkande, since they could only lose from Kimweri Maguvu's victory. As a result, when some of the mission's porters arrived at Pangani they were thrown into prison. Sir John Kirk took the matter to Barghash, and the incident ended with the Wali of Pangani in irons, and a considerable sum in compensation paid by the Sultan. Another description of the war is in J. P. Farler, "Other Troubles at Magila," *Central Africa* 2 (September 1884): 147–49. T. H. R. Cashmore gives a useful sketch of Mbaruk's life (omitting this incident) in "Sheikh Mbaruk bin Rashid bin Salim el Mazrui," in *Leadership in Eastern Africa*, ed. Norman R. Bennett (Boston, 1968), pp. 109–37. The main source is Historical traditions: Jaha Mtoi, 28 November 1967; Kasimu Kimweri, 1 February 1968; Kwavi Senkunde, 28 May 1968, text 2; Kimweri Magogo, 3 April 1967; Kimweri Magogo and Mbwana Mkanka Mghanga, 19 May 1967; Mahimbo Kihedu, 1 February 1968; Ng'wa Paula s/o Ng'wa Kimungu, 12 July 1967. Baumann gives the incorrect date of 1886 for the event (*Usambara*, p. 190).

whole days picking lice, unable to fight. They fought for a long time but they simply were not able to enter Mghambo." The western forces returned to their homes, and before the war could be resumed the Germans entered Pangani.[15]

## The Regional Culture of Mazinde

In a period when the major war for power in Shambaai was fought by the Wali of Pangani, chiefs of Bondei and Zigula, and the most prominent family of Mombasa, it is clear that the most important political events were no longer local in scale, but regional. In this setting the traditional Shambaa concern with maintaining the culture of the ancestors was clearly out of step. At Mazinde, as at other centers of regional politics and economics, there was a spirit of eclecticism. Languages, religious concepts, elements of material culture were adopted in great numbers. Mazinde developed a culture which drew on the entire region in much the same way its politics drew on the region.

While rectangular coastal style houses at Vugha were placed just outside town, as visitors' quarters, at Mazinde the rectangular houses were Semboja's court, in the center of a mass of round commoners' houses. The rectangular houses, which were tangential at Vugha, were central at Mazinde; the round houses which were central at Vugha, were tangential at Mazinde.[16]

Semboja's house at Mazinde, as described by a missionary-explorer, was filled with objects that had come from other cultures. "Sultan Semboja's room," the missionary wrote "was like a used furniture shop. There were plates, cloths, silver, writing desks, chairs." The most surprising thing was the presence of several issues of *Petermanns Mitteilungen*. The missionary "asked whether Semboja subscribed to this excellent geographi-

15. The description quoted is from Historical traditions: Salehe Ali, 11 November 1967. See also Jaha Mtoi, 28 November 1967; Ng'wa Paula s/o Ng'wa Kimungu, 12 July 1967; Mahimbo Kihedu, 1 February 1968. Magila Logbook, 1884–1890 (TNA, UMCA-CPEA), pp. 127, 147–51; Farler to Penney, 9 December 1887.
16. Baumann, *Deutsch-Ostafrika*, p. 96.

cal journal. 'Ah,' he said casually, 'it's a souvenir of Hans Meyer' [whose caravan Semboja had plundered]."[17]

The need to expand his cultural universe extended to all spheres of Semboja's life. One oral informant reported that Semboja brought two coastal women of good family to Mazinde to teach his wives Swahili cuisine.[18]

Semboja affected the dress of an Arab. According to New:

> I was surprised to find Semboja in appearance and dress an Arab; with white kanzu, black surtout braided over the shoulders with tinsel, coloured girdle and turban, sword and dagger mounted in silver, an oblong case of silver like a large snuff-box, and stuffed with charms, at his breast, he presented a great contrast to his poorly-clad brigand-like followers. I expected to have met a tall, fine, black, shaggy, fierce, lion-like sort of man; yet here was a short, stooping, yellow, haggard, tame-looking fellow, not at all imposing or impressive at first sight. But I soon found out that, with a high nervous temperament, he was sharp, short, active, energetic, and resolute.[19]

Semboja surrounded himself with exotic objects: he wore them on his person, kept them in his quarters—even his house was foreign.

Vugha retained its original shape, even in this period of rapid change, because of the strength of ritual prohibitions. But Semboja's son Kimweri Maguvu, ruler of Vugha, made innovations in much the same way as his father at Mazinde. J. P. Farler, the UMCA missionary, met Kimweri, who was dressed for the meeting in a suit of European clothes, with a sun hat and patent leather shoes. Kimweri asked Farler for pepper seed, curry powder, petroleum, coffee seed, and the seeds of various fruits which the missionaries grew at their station in Bondei. Kimweri was able to read and write Swahili in Arabic characters.[20]

17. A. Le Roy, *Au Kilima-Ndjaro* (Paris, n.d.), p. 438.

18. Historical traditions: Mdoembazi Guga, 29 November 1967.

19. Charles New, "Journey from the Pangani, via Wadigo, to Mombasa," *Proceedings of the Royal Geographical Society* 19 (1874–75): 319.

20. J. P. Farler, "News from Magila," *Central Africa* 6 (June 1888): 82–85.

It is tempting but wrong to accept Kimweri's mastery of written Swahili as evidence that the culture of the trading chiefs was coastal culture. The argument that Swahili was the trade language of precolonial Tanzania is an example of reasoning that the unknown must have been similar to the known: that because Swahili was the language for communication between ethnic groups in the colonial period, the same must have been true earlier.

Mazinde was not a Swahili town; it was a multilingual town. Many languages were spoken, and many cultures absorbed. The point is one of some importance, because the linguistic usage was a reflection of political and economic realities in this period. From the point of view of Semboja it was important to integrate all the peoples of the region, including Swahili speakers, into a coherent economic, political, and cultural system.

Each of the trading towns in the plains near the edges of Shambaai had a predominant language, and those who planned to trade regularly in a given town learned the language. The *lingua franca* of Mazinde was Zigula. This was the language in which the Shambaa, Pare, Iloikop Maasai, Zigula, and Swahili communicated with one another. Similarly, at the Kitivo market to the north of Shambaai, when Pare, Segeju, Zigula, and Swahili traders met they conversed in Shambaa. Vugha was served by the trading town Makuyuni, where Zigula was the language of common usage. The men who came from the coast to trade at Makuyuni spoke Zigula.[21]

While each town had a dominant language, the entrepreneurs of the period were multilingual. Semboja spoke Zigula, Shambaa, Swahili, Maasai, and probably other languages. A number of Iloikop Maasai at Mazinde spoke fluent Shambaa and Zigula. Harry Johnston, one of the few explorers interested enough in

21. For the linguistic usages at Mazinde and Makuyuni, see Historical traditions: Barua Makange, 22 February 1968; Jaha Mtoi, 28 November 1967; Kimweri Magogo, 1 December 1967; Kwavi Senkunde, 28 May 1968, text 2; Mdoembazi Guga, 29 November 1967; Semnguu Koplo, 27 November 1967. Lemenye, *Sameni Ole Kivasis,* pp. 1–5. The language of the Kitivo market is described in E. Johanssen, "Ein Ausflug nach Kitivo," *Nachrichten* 6 (July 1892): 130.

language to note the complexity of the local situation, reported of the notables at the Pare trading town of Gonja that "not only they but the people they governed were great linguists. They spoke Ki-zeguha, Ki-pare, Ki-swahili, a little Arabic, and Masai. The latter language they were quite versed in."[22]

The people of the trading towns learned new religions in much the same way that they learned new languages—one could learn Islam without taking it as seriously as the Shambaa religion of the ancestors. Semboja and his son Kimweri Maguvu of Vugha probably called themselves Muslims at times, but they continued to eat pork, and they were central figures in the cult of the royal ancestors. The oral traditions state that no one in Shambaai recited Islamic prayers or fasted during Ramadhan until well into the colonial period. Islam was spreading more rapidly during this period in Bondei, where there was a longer period of contact. The agents of Islamization at this time in Bondei, and during the colonial period in Shambaai, were, for the most part, not Arabs or coastal townsmen but Zigula.[23]

Islam was not the only religion being learned at Mazinde and the other trading towns. The religious picture, like the linguistic situation, was characterized by wide-ranging eclecticism. The Mazinde people, and those in other parts of southern Shambaai, were suffering from what they thought of as new illnesses—illnesses caused by evil spirits (*mpepo* or *mizuka*).

The concepts of spirit illness which existed at that time, and which survive in some places today, described the tensions of life in a period of intensified contact with the outside world. Some nature spirits which are thought to cause illnesses were part of Shambaa culture long before the period under discussion. Most spirit illnesses, however, are thought to be caused by the spirits of foreigners. At a cult meeting I attended, a woman was present who had reached the point of despair because she hated going to her gardens day after day, although it is the duty of

22. Johnston, *Kilima-Njaro*, pp. 307f.
23. Historical traditions: Jaha Mtoi, 28 November 1967; Mdoembazi Guga, 29 November 1967; Rashidi Beleko, 30 November 1967. Baumann, *Usambara*, pp. 121, 141; Baumann, *Deutsch-Ostafrika*, p. 168; Farler, "News from Magila," p. 85; Steere, *Central Africa Mission*, p. 9.

every Shambaa woman to farm. When possessed, she sang, "I am an Arab and I don't like to farm." Not only was the concept of the disease seen as coming from outside Shambaai, but the illness was caused by a foreign spirit.[24]

It has been shown that the earliest intense contact with the new economic forces came through Zigula. On the basis of limited current knowledge, it appears that the earliest alien spirit, *handia,* came from Zigula as early as the 1870s. It was said to cause women to want to eat their own babies. The disease does seem appropriate as the symbolic expression of the character of life in the period called "rapacity" (see p. 165). The Zigula disease had its greatest impact at the southern tip of Shambaai, in the area nearest the Zigula trading town of Makuyuni. The spirit called *bahari,* "the ocean," existed in both Shambaai and Bondei. Outbreaks of *bahari* possession occurred most frequently after the departure of visiting coastal traders. There were other spirits associated with most of the ethnic groups with whom the Shambaa came into contact: the Pare, Digo, Taita, Maasai, Iloikop, Bondei, Ng'indo. Often it was impossible to distinguish between the symptoms of diseases caused by the different ethnic spirits, in which case the medical practitioner would inquire about the identity of the most recent alien visitors to a village, and attribute the disease to the appropriate spirit.[25]

The spirit-possession diseases were pathological results of the expansion of the scale of communications. Soon after the diseases came to the Shambaa trading towns, they moved on along the trade route to Pare. Because of the foreign nature of the diseases, the doctors who treat them speak in foreign languages. Kimambo reports that Pare doctors, when they make incanta-

24. The writer has attended a number of possession ceremonies. The historical materials include: Kimambo, *Political History of the Pare,* pp. 189–190; Baumann, *Deutsch-Ostafrika,* p. 169; P. Wohlrab, "Ein Neuer Dämonen-Kultus in Usambara," *Nachrichten* 27 (December 1913):186–189; W. Hosbach, "Eine Geistergeschichte," *Nachrichten* 25 (November 1911):209–213; Karl Wohlrab, *Die christliche Missionspredigt unter den Schambala* (Tübingen, 1929), pp. 48–50; Karasek, "Beiträge zur Kenntnis der Waschambaa," *Baessler-Archiv* 8:40–45.

25. The materials for this paragraph are taken mostly from Karasek, "Beiträge zur Kenntnis der Washchambaa," *Baessler-Archiv* 8:40–45.

tions, speak Shambaa; Shambaa doctors speak Swahili. Each
group attributes its illnesses to strangers, but in reality the disease is a regional one.

The spread of spirit-possession diseases shows, then, that even
before colonial rule began the people of Shambaai, as well as the
rest of the Pangani Valley, were disturbed to the point of personal illness by the rapidity of social change. The continuity between the last decades of precolonial rule and the first decades
after conquest is shown by the fact that no new disease concept
was added after conquest; German spirits were simply added to
the catalogue of foreign causes of disease. Shortly after a rail-
road was built in the plains, the spirit of the locomotive began to
cause disease. Belief in the diseases not only allowed the Shambaa to give their sense of disturbance a concrete expression, it
enabled them to learn the characteristics of the foreigners, to integrate them into the Shambaa cultural knowledge, by acting the
part of the alien while possessed by his spirit.

The Shambaa lost control of their own political fate after ob-
serving, and participating as marginal actors in, the Bushiri uprising which followed the German occupation of the coast in the
middle of 1888. The rising which was led by Bushiri bin Salim
el-Harthi was remarkable proof that a regional scale of action
had been achieved, for the forces which fought against the European invasion included coastal Swahili speakers, Zigula, Ngulu,
Zaramo, Hehe, Bondei, Mbugu, Shambaa, slaveholders and
slaves, Muslims and those who practiced the religion of the ancestors. It is significant that the political leaders of the Shambaa
responded to the German presence only once they had observed
the defeat of this grand coalition of the peoples of the wide
coastal zone opposite Zanzibar and Pemba.[26]

The Shambaa participated only at the periphery of the rising.
Semboja used the occasion of the start of fighting to seize 250
valuable loads from Baumann and Meyer—two German explorers who were passing through Mazinde at the end of September

26. The fullest account of the rising is given in Fritz Ferdinand Müller,
*Deutschland—Zanzibar—Ostrafrika* (Berlin, 1959).

1888, unaware of what was happening at the coast. With this, Semboja's action against the Germans ended. According to the oral traditions, Kimweri Maguvu at Vugha wanted to fight against the Europeans, but Semboja responded to his son that he had dreamed about the Germans, and had seen that resistance was hopeless. If some were killed, others would follow. The eastern Kilindi chose to make a modest contribution toward Bushiri's resistance forces. There are reports of small bodies of Shambaa fighting men under the leadership of the eastern Kilindi going down to the coast in October 1888. Some Mbugu also went to the coast to fight at Bushiri's side.[27]

Bushiri was decisively defeated in the hinterland of Bagamoyo, south of the Pangani Valley, in May 1889. It must have been clear to Shambaa leaders by this point that resistance to the Germans could not win. By November 1889, Bushiri was heading north in full retreat with only forty men left. He begged Semboja to be allowed to pass through Shambaai in order to reach the British sphere. Semboja refused.[28]

By early 1890, the wishes of the Shambaa leaders and of the Germans were converging. The Shambaa had no desire to resist, and the Germans wanted to secure the cooperation of the local leaders wherever possible, so that they could complete operations against the few remaining pockets of resistance. In February 1890 Kibanga went to visit the Germans at Tanga, where he was named chief of all East Usambara and Bondei. In the same month Semboja paid a substantial fine for his seizure of Bau-

27. The seizure of Baumann and Meyer's property is described in Baumann, *Deutsch-Ostafrika*, pp. 97–98; and Baumann, *Usambara*, p. 192. The discussion between Kimweri Maguvu and Semboja is given in Historical traditions: Kimweri Magogo and Mbwana Mkanka Mghanga, 19 May 1967; Kwavi Senkunde, 28 May 1967, text 2; Mdoembazi Guga, 15 June and 29 November 1967; Ng'wa Paula s/o Ng'wa Kimungu, 12 July 1967. On the role of the eastern Kilindi, see Umba Logbook 1886–1894 (October 6, 1888) (TNA, UMCA-CPEA), p. 38; Mkuzi Logbook 1881–1892 (October 20–22, 1888) (ibid.). On Mbugu participation, see *Nachrichten* 6 (March 1892), p. 53. I have no doubt that my own knowledge of Shambaa participation is incomplete because I have not consulted the Potsdam archives.

28. Müller, *Deutschland*, pp. 447–48.

mann and Meyer's property, and was then paid a monthly wage for going over to the victors. The German flag was raised at Mazinde, which became a station for keeping the caravan route open into the interior.[29]

Kimweri Maguvu died at the end of November 1893, and his brother Mputa became king of Vugha. Then in March 1895 Semboja died. Soon after his death, in the period when leadership in Shambaai was still uncertain, the German officer at Mazinde declared the king of Vugha guilty of murder for having exercised the sovereign duty of a Shambaa king by killing the lover of one of his wives. On 30 April 1895 the Kilindi of Shambaai and the elders of Vugha were forced to watch at Mazinde while their king was hanged. With this act, power passed from the hands of the Kilindi.[30]

29. Ibid., p. 451; Baumann, *Usambara,* p. 194; Rochus Schmidt, *Deutschlands Kolonien: ihre Gestaltung, Entwickelung und Hilfsquellen,* I, *Ost-Afrika* (Berlin, n.d.), pp. 107–8; Magila Logbook 1884–1890 (22 February 1890) (TNA, UMCA-CPEA), p. 289.

30. The hanging is described by Lieutenant E. Storch, the Mazinde officer, in *Nachrichten* 9 (September 1895): 138–40. The events of the period are described in Vugha's station diary in the Bethel Mission archives. See also the account of the period compiled from German sources by R. W. Gordon, keeper of the German records for the British in Tanganyika, in the papers of W. S. G. Barnes (Rhodes House, MSS Afr. s. 462).

# REFERENCE MATTER

# BIBLIOGRAPHY

DOCUMENTARY SOURCES

*Historical Traditions*

The historical traditions are those that I collected in Shambaai between May 1966 and July 1968. These include transcripts of both oral narratives and conversations on social organization. About half are transcripts of tape recordings, and half are direct transcripts of conversations, made in an improvised shorthand. All the traditions are in the Shambaa language, except for a small body of Mbugu texts with Shambaa translations. Each transcript is headed by the name of the informant, the date of the conversation, and the place. Other pertinent information about the informant is given in the body of the text. All the traditions are in my possession at the present time.

*Archives*

Bethel Mission, Bethel bei Bielefeld, Federal Republic of Germany. The mission began work in Shambaai in 1891, and so the collection is of especial interest for the period of German colonial rule. The missionaries were deeply interested in Shambaa culture, however. The papers include descriptions of indigenous society, as well as some mention of the historical reminiscences of the people of Shambaai. The collection includes mission correspondence, station diaries, and the manuscript reminiscences of some of the missionaries.

Church Missionary Society (CMS), London. The Society's archives, of which there is a microfilm copy at Memorial Library, the University of Wisconsin, Madison, include the letters and journals of missionaries who lived at Mombasa from the 1840s on, some of whom visited Shambaai. Most important for this work are the letters and journals of Dr. J. L. Krapf (CA5/016), who visited Shambaai in 1848 and 1852 and Kamba country in 1849 and 1851, and who also wrote a memoir on the East African slave trade based on his observations. The papers of J. Erhardt (CO5/09) include the journal of a visit to Shambaai in 1853, and another of a stay at Tanga in 1854. The records of J. Rebmann (CA5/024) include journals of visits to Taita and Chagga. The writings of Krapf and Rebmann provide important evidence for the history of the region as seen from Mombasa between 1844 and 1853.

Rhodes House, Oxford. The Rhodes House collection holds the diaries and some letters of Richard Thornton, the nineteenth-century explorer (MSS Afr. s. 27). There are several letters by J. P. Farler to the British Anti-Slavery Society, on the slave trade in Bondei (MSS Brit. Emp. s. 22). The collection also holds the papers of W. S. G. Barnes on the reconstruction of traditional forms of government at the time of the imposition of indirect rule (MSS Afr. s. 462).

Tanzania National Archives, Dar es Salaam. The Tanzania National Archives contain voluminous records of the colonial period. There are two sets of records which are relevant to the period of this study. First, the collection contains the logbooks of the separate stations of the Universities Mission (Church of the Province of East Africa) for the 1880s; they are referred to in the notes as TNA, UMCA-CPEA. Second, the National Archives is microfilming the district books of Tanzania. These are typescript volumes on the history and local customs of the separate districts. The microfilms are available at the Center for Research Libraries, Chicago.

United Society for the Propagation of the Gospel, London. The records of the former Universities Mission to Central Africa are located in the collection of the Society. The correspondence of the missionaries in Bondei, which dates back to 1875, is relevant to this study. The most useful boxes of correspondence were marked A 1 VI, A 1 VIII, Wo, and LMN. The collections is referred to in the notes as USPG-UMCA.

UNPUBLISHED MANUSCRIPTS

Cory, Hans. "Sambaa Law and Custom." Revised and edited by E. B. Dobson. Typescript. Cory Collection, University College, Dar es Salaam, 1951.

Döring, Paul. "Unter seinen Flügeln." Typescript. Deposited in the Bethel Mission Archives, Bethel bei Bielefeld, 21 December 1948.

Dupré, H. "Land und Volk in Usambara. Selbstgeschautes und Selbsterlebtes." Manuscript. Bethel Mission Archives, Bethel bei Bielefeld, n.d.

Feierman, Steven. "Concepts of Sovereignty among the Shambaa and Their Relation to Political Action." D.Phil. dissertation, Oxford University, 1972.

Hoza, Yohana. "Sheuta: Dini ya Kishambala, au Miviko ya Kishambala." Manuscript. In the possession of Yohana Hoza, Vugha, Lushoto Area, Tanzania, n.d.

Iliffe, John. "Kingship and Rebellion in Pre-Colonial Africa: The Kiva Rising of 1869." Typescript. Cambridge, 1972.

Jacobs, Alan H. "The Traditional Political Organization of the Pastoral Masai." D.Phil. dissertation, Oxford University, 1965.

Kimambo, Isaria N. "Enlargement of Scale among the Pare c. 1750–1890." Paper presented to the Social Science Conference of the University of East Africa, University College, Dar es Salaam, 2–5 January 1968. Mimeographed.

LangHeinrich, F. "Wie ich Missionar wurde." Typescript. Copy in Bethel Mission Archives, Bethel bei Bielefeld, n.d.

Miers, Suzanne. "Great Britain and the Brussels Anti-Slave Trade Act of 1890." Ph.D. dissertation, University of London, 1969.

Mkufya, Marko. "Ereignisse aus dem leben des Lehrers Marko Mkufya." Recorded by Nünneke. Manuscript. Bethel Mission Archives, Bethel bei Bielefeld, n.d.

Msami, U. S. Abduel. "Historia ya Upare." Manuscript. Tanzania National Archives, Dar es Salaam, n.d.

Omer-Cooper, John. "Kingdoms and Villages, a Possible New Perspective in African History." Paper presented to the Social Science Conference of the University of East Africa, University College, Dar es Salaam, 2–5 January 1968. Mimeographed.

Riese, F. "Die Opfer der Schambala." Manuscript. Bethel Mission Archives, Bethel bei Bielefelt, n.d.

Soper, R. C. "Report on an Archaeological Reconnaissance of the Area of the Usambara Mountains, Tanzania: 14th January—13th

February 1967." British Institute of History and Archaeology in East Africa, Nairobi, n.d. Mimeographed.

Winans, Edgar V. "The Structure of Shambalai." Paper presented to the Conference of the East African Institute of Social Research at Moshi, Tanganyika, June 1957. Mimeographed.

### SELECT PUBLISHED SOURCES

This select bibliography concentrates on sources for the study of precolonial Shambaa history and society. For this reason, the numerous primers and religious texts published in the Shambaa language by missionaries are excluded. The works by Lutheran missionaries are carefully described by Ernst Dammann, in "Sprachliche Bemühungen von Betheler Missionaren um das Schambala," listed below. Those by the Trappist missionary Erasmus Hörner are listed by Robert Streit and Johannes Dindinger, in *Bibliotheca Missionum,* vol. 18, Freiburg, 1953. Also excluded is the large literature on Shambaa geography, natural history, and the development of plantations. The dozens of references on these subjects are largely irrelevant to the main thrust of this work. An extensive bibliography may be found in Manfred Attems, *Bauernbetriebe,* for which the full reference is given below. A comprehensive bibliography of the Shambaa which I have compiled will be published in a forthcoming volume of the Ethnographic Survey of Africa. The most important sources for the history of the Doe, Kamba, Zigula, and other neighboring peoples, as they relate to Shambaa history, may be found in the appropriate notes above.

Abdallah bin Hemedi 'lAjjemy. *Habari za Wakilindi.* Edited by J. W. T. Allen and William Kimweri bin Mbago. Nairobi, 1962. *Habari za Wakilindi* was originally published by the UMCA Press in German East Africa, in three parts. The manuscripts of parts 2 and 3 are in the library of the School of Oriental and African Studies, London. A translation of part 1 by Roland Allen was published as "The Story of Mbega," in *Tanganyika Notes and Records,* no. 1 (March 1935), pp. 38–51; no. 2 (October 1936), pp. 80–91; no. 3 (April 1937), pp. 87–98. The first part has also been published in Swahili in the *Journal of the East African Swahili Committee,* no. 27 (1957), pp. 13–63, as "Habari za Wakilindi." The work has also been published in English in its entirety as *The Kilindi* by J. W. T. Allen and William Kimweri bin Mbago, Nairobi, 1963.

Ankermann, Bernhard. *Ostafrika.* Das Eingeborenenrecht, edited by Erich Schultz-Ewerth and Leonard Adam, vol. 1. Stuttgart, 1929.

Attems, Manfred. *Bauernbetriebe in tropischen Höhenlagen Ostafrikas.* IFO Institut für Wirtschaftsforschung, Afrika Studien, no. 25. Munich, 1967.

Baker, E. C. *Report on Social and Economic Conditions in the Tanga Province.* Dar es Salaam, 1934.

Baumann, Oscar. *In Deutsch-Ostafrika während des Aufstandes.* Vienna and Olmütz, 1890.

Baumann, Oscar. "Karte von Usambara." *Dr. A. Petermanns Mitteilungen aus Justus Perthes Geographischer Anstalt* 35 (1889): 257–61.

Baumann, Oscar. "Usambara." *Dr. A. Petermanns Mitteilungen aus Justus Perthes Geographischer Anstalt* 35 (1889): 41–47. The description given here is repeated in Chapter Five of *In Deutsch-Ostafrika während des Aufstandes.*

Baumann, Oscar. *Usambara und seine Nachbargebiete.* Berlin, 1891.

Baumann, Oscar, and Meyer, Hans. "Dr. Hans Meyers Usambara-Expedition." *Mittheilungen von Forschungsreisenden und Gelehrten aus den Deutschen Schutzgebieten* 1 (1888): 199–205.

Becker, Dr. A. *Aus Deutsch-Ostafrikas Sturm und Drangperiode.* Halle. 1911.

Bellville, Alfred. "Journey to the Universities' Mission Station of Magila on the Borders of the Usambara Country." *Proceedings of the Royal Geographical Society* 20 (1875–76): 74–78.

Beidelman, T. O. "Correspondence: Shambala." *Tanganyika Notes and Records,* no. 62 (March 1964), pp. 106–8.

Bennigsen, Rudolf von. "Bericht des Finanzdirektors v. Benningsen über seine Reise nach Westusambara und dem Pare Gebirge." *Deutsches Kolonialblatt* 8 (1897): 486–89.

Bethel Mission. *Ushimolezi: Schambala Lesebuch.* 4th ed. Vuga, 1930. The first edition of this work was published in 1894 at Gütersloh as *Ushimulezi wa Washambala.* The second edition was published with substantial additions at Gütersloh in 1898. The work was substantially revised for the fourth edition.

Bleek, W. H. I. *A Comparative Grammar of South African Languages.* Cape Town, 1869.

Boteler, Capt. Thomas. *Narrative of a Voyage of Discovery to Africa and Arabia Performed in His Majesty's Ships Leven and Barracouta from 1821 to 1826 under the Command of Capt. F. W. Owen.* 2 vols. London, 1835.

Burton, Richard F. *Zanzibar: City, Island, and Coast.* 2 vols. London, 1872.

Burton, Richard F., and Speke, J. H. "A Coasting Voyage from Mombasa to the Pangani River; Visit to Sultan Kimwere; and Progress of the Expedition into the Interior." *Journal of the Royal Geographical Society* 28 (1858): 188–226.

Copland, B. D. "A Note on the Origin of the Mbugu with a Text." *Zeitschrift für Eingeborenen Sprachen* 24 (1933–34): 241–45.

Copland, B. D. "Note on the Officials of the Kilindi Kingdom and the First Rulers," *Journal of the East African Swahili Committee,* no. 27 (1957) pp. 64–65.

Cory, Hans. *African Figurines: Their Ceremonial Use in Puberty Rites in Tanganyika,* London, 1956.

Cory, Hans. "The Sambaa Initiation Rites for Boys." *Tanganyika Notes and Records,* nos. 58–59 (March–September 1962), pp. 2–7.

Cory, Hans. "Tambiko (*Fika*)." *Tanganyika Notes and Records,* nos. 58–59 (March–September 1962), pp. 274–82.

Coupland, Sir Reginald. *The Exploitation of East Africa.* 2d ed. London, 1968.

Dahlgrün, M. "Heiratsgebräuche der Schambaa." *Mittheilungen von Forschungsreisenden und Gelehrten aus den Deutschen Schutzgebieten* 16 (1903): 219–30.

Dale, Godfrey. *An Account of the Principal Customs and Habits of the Natives Inhabiting the Bondei.* London, 1896. Also published as an article in the *Journal of the Anthropological Institute* 25 (1896): 181–239.

Dammann, Ernst. "Bonde Erzählungen." *Zeitschrift für Eingeborenen-Sprachen* 28 (1937–38): 299–318.

Dammann, Ernst. "Sprachliche Bemühungen von Betheler Missionaren um das Schambala." In *Ostafrikanische Studien.* Vol. 8. Nürnberger Wirtschafts- und Sozialgeographische Arbeiten. Nuremberg, 1968.

Dobson, E. B. "Comparative Land Tenure of Ten Tanganyika Tribes." *Journal of African Administration* 6 (April 1954): 80–91.

Dobson, E. B. "Land Tenure of the Wasambaa." *Tanganyika Notes and Records,* no. 10 (December 1940), pp. 1–27.

Döring, P. *Hohenfriedeberg: eine Missionsstation in Usambara.* Berlin, 1900.

Döring, P. *Lehrlingsjahre eines jungen Missionars in Deutsch-Ostafrika.* Berlin, 1900.

Döring, P. *Morgendämmerung in Deutsch-Ostafrika.* Berlin, 1901.

Ekemode, G. O. "Arab Influence in the 19th Century Usambara." *African Historian* 2 (1968): 14–20.

Ekemode, G. O. "Kimweri the Great: Kilindi King of Vuga." *Tarikh* 2 (1968): 41–51.

Farler, J. P. "England and Germany in East Africa." *The Fortnightly Review* n.s. 45 (1889): 157–65.

Farler, J. P. Letters to the Editor, *The Times* (London), 16 October and 13 November 1885.

Farler, J. P. "Native Routes in East Africa from Pangani to the Masai Country and the Victoria Nyanza." *Proceedings of the Royal Geographical Society,* n.s. 4 (1882): 730–42, 776.

Farler, J. P. "The Usambara Country in East Africa." *Proceedings of the Royal Geographical Society,* n.s. 1 (1879): 81–97.

Farler, J. P. *The Work of Christ in Central Africa: A Letter to the Rev. H. P. Liddon.* London, 1878.

Feierman, Steven. "The Shambaa." In *Tanzania before 1900,* edited by Andrew Roberts, pp. 1–15. Nairobi, 1968.

Fischer, G. A. "Bericht über die im Auftrage der Geographischen Gesellschaft in Hamburg unternommene Reise in das Massai–Land." *Mitteilungen der Geographischen Gesellschaft in Hamburg* 5 (1882–83): 36–99.

Frere, Bartle. *Eastern Africa as a Field for Missionary Labour.* London, 1874.

Gissing, C. E. "A Journey from Mombasa to Mounts Ndara and Kasigao." *Proceedings of the Royal Geographical Society,* n.s. 6 (1884): 551–66.

Gleiss, Franz. *Luka Sefu.* Bethel bei Bielefeld, Westphalia, 1911.

Gleiss, Franz. "Magili, der Herr der Heuschrecken." *Nachrichten aus der ostrafrikanischen Mission* 12 (August 1898): 128–30.

Gleiss, Franz. *Schambala-Sprachführer.* Tanga (Deutsch-Ostrafrika), 1908.

Gleiss, Franz. *An meinen Hirten!* Bethel bei Bielefeld, 1926.

Gleiss, Franz. *Vor den Toren von Wuga.* Bethel bei Bielefeld, 1928.

Goodman, Morris. "The Strange Case of Mbugu." In *Pidginization and Creolization of Languages,* edited by Dell Hymes, pp. 243–54. Cambridge, 1971.

Green, E. C. "The Wambugu of Usambara." *Tanganyika Notes and Records,* no. 61 (September 1963), pp. 175–89.

Greenberg, Joseph H. "The Mogogodo, a Forgotten Cushitic People." *Journal of African Languages* 2 (1963): 29–43.

Guillain, Charles. *Documents sur l'histoire, la geographie et le commerce de l'Afrique orientale.* 3 vols. Paris, 1856.

Haberlandt, M. "Dr. Oskar Baumann, ein Nachruf (mit Bild)." *Abhandlungen der K. K. Geographischen Gessellschaft in Wien* 2 (1900): 1–20.

Heanley, R. M. *A Memoir of Edward Steere*. London, 1909.

Hobley, C. W. *Ethnology of the A-Kamba and other East African Tribes*. Cambridge, 1910.

Hollis, A. C. "Notes on the History of Vumba, East Africa." *Journal of the Anthropological Institute*, n.s. 30 (1900): 275–98.

Hörner, Erasmus. *Grammatik der Schambalasprache*. Natal, 1899. [Not consulted.]

Hörner, Erasmus. *Kleiner Leitfaden zur Erlernung des Kishambala*. Mariannhill, Natal, 1900. [Not consulted.]

Hosbach, W. *Abraham Kilua, der schwarze Vikar von Neu–Bethel*. Bethel bei Bielefeld, Westphalia, 1925.

Hosbach, W. "Eine Geistergeschichte." *Nachrichten aus der ostafrikanischen Mission* 25 (1911): 209–13.

Johanssen, Ernst. *Führung und Erfahrung in 40 jährigem Missionsdienst*, vols. 1 and 2. Bethel bei Bielefeld, n.d.

Johanssen, Ernst, and Döring, Paul. "Das Leben der Schambala, beleuchtet durch ihre Sprichwörter." *Zeitschrift für Kolonialsprachen* 5 (1914–15): 137–50, 190–226, 306–18.

Johnston, H. H. *The Kilima-Njaro Expedition*. London, 1886.

Johnston, Keith. "Notes of a Trip from Zanzibar to Usambara, in February and March 1879." *Proceedings of the Royal Geographical Society*, n.s. 1 (1879): 545–64, 616.

Kähler-Meyer, E. "Studien zur tonalen Struktur der Bantusprachen." *Afrika und Übersee* 46 (1962): 1–42.

Kallenberg, Friedrich. *Auf dem Kriegspfad gegen die Massai*. Munich, 1892.

Karasek, A. "Beiträge zur Kenntnis der Waschambaa," edited by August Eichhorn, *Baessler-Archiv* 1 (1911): 155–222; 3 (1913): 69–131, 131; 7 (1918–22): 56–98; 8 (1923–24): 1–53.

Karasek, A. "Tabakspfeifen und Rauchen bei den Waschambaa." *Globus* (1908): 285–87.

Kelly, J. B. *Britain and the Persian Gulf, 1795–1880*. Oxford, 1968.

Kersten, Otto. *Baron Carl Claus von der Decken's Reisen in Ost-Afrika in den Jahren 1859 bis 1861*, vol. 1. Leipzig and Heidelberg, 1869.

Kimambo, Isaria N. *A Political History of the Pare of Tanzania. c 1500–1900*. Nairobi, 1969.

Kirk, John. "Visit to the Coast of Somali-land." *Proceedings of the Royal Geographical Society* 17 (1873): 340–41.

Kiro, Selemani. "The History of the Zigua Tribe," translated by Petro Sh. Mntambo. *Tanganyika Notes and Records,* no. 34 (1953), pp. 70–74.

Koch, Robert. "Report on West Usambara from the Point of View of Health (5/8/1898)." *Tanganyika Notes and Records,* no. 35 (July 1953), pp. 7–13.

Kohler, J. "Das Banturecht in Ostafrika." Part 4 of "Rechte der deutschen Schutzgebieten." *Zeitschrift für vergleichende Rechtswissenschaft* 15 (1901): 1–83.

Koritschoner, Hans. "Details of a Native Medical Treatment." *Tanganyika Notes and Records,* no. 2 (1936): pp. 67–71.

Krapf, Johann Ludwig. *Reisen in Ostafrika.* Stuttgart, 1964.

Krapf, Johann Ludwig. *Travels, Researches, and Missionary Labours, during an Eighteen Years' Residence in Eastern Africa.* London, 1860.

Lamphear, John. "The Kamba and the Northern Mrima Coast." In *Pre-Colonial African Trade,* edited by Richard Gray and David Birmingham, pp. 75–101. London, 1970.

LangHeinrich, F. "Die Entwickelung des Verkehrs in Westusambara." *Nachrichten aus der ostafrikanischen Mission* 27 (1913): 7–12.

LangHeinrich, F. *Schambala-Wörterbuch.* Abhandlungen des Hamburgischen Kolonialistituts, vol. 43. Hamburg, 1921.

LangHeinrich, F. "Vergangene Pracht." *Nachrichten aus der ostafrikanischen Mission* 16 (1902): 73–78.

LangHeinrich, F. "Die Waschambala." In *Rechtsverhältnisse von eingeborenen Völkern in Afrika und Ozeanien,* edited by S. R. Steinmetz, pp. 218–67. Berlin, 1903.

Last, J. T. *Polyglotta Africana Orientalis.* London, 1885.

Latham, R. G. *Comparative Philology.* London, 1862.

Liebert. "Bericht über die Inspektionsreise des Kaiserlichen Gouverneurs." *Deutsches Kolonialblatt* 8 (1897): 313–19. A part of this report, on Usambara, was reprinted in *Der Tropenpflanzer* 1 (1897): 171–72.

Lemenye, Justin. *Maisha ya Sameni Ole Kivasis, yaani Justin Lemenye.* Edited by H. A. Fosbrooke. Nairobi, 1953. Translated into English by H. A. Fosbrooke as "The Life of Justin: an African Autobiography." *Tanganyika Notes and Records,* no. 41 (1955), pp. 31–57; no. 42 (1956), pp. 19–30.

Le Roy, Alexandre. *Au Kilima-Ndjaro.* Paris, n.d. (1893?).

Mauss, Marcel, and Hubert, H. "Etude sommaire de la représentation du temps dans la religion et la magie." In *Mélanges d'histoire des religions,* edited by H. Hubert and M. Mauss, pp. 190–229. Paris, 1929.

Meeussen, A. E. "Tonunterschiede als Reflexe von Quantitätsunterschieden im Schambala." In *Afrikanistische Studien,* edited by J. Lukas, pp. 154–56. Berlin, 1955.

Meinhof, Carl. "Linguistische Studien in Ostafrika." Parts 2, 8, 10, 11. *Afrikanische Studien.* Part 3 of Mitteilungen des Seminars für Orientalische Sprachen zu Berlin. 1904, pp. 217–36; 1906, pp. 278–84, 294–323, 324–33.

Meyer, Hans. *Das Deutsche Kolonialreich,* vol. 1. Leipzig and Vienna, 1909.

Meyer, Hans. *Das Kilimanjaro.* Berlin, 1900.

Meyer, Hans. *Ostafrikanische gletscherfahrten.* Leipzig, 1890.

Moreau, R. E. "Bird Names used in Costal North-Eastern Tanganyika Territory." *Tanganyika Notes and Records,* no. 10 (December 1940), pp. 47–72; no. 11 (April 1941), pp. 47–60.

Moreau, R. E. "Bird-Nomenclature in an East African Area." *Bulletin of the School of Oriental and African Studies* 10 (1939–42): 998–1006.

Moreau, R. E. "Suicide by 'Breaking the Cooking Pot.'" *Tanganyika Notes and Records,* no. 12 (December 1941), pp. 49–50.

Müller, Fritz Ferdinand. *Deutschland—Zanzibar—Ostafrika: Geschichte einer deutschen Kolonialeroberung.* Berlin, 1959.

Mwakyosa, D. A. "The Rule of Witch–Craft among the Wasambaa." *Makerere* 1 (1947): 121–23.

New, Charles. "Journey from the Pangani, via Wadigo, to Mombasa." *Proceedings of the Royal Geographical Society* 19 (1875): 317–23. An article which is essentially the same may be found in the *Journal of the Royal Geographical Society* 45 (1875): 414–20.

New, Charles. *Life, Wanderings, and Labours in Eastern Africa.* London, 1873.

Oliver, Roland. "Discernible Developments in the Interior, *c.* 1500–1840." In *History of East Africa,* vol. 1, edited by Roland Oliver and Gervase Mathew, pp. 169–211. Oxford, 1963.

Owen, W. F. W. *Narrative of Voyages to Explore the Shores of Africa, Arabia, and Madagascar.* Edited by Heaton Bowstead Robinson. 2 vols. London, 1833.

Peters, Karl. *Das Deutsch-Ostafrikanische Schutzgebiet.* Munich and Leipzig, 1895.

Picarda, Père. "Autour de Mandéra: Notes sur l'Ouzigoua, l'Oukwere, et l'Oudoé (Zanguebar)." *Les Missions Catholiques* (Lyon) 18

(1886): 184–89, 197–201, 208–11, 225–28, 234–37, 246–49, 258–61, 269–74, 281–85, 294–97, 322–24, 332–34, 342–46, 356–57, 365–69.

Riese, F. *Etwas über die Mysterien der Schambala.* Bethel bei Bielefeld, 1911.

Roehl, Karl. "Eine fast verloren gegangene Klasse des Ur–Bantu." In *Festschrift [Carl] Meinhof,* pp. 233–40. Glückstadt and Hamburg, 1927.

Roehl, Karl. *Versuch einer systematischen Grammatik der Schambalasprache.* Abhandlungen des Hamburgischen Kolonialinstituts, vol. 2. Hamburg, 1911.

Rösler, O., and Gleiss, Franz. *Schambala-Grammatik: mit Übungssätzen nebst einer Sammlung von Redensarten in Gesprächsform von Frau Missionar O. Rösler in Wuga und Wörterbuch schambala-deutsch und deutsch-schambala von Franz Gleiss.* Archiv für das Studium deutscher Kolonialsprachen, vol. 13. Berlin, 1912.

"Salt Production among the Wasambaa." *Tanganyika Notes and Records,* no. 8 (December 1939), pp. 102–3.

Sangai, G. R. Williams. *Dictionary of Native Plant Names in the Bondei, Shambaa, and Zigua Languages with Their English and Botanical Equivalents.* Nairobi, 1963.

Seidel, A. "Beiträge zur Kenntnis der Schambalasprache in Usambara." *Zeitschrift für afrikanische und oceanische Sprachen* 1 (1895): 34–82, 105–17.

Seidel, A. "Eine Erzählung der Wa–Schambala." *Zeitschrift für afrikanische und oceanische Sprachen* 2 (1896): 145–9.

Seidel, A. *Handbuch der Schambalasprache in Usambara.* Dresden–Leipzig, 1895.

Smith, Charles Stewart. "Explorations in Zanzibar Dominions." *Royal Geographical Society Supplementary Papers* 2 (1889): 101–25.

Soper, R. C. "Iron Age Sites in North-Eastern Tanzania." *Azania* 2 (1967): 19–36.

Soper, R. C.: "Kwale: an Early Iron Age Site in South–Eastern Kenya." *Azania* 2 (1967): 1–17.

Speke, John Hanning. *What Led to the Discovery of the Source of the Nile.* London, 1967.

Steere, E. *Collections for a Handbook of the Shambala Language.* Zanzibar, 1867.

Steere, E. *First Freed Slave Settlement in Central Africa.* Central African Mission, Occasional Paper, no. 7. London, n.d. (1876?).

Steuber, W. "Die Unterwerfung des Kilima-Ndjaro Gebietes." In *Hermann von Wissman: Deutschlands grösster Afrikaner,* edited by C. von Perbrandt, G. Richelman, and Rochus Schmidt, pp. 341–77. Berlin, 1906.

Storch, E. "Sitten, Gebräuche und Rechtspflege bei den Bewohnern Usambara und Pares." *Mitteilungen aus den Deutschen Schutzgebieten* 8 (1895) : 310–31.

Storch, E. "Über das Strafverfahren gegen des Jumben Mputa von Wuga und über die Einsetzung des Jumben Kipanga von Handei in Wuga." *Nachrichten aus der ostafrikanischen Mission* 9 (1895): 138–40.

Sykes, Colonel. "Notes on the Possessions of the Imaun of Muskat, on the Climate and Productions of Zanzibar, and on the Prospects of African Discovery from Mombas." *Journal of the Royal Geographical Society* 23 (1853): 101–19.

Thornton, Richard. "Notes on a Journey to Kilima-ndjaro, made in the Company of the Baron von der Decken," *Journal of the Royal Geographical Society* 35 (1865): 15–21.

Thurnwald, Richard C. *Black and White in East Africa.* London, 1935.

Trittelvitz, W. *Nicht so Langsam.* Bethel bei Beilefeld, Westphalia, n.d. [Not consulted.]

United Republic of Tanzania, Ministry of Economic Affairs and Development Planning, Bureau of Statistics. *1967 Population Census.* 5 vols. Dar es Salaam, 1969–71.

Universities Mission to Central Africa. *Bluebooks.* London, 1867–1873.

Vickers-Haviland, L. A. W. "The Making of an African Historical Film." *Tanganyika Notes and Records,* no. 6 (1938), pp. 82–86.

Wakefield, T. "Routes of Native Caravans from the Coast to the Interior of Eastern Africa, Chiefly from Information Given by Sádi Bin Ahedi, a Native of a District Near Gazi, in Udigo, a Little North of Zanzibar." *Journal of the Royal Geographical Society* 40 (1870): 303–28.

Ward, Gertrude. *The Life of Charles Alan Smythies.* Edited by Edward Francis Russell. London, 1898.

Werner, Alice. *Myths and Legends of the Bantu.* London, 1933. Chapter 9, "The Wakilindi Saga," is drawn from *Habari za Wakilindi.*

Werner, Alice. "Notes on the Shambala and Some Allied Languages of East Africa." *Journal of the African Society* 5 (1906): 154–66.

Whiteley, W. H. "Linguistic Hybrids." *African Studies* 19 (1960): 95–97.

Whiteley, W. H. *A Short Description of Item Categories in Iraqw.* Kampala, 1958.

Wilson, George Herbert. *The History of the Universities Mission to Central Africa.* London, 1936.

Winans, Edgar V. *Shambala: the Constitution of a Traditional State.* London, 1962.

Winans, Edgar V. "The Shambala Family." In *The Family Estate in Africa,* edited by Robert F. Gray and P. H. Gulliver, pp. 35–61. London, 1964.

Wohlrab, Karl. *Die christliche Missionspredigt unter den Schambala.* Tübingen, 1929.

Wohlrab, Paul. "Ein Neuer Dämonen-Kultus in Usambara." *Nachrichten aus der ostafrikanischen Mission* 27 (1913): 186–89.

Wohlrab, Paul. "Das Recht der Schambala," *Archiv für Anthropologie* (1918), pp. 160–81.

Wohlrab, Paul. *Usambara: Werden und Wachsen einer heidenchristlichen Gemeinde in Deutsch-Ostafrika.* Bethel bei Bielefeld, 1915.

PERIODICALS

*Central Africa: a Monthly Record of the Universities Mission.* London, 1833–1914.

*Nachrichten aus der ostafrikanischen Mission.* Berlin, 1887–1914.

# INDEX

Abdallah bin Hemedi 'lAjjemy, 106, 158. *See also Habari za Wakilindi*

Abolition of slave trade, 168, 169–71

Accession rite, 58, 95–96

*Alama* (Bondei initiation rite), 86n

Alington, C. A., 159

Alliance: networks, 37–39, 78; Mbegha's use of, 84–86; and political scale, 188, 190

Altitude of Shambaai and *nyika*, 17, 20

Amboni (market), 126

American trade, 142, 169

Ancestors: sacrifice to, 51; and early village leadership, 78; and culture of Vugha, 91–92. *See also* Ghosts

Animality, in Shambaa thought, 52, 61

Animals, categories of, 41, 48, 55–59, 61, 62

Arabia, 136

Arabic, and regional language usage, 200

Arabs, 136, 137, 183, 193, 201

Asu, 19

Avuniwa (oral informant), 49

Bagamoyo: Kamba at, 127–28; coast-hinterland relations, 133; Bushiri defeated near, 203

Bagha: during reigns of Bughe, Kinyashi Muanga Ike, and Kimweri ye Nyumbai, 98, 113; in War of Kimweri and Kibanga, 193, 195

Baghai (Mlalo subchiefdom), 119

Baghai (village in Vugha chiefdom), 111–12

Balangai: Mbegha's influence at, 65; in succession dispute after Bughe's death, 93–96

Banana gardens: locations at villages, 37; location at Vugha, 92

Bananas: growth of, in Shambaai, 18, 20, 26; as town food supply, 29–30; defined, 30n; as trade item, 131

Bangwe, 67

Bantu, 17, 74

Banyan, 158

Barawa, 137

Barghash ibn Said (Sultan of Zanzibar), 192, 195, 196

Baumann, Oscar, 16, 151n, 172, 173, 202–3, 204

Beans, 26, 27

Beidelman, T. O., 85n, 128n

Bethel Mission, archival sources, 16

ler, 198; religion of, 200; death
of, 204
**Kimweri Mbegha.** *See* Maua
**Kimweri ye Nyumbai:** traditions
about, 10, 102–4, 107, 182; and
chronology of early kingdom,
93–94*n;* dates of reign, 101–2*n*,
151–52*n;* governed chiefdoms,
101–8, 109–19, 146 (*see also* under names of chiefdoms); Bondei
revolts, 108, 162; trade and politics, 1836–1862, 123–24, 135,
138–44; use of father-son relationship, 146; dispute among
Kimweri's successors, 146–53;
appointment of Shekulwavu as
successor, 149–51; death of, 151–
52; sons of united against Shekulwavu, 157; population movement during reign, 166; reign
characterized, 167; support from
common people, 185; mentioned,
104, 105, 120, 147, 172, 189, 190
**Kingship ideals,** 53, 58–59, 64
**Kinyashi (son of Shekulwavu, ninth
king):** sons of, reticence of, 14;
as child, 160; in genealogy, 190;
held Hundu in War of Kimweri
and Kibanga, 191; visited Zanzibar after War of Mbaruk, 196
**Kinyashi Muanga Ike (fourth
king):** and royal chronology,
94*n;* succession dispute, 94–99;
government of chiefdoms, 97–
101, 105–6; death of, 101; traditions about, 103; in genealogy,
104, 105; guns unknown to, 140–
41; mentioned, 117–18, 172, 173
**Kirk, John,** 165, 192, 196*n*
**Kisabengo (founder of Simba
Mwene),** 138
**Kishasha (commoner of Vugha),**
181
**Kisiwani (Pare trading town),** 186
**Kitivo (trading village),** 124–25,
199

*Kitundu wantu* (forest for disposal
of dangerous corpses), 47
**Kiunguia (son of Kimweri ye
Nyumbai, chief of Ngulwi),** 110
**Kiva (Bondei movement),** 163–65
**Kivo (son of Mshuza, Ubii sub-
chief),** 110
**Kivoi (Kamba trader),** 128*n*
**Kivui Mwenda (Kamba trader),**
128
**Kivuma (Zigula chief),** 143
**Kiwanda,** 159–60
*Kiza* (Hea rain magic), 87
**Kolowa (son of Dafa, chief of
Gare),** 110
**Korogwe,** 143
**Krapf, Johann Ludwig:** described
government of eastern territories,
100; on age of Kimweri ye
Nyumbai, 101–2*n;* observations
of, at Mponde, 113; evidence of,
on Kamba, 127–28; on Shambaa
relations with Zigula and Zanzi-
bar, 138–39, 140*n*, 141, 142;
and date of Kimweri ye Nyu-
mbai's death, 151–52*n*
**Kunguu (son of Kimweri ye
Nyumbai, chief of Mahezan-
guu),** 116–17
**Kwa Doe (Vugha subchiefdom),**
114
**Kwa Mbiu (village in Zigula),** 48–
49, 65, 83
**Kwamkoro,** 187*n*
**Kwa Mongo, Mount (near Vugha),**
152
**Kwavi.** *See* Maasai
**Kwere (ethnic group),** 138
**Kwe Tango,** 158, 159, 160
**Kwizu (descent group at Mlalo),**
119

**Laikipiak,** 75
**Laikipya,** 74–75
**Legitimate commerce,** 168, 170

DESIGNED BY AUDREY SINNOTT

MANUFACTURED BY GEORGE BANTA CO., INC., MENASHA, WISCONSIN

TEXT AND DISPLAY LINES ARE SET IN TIMES ROMAN

ШU

Library of Congress Cataloging in Publication Data

Feierman, Steven, 1940–
The Shambaa kingdom.

Bibliography: p. 207–219
1. Shambala (Bantu tribe) I. Title.
DT443.F44   1974        916.78'22        73–2044
ISBN 0–299–06360–7